ARCO

POSTAL EXAMS

John Gosney
Dawn Rosenberg McKay

IDG Books Worldwide, Inc.
An International Data Group Company
Foster City, CA • Chicago, IL • Indianapolis, IN • New York, NY

5th Edition

IDG Books Worldwide, Inc.
An International Data Group Company
919 E. Hillsdale Boulevard
Suite 400
Foster City, CA 94404

For general information on IDG Books Worldwide's books in the U.S., please call our Consumer
Customer Service department at 800-762-2974. For reseller information, including discounts and
premium sales, please call our Reseller Customer Service department at 800-434-3422.

International Standard Serial Number information available upon request

ISBN: 0-02-863538-8

Manufactured in the United States of America

10 9 8 7 6 5 4 3 2 1

C O N T E N T S

Score Higher: Address-Checking Strategies 43

Score Higher: Memory for Addresses 55

Score Higher: Strategies for Working with Number Series 63

Score Higher: Strategies for Following Oral Instructions 73

PART TWO
Model Examinations

Model Examination I: Exam 470 and Exam 460 97

Model Examination II: Exam 710 (Parts A & B) and Exam 711 (Part C) 139

Model Examination III: Exam 911 185

Model Examination IV: Exam 91 201

Model Examination V: Exam 630 229

Glossary 273

Dedication

To my parents, Richard and Marilyn Gosney

Introduction

Congratulations on selecting *ARCO Postal Exams Handbook, 5th Edition*. You have in your hands a powerful tool to ensure your best chances at getting a great score on the United States Postal Service exam. By working through this book, taking time to practice the sample exercies, and studying the various tips and techniques for tackling various question types, you can put yourself at a significant advantage for achieving your best score.

This book also contains up-to-date information on various positions with the United States Postal Service, including job requirements, benefits, working conditions, and salaries. The *Handbook* is *your* book, written with *your success* in mind—enjoy reading it, and good luck on your exam!

How to Use this Book

Unlike many test preparation books, you don't have to read through this handbook from front to back. If you prefer, you can jump right into the sample tests (Chapters 8–12). Or, maybe you'd like to see some strategies for approaching the various exam questions—you can find these in Chapters 4–7. Finally, detailed, current information on jobs with the USPS can be found in the first several chapters (including World Wide Web addresses for more detailed information). Again, this is *your* book—use it as you like!

Acknowledgements

Thanks to everyone at ARCO for their outstanding support and professionalism on this and other projects. Thanks to Dave Henthorn for keeping everything on track during some wild organizational changes. A special thanks to Lorna Gentry, who, more than anyone, is responsible for this in the first place and who is always a pleasure to work with. Thanks, Lorna!

Also, a special nod of appreciation to Dawn Rosenberg McKay for providing great research material and ensuring that the information contained in the book was current.

Finally, thanks to Melissa, Genna, and Jackson. You know who you are!

—John Gosney

ONE

A Job with the U.S. Postal Service

CONTENTS

WORKING FOR THE POSTAL SERVICE

Welcome to the U.S. Postal Service

Remember when you were a kid and you took a field trip to your local post office? More than likely, a friendly employee gave you a tour of the mail-sorting area, demonstrated how the various computers are used (depending, of course, on your age at the time of the tour) and perhaps gave you a peek into one of the mail trucks. And, if you're like many people, you left with the impression that the only thing postal employees do is sort the mail. Maybe this impression stayed with you into adulthood.

Most people are familiar with the duties of the city carrier and window clerk, the same friendly employees who may have given you the tour when you were young. However, very few people are aware of the many different tasks required in "sorting the mail," not to mention the enormous variety of occupations in the U.S. Postal Service.

Twenty-four hours a day, mail (and, by mail, we mean letters, packages, magazines, and other assorted papers) moves through the typical large post office. It takes a lot of hard work to keep that mail moving, and all that hard work requires the involvement of many different people performing many different tasks:

- City carriers collect some of this mail from neighborhood mailboxes; some is trucked in from surrounding towns or from the airport. When a truck arrives at the post office, mail handlers unload the mail.
- Postal clerks then sort the mail according to destination. After being sorted, outgoing mail is loaded into trucks for delivery to the airport or to nearby towns. Local mail is left for carriers to deliver the next morning.
- To keep buildings and equipment clean and in good working order, the Postal Service employs a variety of service and maintenance workers, including janitors, laborers, truck mechanics, electricians, carpenters, and painters. Some workers specialize in repairing machines that process mail.
- Postal inspectors audit the operations of post offices to see that they are run efficiently, that funds are spent properly, and that postal laws and regulations are observed. They also prevent and detect crimes such as theft, forgery, and fraud involving use of the mail.
- Postmasters and supervisors are responsible for the day-to-day operation of the post office, for hiring and promoting employees, and for setting up work schedules.

Almost 85 percent of all postal workers are in jobs directly related to processing and delivering mail. This group includes postal clerks, city careers, mail handlers, rural carriers, and truck drivers. Postmasters and supervisors make up nearly 10 percent of total employment, and maintenance workers comprise about 4 percent. The remainder includes such workers as postal inspectors, guards, personnel workers, and secretaries.

As you can see, there are lots of exciting positions within the U.S. Postal Service. Within the pages of this book, we'll explore these positions, from the requirements of the position to what test you'll need to take to qualify.

Salary, Benefits, and Employment Opportunities with the U.S. Postal Service

The United States Postal Service is an independent agency of the federal government. As such, employees of the Postal Service are federal employees who enjoy the very generous benefits offered by the government. These benefits include an automatic raise at least once a year, regular cost-of-living adjustments, liberal paid vacation and sick leave, life insurance, hospitalization, and the opportunity to join a credit union.

At the same time, the operation of the Postal Service is businesslike and independent of politics. A postal worker's job is secure even though presidential administrations may change. An examination system is used to fill vacancies. This system provides opportunities for those who are able and motivated to enter the Postal Service and to move within it.

BENEFITS

Table 1.1 illustrates the general benefits offered by the USPS.

> Postal Service employees are covered by the same benefits as other employees of the federal government, including Federal Employees Health Benefits (FEHB), Federal Employees Retirement System (FERS), and life insurance.

TABLE 1.1

Type of Benefits	Who Is Covered	Available Options
Health: *Federal Employees Health Benefits (FEHB)*	Postal employees and retirees, and their survivors. Coverage may include: • Self only (HMOs) • Family coverage for yourself, your spouse, and unmarried dependant children under age 22	• Managed fee for service plans • Point of service (POS) options • Health maintenance organizations
Retirement: *Federal Employees Retirement System (FERS)*	Almost all new employees hired after 1983 are automatically covered. Employees who leave may still qualify for benefits. Retirement funds build on the Social Security benefits employees may earn in the future or those already earned from nonfederal work.	FERS is a three-tiered retirement plan consisting of these components: • Social Security benefits (available for those age 62 and retired) • Basic Benefits Plan (financed by a small contribution from the employee and the government) *A special retirement supplement, for employees who meet the criteria, is paid as a monthly benefit until the employee reaches age 62.*

Type of Benefits	Who Is Covered	Available Options
Life: *The Federal Employees' Group Life Insurance Program (FEGLI)*	Postal employees and retirees, as well as many of their family members, are eligible for this group life insurance program.	• Thrift Savings Plan (tax-deferred retirement savings and investment plan; similar to 401(k) plans) • Basic insurance (automatic unless employee opts out; insured pays $2/3$ of the cost, government pays $1/3$) • Optional insurance (not automatic; insured pays 100% of the cost)

SALARIES

Salaries within the USPS are graded. Depending on amount of time you've been employed, any promotions you might have achieved, and whether you work full- or part-time all determine your salary.

The following tables illustrate salary levels for various positions with the USPS. You are assigned a grade (for example, Grade 5) depending on the type of position you fill (note that each position has different grade levels). To move between steps (such as from Grade B to Grade C), you must be in the previous position for a specified number of weeks. (More details on these step requirements are defined later.)

LETTER CARRIER PAY SCHEDULE: 3/14/1998 (YEARLY)

	A	B	C	D	E
Grade 5	$27,011	$29,895	$32,210	$34,443	$34,731
Grade 6	$28,585	$31,665	$32,859	$35,147	$35,462
	F	G	H	I	J
Grade 5	$35,022	$35,309	$35,600	$35,888	$36,177
Grade 6	$35,777	$36,088	$36,404	$36,718	$37,029
	K	L	M	N	O
Grade 5	$36,468	$36,755	$37,046	$37,334	$37,623
Grade 6	$37,345	$37,660	$37,973	$38,290	$38,604

MAIL HANDLERS PAY SCHEDULE: 3/13/1999 (YEARLY)

	A	B	C	D	E
Grade 4	$23,808	$28,512	$30,721	$33,975	$34,237
Grade 5	$25,122	$30,149	$32,419	$34,618	$34,900
	F	G	H	I	J
Grade 4	$34,503	$34,766	$35,029	$35,293	$35,559
Grade 5	$35,187	$35,467	$35,753	$36,039	$36,320
	K	L	M	N	O
Grade 4	$35,823	$36,087	$36,350	$36,614	$36,877
Grade 5	$36,606	$36,886	$37,171	$37,455	$37,739

RURAL CARRIER EVALUATED SCHEDULE: 3/13/1999
FULL-TIME ANNUAL BASIC RATES (PARTIAL SCHEDULE)

Hours	A	B	C	1	2	3	4
12	$7,768	$8,590	$9,220	$9,859	$9,952	$10,043	$10,135
18	$11,649	$12,887	$13,832	$14,788	$14,926	$15,066	$15,203
24	$15,533	$17,178	$18,439	$19,719	$19,900	$20,082	$20,266
30	$19,415	$21,480	$23,056	$24,651	$24,878	$25,111	$25,337
40	$25,887	$28,633	$30,735	$32,862	$33,167	$33,475	$33,779
48	$33,655	$37,223	$39,955	$42,721	$43,119	$43,518	$43,914
Hours	**5**	**6**	**7**	**8**	**9**	**10**	**11**
12	$10,226	$10,321	$10,413	$10,503	$10,597	$10,688	$10,781
18	$15,343	$15,479	$15,618	$15,756	$15,896	$16,034	$16,172
24	$20,449	$20,633	$20,817	$21,000	$21,182	$21,368	$21,550
30	$25,566	$25,796	$26,026	$26,255	$26,484	$26,714	$26,945
40	$34,087	$34,392	$34,698	$35,006	$35,310	$35,618	$35,923
48	$44,313	$44,713	$45,111	$45,509	$45,907	$46,306	$46,704

FULL-TIME REGULAR APWU SALARY SCHEDULE (PS): 9/12/1998
(MAINTENANCE EMPLOYEES, MOTOR VEHICLE EMPLOYEES, POSTAL CLERKS, MAIL EQUIPMENT SHOPS EMPLOYEES, MATERIAL DISTRIBUTION CENTERS EMPLOYEES)

Grade	AA	A	B	C	D	E	F	G
1	$22,715	$25,041	$27,128	$29,216	$32,323	$32,536	$32,750	$32,962
2	$23,000	$25,393	$27,533	$29,667	$32,837	$33,067	$33,297	$33,527
3	$23,364	$25,771	$27,964	$30,155	$33,393	$33,641	$33,893	$34,138
4	—	$25,738	$28,434	$30,688	$33,997	$34,265	$34,536	$34,805
5	—	$27,219	$30,103	$32,418	$34,651	$34,939	$35,230	$35,517
6	—	$28,793	$31,873	$33,067	$35,355	$35,670	$35,985	$36,296
7	—	$29,392	$32,545	$33,774	$36,119	$36,457	$36,794	$37,133
8	—	—	—	$34,365	$36,937	$37,304	$37,670	$38,037
9	—	—	—	$35,191	$37,829	$38,228	$38,624	$39,021
10	—	—	—	$36,062	$38,771	$39,199	$39,625	$40,054
Grade	**H**	**I**	**J**	**K**	**L**	**M**	**N**	**O**
1	$33,174	$33,387	$33,600	$33,813	$34,027	$34,236	$34,451	$34,663
2	$33,760	$33,988	$34,219	$34,451	$34,679	$34,912	$35,142	$35,370
3	$34,389	$34,635	$34,887	$35,134	$35,383	$35,630	$35,879	$36,126
4	$35,071	$35,340	$35,609	$35,879	$36,150	$36,418	$36,686	$36,953
5	$35,808	$36,096	$36,385	$36,676	$36,963	$37,254	$37,542	$37,831
6	$36,612	$36,926	$37,237	$37,553	$37,868	$38,181	$38,498	$38,812
7	$37,474	$37,809	$38,149	$38,485	$38,823	$39,163	$39,500	$39,837
8	$38,406	$38,771	$39,141	$39,505	$39,873	$40,239	$40,605	$40,974
9	$39,415	$39,810	$40,206	$40,605	$40,999	$41,399	$41,765	$42,191
10	$40,483	$40,909	$41,337	$41,766	$42,192	$42,621	$43,049	$43,476

Again, as you advance in your selected position within the USPS, you will become eligible for pay increases.

To be eligible for a periodic step increase, an employee must meet the following criteria:

• Must have received and currently be serving under a career appointment
• Must have performed in a satisfactory or outstanding manner during the waiting period
• Cannot have received an equivalent increase during the waiting period
• Must have completed the required waiting period (see the following tables)

STEP INCREASE WAITING PERIODS FOR BARGAINING UNIT POSITIONS. (THE NUMBER UNDER EACH GRADE COLUMN INDICATES THE WAITING PERIOD IN NUMBER OF WEEKS.)

POSTAL SERVICE (PS) SCHEDULE

Steps (From → To)	Grades 1–3	Grades 4–7	Grades 8–10	Steps (From → To)	Grades 1–3	Grades 4–7	Grades 8–10
A → B	96	—	—	H → I	44	44	44
B → C	88	96	—	I → J	44	44	44
C → D	88	44	—	J → K	34	34	34
D → E	44	44	52	K → L	34	34	34
E → F	44	44	44	L → M	26	26	26
F → G	44	44	44	M → N	26	26	26
G → H	44	44	44	N → O	24	24	24

MAIL HANDLERS' (MH) SCHEDULE

Steps (From → To)	Grade 3	Grades 4–6	Steps (From → To)	Grades 3	Grades 4–6
A → B	96	—	H → I	44	44
B → C	88	96	I → J	44	44
C → D	88	44	J → K	34	34
D → E	44	44	K → L	34	34
E → F	44	44	L → M	26	26
F → G	44	44	M → N	26	26
G → H	44	44	N → O	24	24

MAIL TRANSPORTATION EQUIPMENT CENTERS

Steps (From → To)	Grades 1–3	Grades 4–7	Grades 8–10	Steps (From → To)	Grades 1–3	Grades 4–7	Grades 8–10
A → B	96	—	—	H → I	44	44	44
B → C	88	96	—	I → J	44	44	44
C → D	88	44	—	J → K	34	34	34
D → E	44	44	52	K → L	34	34	34
E → F	44	44	44	L → M	26	26	26
F → G	44	44	44	M → N	26	26	26
G → H	44	44	44	N → O	24	24	24

MAIL EQUIPMENT SHOPS AND AREA SUPPLY CENTERS

Steps (From → To)	Grades 1–3	Grades 4–7	Grades 8–10	Steps (From → To)	Grades 1–3	Grades 4–7	Grades 8–10
A → B	96	—	—	H → I	44	44	44
B → C	88	96	—	I → J	44	44	44
C → D	88	44	—	J → K	34	34	34
D → E	44	44	52	K → L	34	34	34
E → F	44	44	44	L → M	26	26	26
F → G	44	44	44	M → N	26	26	26
G → H	44	44	44	N → O	24	24	24

RURAL CARRIER SCHEDULES

Steps (From → To)	B to C	C to 1	1 to 2	2 to 3	3 to 4	4 to 5	5 to 6	6 to 7	7 to 8	8 to 9	9 to 10	10 to 11	11 to 12
Hours/Miles	96	44	44	44	44	44	44	44	34	34	26	26	24

Waiting periods for these step increases apply to all hours on the Rural Carrier Evaluated Schedule, all miles on the Rural Mileage Schedule, and Grade 5 of the Rural Auxiliary Schedule.

POSTAL POLICE OFFICERS' SCHEDULE

Steps (From → To)	B to C	C to D	D to E	E to F	F to G	G to H	H to I	I to J	J to K	K to L	L to M	M to N	N to O
Grades 1–2	96	44	44	44	44	44	44	44	34	34	26	26	24

HOLIDAYS

The following holidays are observed by all USPS offices:

- New Year's Day
- Martin Luther King, Jr.'s Birthday
- Washington's Birthday
- Memorial Day
- Independence Day
- Labor Day
- Columbus Day
- Veterans' Day
- Thanksgiving Day
- Christmas Day

LEAVE TIME

In addition to the benefits listed previously, employees of the Postal Service are also granted leave time for a variety of purposes. Table 1.2 illustrates the amount of leave time you can expect, depending on the reason for leave and your years of service.

TABLE 1.2

Type of Leave	Use of This Type of Leave	Amount of Time You May Use
Annual Leave	For rest, recreation, and personal and emergency purposes *Must be approved in advance by the appropriate supervisor*	Employees earn 13, 20, or 26 days of annual leave each leave year, according to their years of service.
Sick Leave	• For medical, dental, or optical examination or treatment • If you are incapacitated by physical or mental illness, injury, or pregnancy or confinement • If the employee has a contagious disease or must care for a family member with a contagious disease • Medical leave for disabled veterans	Full-time employee: 13 days per year (employees accrue four hours for each full biweekly pay period, without limitation)

TABLE 1.2 continued

Type of Leave	Use of This Type of Leave	Amount of Time You May Use
Family and Medical Leave	According to the Family and Medical Leave Act of 1993 (FMLA), employees are entitled to 12 weeks of unpaid leave for: • the birth and care of your child • placement of a child with you for adoption or foster care • care of your spouse, child, or parent with a serious health condition • your own serious health condition *You may substitute Annual Leave for unpaid leave*	Twelve administrative work weeks during any 12-month period
Court Leave	For employees who are summoned, in connection with a judicial proceeding, to serve as a juror or to serve as a witness in a nonofficial capacity in a case involving the federal government or Postal Service	
Military Leave	For reservists or for members of the National Guard	Up to 15 days
Leave Sharing	Allows career postal employees to donate their leave to other career postal employees for a medical emergency when the recipient has exhausted his own leave	

Training and Qualifications for U.S. Postal Service Jobs

An applicant for a Postal Service job must pass an examination and meet minimum age requirements. Generally, the minimum age is 18 years, but a high school graduate may begin work at 16 years if the job is not hazardous and does not require use of a motor vehicle. Many Postal Service jobs do not require formal education or special training. Applicants for these jobs are hired on the basis of their examination scores.

Some postal jobs do have special education or experience requirements, and some are open only to veterans. Any special requirements will be stated on the announcement of examination.

Additional Qualifying Issues for USPS Positions

- Male applicants born after December 31, 1959, must be registered with the Selective Service System, unless for some reason they are exempt.
- The Immigration Reform and Control Act of 1986 applies to postal workers. All postal workers must be citizens of the United States or must be able to prove identity and right to work in the United States (permanent resident alien status—Green Card).
- Applicants should apply at the post office where they wish to work and take the entrance examination for the job they want.
- A physical examination, including drug testing, is required as well.
- Applicants for jobs that require strength and stamina are sometimes given a special test. For example, mail handlers must be able to lift mail sacks weighing up to 70 pounds. The names of applicants who pass the examinations are placed on a list in the order of their scores.
- Examinations for most jobs include a written test.
- Five extra points are added to the score of an honorably discharged veteran, and 10 extra points are added to the score of a veteran who was wounded in combat or disabled. Disabled veterans who have a compensable, service-connected disability of 10 percent or more are placed at the top of the eligibility list.

When a job opens, the appointing officer chooses one of the top three applicants. Others are left on the list so that they can be considered for future openings.

New employees are trained either on the job by supervisors and other experienced employees or in local training centers. Training ranges from a few days to several months, depending on the job. For example, mail handlers and mechanics' helpers can learn their jobs in a relatively short time. Postal inspectors, on the other hand, need months of training.

Advancement opportunities are available for most postal workers because a management commitment provides career development. Employees also can get preferred assignments, such as the day shift or a more desirable delivery route, as their seniority increases. When an opening occurs, employees may submit written requests, called "bids," for assignment to the vacancy. The bidder who meets the qualifications and who has the most seniority gets the job.

Finding More Information on USPS Positions

National job listings for the United States Postal Service can be found at the USPS Web site at www.usps.gov or can be obtained from USPS telephone job lines. These jobs include management, supervisory, administrative, professional, and technical positions, not Craft or Bargaining Unit positions, such as clerk, carrier, or processor. The telephone numbers for these job lines are listed here:

Jobs open to the public:
National vacancies: 800-JOB-USPS (800-562-8777)

Jobs open to postal employees:
National vacancies: 800-NATL-VAC (800-628-5822)

There is no centralized listing of Craft or Bargaining Unit job openings for the local offices of the U.S. Postal Service. These job vacancies are posted on the bulletin boards of local post offices and in local newspapers, and are also available from district offices. You can find the district office closest to you by calling the Local Employment Hot Line (800-276-5627).

Several local post offices are accessible from the United States Postal Service Web site, at www.usps.gov. Some post offices list job openings on the Web site. Some also have a job hotline that can be used to access vacancies in that location. Here are the telephone numbers for these job hotlines:

Salt Lake City, Utah	801-974-2209
Washington, D.C.	202-636-1537
Northern Virginia	703-698-6561
Imperial Valley/San Diego, CA	619-674-0577
Riverside/San Bernardino, CA	909-335-4339
Long Island, NY	516-582-7530

You also can visit several Internet sites for more information. While by no means exhaustive, the following list should get you started in the right direction as you learn more about what working for the USPS has to offer.

General Information
- Postal Facts (http://www.usps.gov/history/pfact98.htm). Facts and figures to help you learn more about the USPS.
- USPS Annual Reports (http://www.usps.gov/history/annual.htm)

Job Listings
- Federal Jobs Digest Online: Postal Exams (http://www.jobsfed.com/postal.htm). Job listings and information about how to apply.
- U.S. Postal Service: Human Resources (www.usps.gov/hrisp). Vacancies in management, supervisory, administrative, professional, and technical positions only.

Online Publications
- *The Mail Handler and The Mail Handler Update* (http://www.npmhu.org/Pubs/MailHanler.htm) and (http://npmhu.org/Pubs/Update.htm). Publications from the National Mail Handlers Association.
- *Postal Digest Reference Links from FedForce* (www.clubfed.com/fedforce/fedforce.html). Articles from *FedForce* that were cited in the *Postal Employees News Digest* newsletter.
- *Postal Life* (www.usps.gov/history/plife/welcome.htm). A publication about Postal Service employees.
- *Postal News from FederalTimes.com* (www.federaltimes.com/). News of interest to those in the United States Postal Service.

Unions, Associations, and Contract Information
- American Postal Workers Union (APWU) Locals (http://www.apwu.org/locals.htm)
- American Postal Workers Union (www.apwu.org)
- National Association of Letter Carriers (http://www.nalc.org/)
- National Association of Postal Supervisors (http://www.naps.org/)
- National Postal Mail Handlers Union (http://www.npmhu.org/)
- National Rural Letter Carriers Association (http://home.nrlca.org/nrlcainfo/)

Collective Bargaining Agreements
- American Postal Workers Union 1998–2000 Agreement (http://www.apwu.org/IndRel/contractpage.htm)
- National Association of Letter Carriers 1994–1998 Agreement (http://www.rollanet.org/~gary/contract.html)
- National Rural Letter Carriers Association 1995–1999 Agreement (http://www.nemisys.com/RCIGinc/95-cont.htm)

Other Information About Working for the U.S. Postal Service
- Letter Carrier Stuff (http://www.rollanet.org/~gary/index.html). Promotes the sharing of information among letter carriers.
- Post Office Locator (http://www.usps.gov/ncsc/locators/find-po.html). Find your local post office.
- Postal Workers Web Ring (http://www.webring.org/cgi-bin/webring?ring=postalring;list). Provides links to postal employees' Web sites.
- The Postal Zone (http://www.geocities.com/CapitolHill/9285). Provides links to information of interest to USPS employees.
- What Does a Letter Carrier Do? (http://home.columbus.rr.com/angelx3/postal/faq.html). Provides a day in the life account written by a city carrier.

POSTAL SERVICE JOB DESCRIPTIONS

A Variety of Positions with the USPS

Deciding on a job within the USPS is like deciding on any other job. Each position is unique and will appeal to different individuals for different reasons. Do you enjoy a specific type of work? If you don't really like being outdoors, then a courier route is probably not the right position for you. Perhaps you enjoy a position that is more routine from day to day, as compared to one that changes every minute. If that's the case, a mail sorting position might be the best fit for you.

The point is that you should try to match the job descriptions listed in this chapter with your own interests. Keep in mind, however, that all positions within the USPS are competitive, so you may need to find two or three positions that interest you, in case your position of choice doesn't happen right away.

> Remember, your goal of landing your first-choice job must be tempered with the realities of the real world. However, career advancement is encouraged within the USPS, so you can always work your way up to that great job you've been dreaming of, even if you don't get it when you first start.

Post Office Clerk

JOB DUTIES

Remember that trip to the post office when you were a kid (we're not letting you forget, are we)? You might remember thinking that the only duties of a postal clerk are to sell stamps and to take your packages.

Actually, the majority of postal clerks are distribution clerks (covered later in this chapter) who sort incoming and outgoing mail in workrooms. Only in a small post office will a postal clerk perform double duty of sitting behind the counter *and* sorting mail.

Generally speaking, a post office clerk performs the following tasks:

- Sort and distribute mail to post offices and to carrier routes
- May perform a variety of services at public windows of post offices, post office branches, or stations (again, usually only in small post offices)
- Perform related duties, as assigned

WORKING CONDITIONS

The postal clerk may have to perform manual work, depending on the size of the post office and the equipment in place (such as chutes and sorting machines) to help with this task. Generally speaking, work involves continuous standing, stretching, and reaching. Additionally, the postal clerk may be required to handle heavy sacks of letter mail or parcel post weighing up to 70 pounds.

As we mentioned at the beginning of this chapter, different jobs will appeal to different people, all for different reasons. However, you should be aware that some distribution clerks (which again can be the primary role of the postal clerk) can become bored with the routine of sorting mail. Also, postal clerks may be required to work at night (especially in large post offices, where sorting and distributing the mail is a "24/7" activity).

However, if your duties also include those of a window clerk, you will more than likely experience a wider variety of duties. You will have frequent contact with the public (which may be viewed as a benefit or drawback, depending on the type of person you are), your work will (usually) be less physically strenuous, and you won't have to work much at night. Again, each post office differs in what duties are assigned to the postal clerk.

QUALIFICATION REQUIREMENTS

Qualification requirements for the position of postal clerk closely mirror the working conditions just described. Candidates must demonstrate the following:

No experience is necessary for the position of postal clerk.

- The ability to perform the physical duties of the position, including these:
  - Prolonged standing, walking, and reaching
  - Handling of heavy sacks of mail
- Distance vision of 20/40 (Snellen) in one eye (corrective lenses permitted)
- The ability to read, without strain, printed material the size of typewritten characters (corrective lenses permitted)
- The ability to hear the conversational voice, with or without a hearing aid (for window positions)
- Emotional and mental stability
- No irremediable defect or incurable disease that prevents efficient performance of duty, or that renders them a hazard to themselves, fellow employees, or others

TESTING REQUIREMENT

The testing requirements for postal clerks are Postal Service Test 470, Configuration 1. You must attain a rating of at least 70 out of 100.

The subjects you will be tested on include these:

- Memory for addresses
- Address checking

ADDITIONAL PROVISIONS

You should also be aware of the following additional provisions for postal clerks:

- Duties of newly appointed part-time clerks and carriers are interchangeable.
- Postal clerks must maintain pleasant and effective public relations with customers and others. This requires a general familiarity with postal laws, regulations, procedures commonly used, and the geography of the area.
- Postal clerks must maintain neat and proper personal attire and grooming, including wearing a uniform when required.

Postal clerks are represented by this organization:

The American Postal Workers Union, AFL-CIO
1300 L St. NW
Washington, D.C. 20005
202-842-4200
www.apwu.org

City or Special Carrier/Special Delivery Messenger

Perhaps the most familiar of the positions within the Postal Service, the role of "mailperson" brings to mind a wealth of feelings. How many times have you anxiously waited for the postman to deliver a letter or package? Maybe it was the results of your college entrance exams, or perhaps one of the many items (and items of exceptionally high quality, of course) that you impulsively purchased from an advertisement you saw on television.

Indeed, the postman is a fixture in our culture, the bringer of good and bad news (and lots of junk mail, too!). All kidding aside, this is an exceptionally crucial job. Despite the rise in popularity of e-mail, can we really imagine a world in which there was no daily postal delivery? Postal couriers definitely are worthy of the attention they receive.

You might be surprised to learn, however, that much of the postal carrier's work is done at the post office. Often starting as early as 6 AM, carriers start their day at the post office, where they spend a few hours arranging their mail for delivery, readdressing letters to be forwarded, and taking care of other details.

JOB DUTIES

A carrier typically covers a route on foot, toting a heavy load of mail in a satchel or pushing it in a cart. In outlying areas, a carrier may drive a car or small truck. Carriers and special delivery messengers perform the following tasks:

- Promptly and efficiently deliver and collect mail on foot or by vehicle under varying conditions in a prescribed area or on various routes
- Deliver parcel post from trucks and make collections of mail from various boxes or other locations
- Maintain pleasant and effective public relations with customers

WORKING CONDITIONS

The mail is always delivered, come rain or shine—and probably fire, floods, and locusts, if the truth be told. Seriously, there must be an extreme weather situation for the mail to be postponed for an entire day (it may be late, of course, but that's a big difference from not going out at all).

With that thought in mind, carriers must be able to carry out the following tasks:

- Drive motor vehicles in all kinds of traffic and road conditions (obviously, you'll need a driver's license)
- Carry mail in shoulder satchels weighing as much as 35 pounds
- Load and unload sacks of mail weighing up to 70 pounds
- Serve in all kinds of weather

Despite these tough requirements, the job does have some key advantages. Carriers who begin work early in the morning are through by early afternoon. They are also free to work at their own pace as long as they cover their routes within a certain period of time.

QUALIFICATION REQUIREMENTS

As with many positions with the USPS, carriers must be in such physical condition as to allow them to do potentially strenuous and physically taxing work. Upon physical examination, you must be able to demonstrate the following:

- The ability to undergo prolonged standing, walking, and reaching
- The ability to handle heavy sacks of mail
- Distance vision of 20/40 (Snellen) in one eye (corrective lenses permitted)
- The ability to read, without strain, printed material the size of typewritten characters (corrective lenses permitted)
- Emotional and mental stability
- No irremediable defect or incurable disease that prevents efficient performance of duty or that renders you a hazard to yourself, fellow employees, or others

- If driving a vehicle weighing less than 10,000 pounds (GVW), vision of 20/40 in one eye and the ability to read, without strain, printed material the size of typewritten characters (corrective lenses permitted). The ability to hear is not required to operate a vehicle weighing less than 10,000 pounds (GVW).

> No experience is necessary for the position of city or special carrier.

TESTING REQUIREMENT

The testing requirements for postal clerks are Postal Service Test 470, Configuration 1. You must attain a rating of at least 70 out of 100.

The subjects you will be tested on include these:

- Memory for addresses
- Address checking

ADDITIONAL PROVISIONS

In addition to the information listed previously, you will also be required to adhere to the following requirements, if you wish to be a carrier for the USPS:

- Duties of newly appointed part-time clerks and carriers are interchangeable.
- Carriers must maintain pleasant and effective public relations with customers and others. This requires a general familiarity with postal laws, regulations, procedures commonly used, and the geography of the area.
- Carriers must maintain neat and proper personal attire and grooming, including wearing a uniform when required.
- For positions requiring driving, applicants must have a valid state driver's license and demonstrate and maintain a safe driving record. Applicants must pass the Postal Service road test to show the ability to safely drive a vehicle of the type used on the job.

> City Carriers are represented by this organization:
>
> National Association of Letter Carriers, AFL-CIO
> 100 Indiana Ave. NW
> Washington, D.C. 20001-2144
> 202-393-4695
> www.nalc.org

Distribution Clerk, Machine

JOB DUTIES

The work of the distribution clerk is more routine than that of other postal clerks, but the starting salary is higher. However, you should realize that as a distribution clerk, you may be on your feet all day. Additionally, you must be able to ooccasionally handle sacks of mail weighing as much as 70 pounds.

Perhaps the most challenging aspect of the job (and an aspect that will either greatly appeal to you or greatly discourage you, depending on your personality type) is the way in which you must sort mail. You must memorize a complicated scheme, which will enable you to quickly and efficiently sort mail. For example, these schemes include being able to quickly read a ZIP Code and then determine how the piece of mail is to be directed.

> Increasing automation within the Postal Service has made the job of the distribution clerk quite secure. Although there are never any 100 percent guarantees, this is a fact you might consider when investigating USPS positions (along with your own personal interests, of course).

QUALIFICATION REQUIREMENTS

The distribution clerk, machine, applicant must possess sufficient levels of the following knowledge, skills, and abilities (KSAs):

- Knowledge of multi-position letter sorting machine
- Ability to perform the following:
  - Work without immediate supervision
  - Work in cooperation with follow employees to efficiently perform the duties of the position
  - Observe and act on visual information such as names, addresses, numbers, and shapes
  - Learn and recall pairings of addresses with numbers, letters, or positions
  - Sequence, or place mail in the proper numerical, alphabetical, or geographic order
- Physical ability to efficiently perform the duties of the position
- Vision of 20/40 (Snellen) in one eye, near acuity of 7 or higher in either eye (Titmus or Bausch and Lomb), and the ability to read, without strain, printed material the size of typewritten characters (corrective lenses permitted)
- Ability to distinguish basic colors and shades

TESTING REQUIREMENT

To apply for this poistion, you must

- Take Postal Service Test 470, Configuration 1 as a requirement for the trainee position.
- Successfully complete dexterity training, as required by management.

Distribution Clerks are represented by this organization:

The American Postal Workers Union, AFL-CIO
1300 L St. NW
Washington, D.C. 20005
202-842-4200
www.apwu.org

Flat Sorting Machine Operator

JOB DUTIES

A flat sorting machine operator's work is very similar to that of the distribution clerk. However, as a flat sorting machine operator, you will work with large, bulky packages.

You might guess that, with this requirment, you will have to possess greater physical strength and stamina. As with the machine operator's position, increasing automation adds a good degree of security to this position, which is a definite plus that might offset the physically taxing requirements.

QUALIFICATION REQUIREMENTS

To qualify for this position, you must possess sufficient levels of the following KSAs:

- Ability to work without immediate supervision
- Ability to work in cooperation with fellow employees to efficiently perform the duties of the position
- Ability to observe and act on visual information such as names, addresses, numbers, and shapes
- Ability to learn and recall pairings of addresses with numbers, letters, or positions
- Ability to sequence, or place mail in the proper numerical, alphabetical, or geographic order
- Ability to perform routine troubleshooting, such as removing jams
- Ability to to efficiently perform the physical duties of the position
- Vision of 20/40 (Snellen) in one eye, near acuity of 7 or higher in either eye (Titmus or Bausch and Lomb), and the ability to read, without strain, printed material the size of typewritten characters (corrective lenses permitted)
- Ability to distinguish basic colors and shades

TESTING REQUIREMENT

The testing requirements for this position require that you

- Take the Postal Service Test 470, Configuration 1 as a requirement for the trainee position.
- Successfully complete the appropriate training program for the flat sorting machine operation.
- Demonstrate the ability to key at 45 items per minute with 98 percent accuracy.

Flat Sorting Machine Operators are represented by this organization:

The American Postal Workers Union, AFL-CIO
1300 L St. NW
Washington, D.C. 20005
202-842-4200
www.apwu.org

Mail Handler

JOB DUTIES

As a mail handler, you will unload loads, move bulk mail, and perform other duties incidental to the movement and processing of mail.

QUALIFICATION REQUIREMENTS

To qualify for the position of mail handler, you must demonstrate the following:

- Sufficient levels of KSAs, which include at least minimum competency for senior-qualified positions
- Ability to perform these KSAs by describing examples of experience, education, or training, any of which may be non-postal
- Physical ability to perform efficiently the duties of the position

Because of the extreme physical nature of this job, certain physical conditions can preclude you from taking the strength and stamina test without prior approval from your doctor (which is a requirement for this position). These conditions include hernia or rupture, back trouble, heart trouble, pregnancy, or any other condition that makes it dangerous for you to lift and carry 70-pound weights.

- Vision of 20/40 (Snellen) in one eye and the ability to read, without strain, printed material the size of typewritten characters (corrective lenses are permitted)
- Ability to hear the conversational voice in at least one ear (hearing aid permitted)

TESTING REQUIREMENT

Testing requirements for the position of mail handler demand that you must

- Successfully complete the Postal Service Test 470, Configuration 2, which measures an applicant's ability to understand simple word meanings, check names and numbers, and follow oral directions.
- Pass a test of physical abilities prior to appointment.

If you fail to qualify on the strength and stamina test, you won't be tested again in the same group of hires. If you fail this test a second time, your eligibility for the position is canceled.

Mail Handlers are represented by this organization:

National Postal Mail Handlers Union, AFL-CIO
1101 Connecticut Ave. NW, Suite 500
Washington, D.C. 20036
202-833-9095
www.npmhu.org

Mail Processor

JOB DUTIES

Mail processors perform a combination of tasks that are required to process the mail by utilizing a variety of mail processing equipment.

WORKING CONDITIONS

You won't find the physical requirements for this position as tough as those required for mail handlers (but you also won't start at the same salary as that of a mail handler).

QUALIFICATION REQUIREMENTS

To qualify for the position of mail processor, you must demonstrate the following:

- Ability to perform efficiently the physical duties of the position
- Vision of 20/40 (Snellen) in one eye and the ability to read, without strain, printed material the size of typewritten characters (corrective lenses permitted)
- Ability to distinguish basic colors and shades

TESTING REQUIREMENT

You must successfully complete Postal Service Test 470, Configuration 2, which tests your ability to understand simple word meanings, check names and numbers, and follow oral directions.

Mail Processors are represented by this organization:

The American Postal Workers Union, AFL-CIO
1300 L St. NW
Washington, D.C. 20005
202-842-4200
www.apwu.org

Mark-up Clerk—Automated

JOB DUTIES

A mark-up clerk, automated, operates an electro-mechanical operator-paced machine to process mail that is undeliverable as addressed. In doing this, the clerk operates the keyboard of a computer terminal to enter and extract data to several databases. Although you don't have to be a computer programmer to qualify for this position, you should feel comfortable working with computers, as you will need to work in several potentially different programs to enter, view, and change data.

QUALIFICATION REQUIREMENTS

To qualify for this position, you must demonstrate the following:

- A sufficient level of the following KSAs:
  - Ability to use reference materials and manuals relevant to the position
  - Ability to perform effectively under the pressures of the position
  - Ability to operate any office equipment appropriate to the position
  - Ability to work with others
- Six months of clerical or office machine operating experience

The ability to type will prove invaluable for your role as a mark-up clerk, automated.

- Successful completion of a four-year high school course; successful completion of business school may be substituted for the six months of clerical or office machine operating requirements
- Able to perform efficiently the physical duties of the position
- Vision of 20/40 (Snellen) in one eye and the ability to read, without strain, printed material the size of typewritten characters (corrective lenses permitted)
- Ability to distinguish basic colors and shades

TESTING REQUIREMENT

Given the clerically oriented requirements of this position, you'll need to demonstrate the ability to key data codes on a computer terminal at a rate of 14 correct lines per minute. This is determined by successful completion of Postal Service Test 715. You'll also need to successfully complete Postal Service Test 470, Configuration 2.

Mark-up Clerks are represented by this organization:

The American Postal Workers Union, AFL-CIO
1300 L St. NW
Washington, D.C. 20005
202-842-4200
www.apwu.org

Rural Carrier
JOB DUTIES

The work of the rural carrier combines the work of the window clerk and the letter carrier. However, the job also has special characteristics of its own.

A rural carrier begins the day with sorting and loading the mail for delivery. Then comes the drive, which may be over tough roads and through tough weather. Given the rural nature of the job, the rural carrier delivers most of the mail from the car. At the end of the day, the carrier returns to the post office with outgoing mail and money collected in various transactions.

As you might guess, you'll enjoy a great deal of independence with this position, as there is no one looking over your shoulder. However, the work can be taxing, and you will have to endure the inherent dilemmas that come with spending lots of time in the car.

Because many of the rural carrier's patrons live in remote locations (hence the word *rural* in the job title), this employee will occasionally also be required to perform all the duties of a window clerk, including accepting, collecting, and delivering all classes of mail and selling stamp supplies and money orders.

WORKING CONDITIONS

In general, you should expect the following working conditions:

- You must load and deliver parcels weighing up to 70 pounds.
- You must place letters and parcels in mailboxes, requiring careful handling of the vehicle and frequent shifting from one side of the vehicle to the other.
- Working with the public requires maintaining pleasant and effective working relations with customers and an acceptable appearance.

QUALIFICATION REQUIREMENTS

Requirements for this position include that you demonstrate the following abilities:

- Ability to read, understand, and apply written instructions
- Ability to perform basic arithmetic computations
- Ability to prepare reports and maintain records
- Ability to communicate effectively with customers
- Ability to work effectively without close supervision
- Ability to perform efficiently the arduous physical duties of the position
- Vision of 20/40 (Snellen) in one eye and the ability to read, without strain, printed material the size of typewritten characters (corrective lenses permitted)

> The ability to hear is not required for this position.

TESTING REQUIREMENT

You must successfully complete Postal Service Test 460 to qualify for a rural carrier position.

ADDITIONAL PROVISIONS

In addition to the requirements listed, you must have a valid state driver's license and a safe driving record, and must pass the Postal Service road test, which shows the ability to safely drive the type of vehicle used on the job.

Additionally, rural carriers furnish all necessary vehicle equipment for prompt handling of the mail, unless supplied by the employer (you will be paid for equipment maintenance).

> Rural carriers are represented by this organization:
>
> National Rural Letter Carriers Association
> Fourth Floor
> 1630 Duke St.
> Alexandria, VA 22314-3465
> 703-684-5545
> www.nrlca.org

Clerk-Typist, Clerk-Stenographer, Typist

JOB DUTIES

A clerk-typist types records, letters, memorandums, reports, and other materials from handwritten and other drafts, or from a dictating machine. He or she sets up the material typed in accordance with prescribed format and assembles it for initialing, signing, routing, and dispatch. The clerk-typist also cuts mimeograph stencils and masters for duplication by other processes.

The miscellaneous office clerical duties of the position include: making file folders, keeping them in the prescribed order, and filing in them; making and keeping routine office records; composing routine memorandums and letters relating to the business of the office, such as acknowledgments and transmittals; examining incoming and outgoing mail of the office, routing it to the appropriate persons, and controlling the time allowed for preparation of replies to incoming correspondence; receipting and delivering salary checks and filling out various personnel forms; acting as receptionist and furnishing routine information over the telephone; relieving other office personnel in their absence; and operating office machines such as the mimeograph, comptometer, and adding machine.

The clerk-stenographer performs all the functions of the clerk-typist. Also, the clerk-stenographer takes dictation, in shorthand or on a shorthand writing machine, of letters, memorandums, reports, and other materials given by the supervisor of the office and other employees. He or she then transcribes it on the typewriter or word processor, sets up the material transcribed in accordance with prescribed format, and assembles it for required initialing, signing, routing, and dispatch. In consideration of the extra training and skill required in the taking of dictation, the clerk-stenographer is rated at salary level 5 rather than at the salary level 4 of the clerk-typist.

QUALIFICATION REQUIREMENTS

Requirements for these positions include demonstrating the following abilities:

- Ability to perform basic mathematical computations
- Ability to follow instructions, both written and verbal
- Ability to keep records, such as files, charts, and indexes, in an organized fashion for proper retrieval
- Ability to prepare reports and correspondence in acceptable form
- Ability to operate office machines safely and make any necessary adjustments to these machines
- Ability to perform efficiently the physical duties of the position
- Vision of 20/40 (Snellen) in one eye and the ability to read, without strain, printed material the size of typewritten characters (corrective lenses permitted)
- Ability to hear the conversational voice (hearing aid permitted)

TESTING REQUIREMENT

To qualify for these positions, you'll need to successfully complete Postal Service Test 710, Parts A and B, which demonstrates your clerical and verbal abilities. Additionally, you will need to successfully complete Postal Service Test 712, which demonstrates your ability to type at a net rate of 45 words per minute in a five-minute test.

Successful completion of Postal Service Test 711 is required for clerk-stenographer postions. This test demonstrates the applicant's ability to take dictation at the rate of 80 words per minute and interpret this dictation.

Clerical staff is represented by this organization:

The American Postal Workers Union, AFL-CIO
1300 L St. NW
Washington, D.C. 20005
202-842-4200
www.apwu.org

Data Conversion Operator

JOB DUTIES

Data conversion operators use a computer terminal to prepare mail for automated sorting equipment. They read typed or handwritten addresses from a letter image on the terminal screen and then select and type essential information so that an address bar code can be applied to the letter. Depending on the quality of the address information shown on the image, data conversion operators are prompted to key the five-number ZIP Code or an abbreviated version of the street and city address. Abbreviated addresses must conform to strict encoding rules so that the computer can then expand the abbreviation to a full address and find the correct ZIP + 4 code. Unlike some other types of data entry, this job is not just "key what you see."

Remote Bar Coding System

Data conversion operators are the vital personnel in the Remote Bar Coding System (RBCS), a system designed to allow letter mail that cannot be read by a machine to be bar-coded and processed in the automated mail stream. RBCS technology has created a new operation called a remote encoding center (REC). RBCS has two major elements: an input subsystem (ISS) and an output subsystem (OSS).

At the processing plant, ISS takes a video picture or image of each letter and then attempts to look up the address to find a ZIP + 4 code. For letters for which the ISS computer cannot find a ZIP + 4 code, corresponding images are transmitted by telephone lines to data conversion operators at the remote encoding center for further processing. At the REC, data conversion operators working at video display terminals are presented with images one at a time. Using specific rules, operators key data for each image so that the computers can find the correct ZIP + 4 code.

At the plant, the output subsystem sprays letters with correct ZIP + 4 bar codes and performs initial sorting. Letters are then processed by bar code sorters. These elements are linked by a communication system consisting of cabling and telephone or microwave telecommunications.

QUALIFICATION REQUIREMENTS

Requirements for the position of data conversion operator include demonstrating the following abilities:

- Ability to perform efficiently the physical duties of the position
- Vision of 20/40 (Snellen) in one eye and the ability to read, without strain, printed material the size of typewritten characters (corrective lenses permitted)
- Ability to distinguish basic colors and shades
- Ability to hear the conversational voice (hearing aid permitted)

Remote encoding centers offer a possibility for flexible scheduling. The basic work hours are between 3:00 PM and 1:00 AM. Individual work schedules range between four and eight hours. RECs operate seven days a week.

TESTING REQUIREMENT

This position has specific testing requirements, including these:

- Successful completion of Postal Service Test 710, which demonstrates the applicant's clerical and verbal abilities
- Successful completion of Postal Service Test 714 at the high standard. This demonstrates the applicant's ability to key data on a computer terminal at a rate of 35 correct lines within five minutes.

Data Conversion Operators are represented by this organization:

The American Postal Workers Union, AFL-CIO
1300 L St. NW
Washington, D.C. 20005
202-842-4200
www.apwu.org

Cleaner; Custodian; Laborer, Custodial

JOB DUTIES

Workers who serve as cleaners, custodians, or custodial laborers are charged with the maintenance of postal buildings. These positions include routine and periodic heavy cleaning, routine maintenance (such as replacing light bulbs), and responsibility for noticing when specialized maintenance or repair work is called for and then following through to be certain that this is done at the proper time.

While the work of custodial laborers, cleaners, and custodians is not generally noticed by the public, their work is vital to the operation of post offices and to the health and safety of postal workers and patrons.

Non-U.S. Veterans Need Not Apply

The positions of cleaner, custodian, and custodial laborer are open only to veterans of the United States Armed Services. Applications from nonveterans will be rejected. While these positions are at the low end of the postal pay scale, they afford the veteran an opportunity to earn a steady wage and to enjoy all the fringe benefits and security of all other postal employees.

The person who starts a career with the Postal Service as a cleaner, custodian, or custodial laborer can advance to positions of greater responsibility within the custodial service or can prepare for examinations for other positions, either more specialized jobs within building maintenance or completely different jobs such as mail handler, letter clerk, and others.

People who already work for the Postal Service in any capacity need not wait for an exam that is open to the public to be announced. After being employed at their present position for a year, they may ask to take an exam at any time. Although this request may or may not be granted, this is one special advantage of postal employees that makes the veterans-only feature of this position so valuable. A veteran who wants a postal career can break in at the bottom and rise rapidly.

QUALIFICATION REQUIREMENTS

Individuals who serve in these positions must demonstrate the following abilities:

- The ability to use hand tools, such as power cleaning equipment (waxers, polishers, mowers, and similar equipment) (for laborer, custodian)
- Ability to work without immediate supervision
- Ability to handle weights and loads beyond normal functions of a position (for custodian and laborer, custodian)
- Ability to perform efficiently the physical duties of the position, including standing, walking, climbing, bending, reaching, and stooping for prolonged periods of time
- Vision of 20/40 (Snellen) in one eye and the ability to read, without strain, printed material the size of typewritten characters (corrective lenses permitted)

Cleaners and custodial employees are represented by this organization:

The American Postal Workers Union, AFL-CIO
1300 L St. NW
Washington, D.C. 20005
202-842-4200
www.apwu.org

Motor Vehicle Operator, Tractor Trailer Operator

JOB DUTIES

What's the thing these jobs have in common? The answer is driving various Postal Service vehicles on the highway and within the lots and properties of the Postal Service.

Motor vehicle operators operate a mail truck on a regularly scheduled route to pick up and transport mail in bulk.

Tractor-trailer operators operate a heavy-duty tractor-trailer in over-the-road service, city shuttle service, or trailer spotting operations.

QUALIFICATION REQUIREMENTS

Given the specific technical training inherent to these positions (knowing how to handle a large vehicle), you'll need to have one year or more of full-time, or equivalent, employment driving 7-ton trucks or buses of at least 16 passengers. At least six months must be in driving a tractor-trailer (for the position of tractor-trailer operator).

Additionally, you'll need to demonstrate the following abilities:

- Safety in performance of duties common to the position
- Ability to drive under local driving conditions
- Ability to follow instructions and to prepare trip and other reports
- Ability to perform efficiently the duties of the position
- Vision that tests at least 30/30 (Snellen) in one eye and 20/50 (Snellen) in the other eye, with or without corrective lenses; the ability to read, without strain, printed material the size of typewritten characters (corrective lenses permitted) (for applicants required to drive vehicles 10,000 pounds [CVW] or more)
- Ability to hear the conversational voice in one ear (hearing aids permitted)
- Emotional and mental stability
- No physical condition that would cause the applicant to be a hazard to himself or others

In most instances, an amputation of the leg or foot will not disqualify an applicant, although it may be necessary that this condition be compensated for by use of a suitable prosthesis.

TESTING REQUIREMENT

These positions are filled by rated application:

- Successful completion of Postal Service Test 91, which demonstrates an applicant's ability to understand instructions and fill out forms
- Successful completion of the Postal Service road test to show an applicant's ability to safely drive a vehicle of the type used on the job

ADDITIONAL PROVISIONS

In addition, applicants must meet a few other requirements:

- Must have a valid state driver's license
- Must demonstrate and maintain a safe driving record

Motor vehicle employees are represented by this organization:

The American Postal Workers Union, AFL-CIO
1300 L St. NW
Washington, D.C. 20005
202-842-4200
www.apwu.org

Garageman

JOB DUTIES

The position of garageman requires routine services to properly maintain motor vehicles. Obviously, this position requires an applicant to be comfortable with—and most importantly, enjoy—working on motor vehicles.

QUALIFICATION REQUIREMENTS

To qualify for this position, you must demonstrate the following abilities:

- Ability to assemble and disassemble mechanical equipment
- Ability to work without immediate supervision
- Ability to work with others
- Vision of 20/40 (Snellen) in one eye and the ability to read, without strain, printed material the size of typewritten characters (corrective lenses are permitted)
- Ability to distinguish basic colors and shades

The ability to hear the conversational voice is required (hearing aids permitted).

TESTING REQUIREMENT

This position is filled by rated application:

- Successful completion of Postal Service Test 91, which demonstrates an applicant's ability to understand instructions and fill out forms
- Successful completion of the Postal Service road test, which shows an applicant's ability to safely drive a vehicle of the type used on the job

ADDITIONAL PROVISIONS

In addition, applicants must meet a few other requirements:

- Must have a valid state driver's license
- Must demonstrate and maintain a safe driving record

Garagemen are represented by this organization:

The American Postal Workers Union, AFL-CIO
1300 L St. NW
Washington, D.C. 20005
202-842-4200
www.apwu.org

Building Equipment Mechanic
JOB DUTIES

Building equipment mechanics perform a variety of tasks (some highly specialized), including these:

- Troubleshooting and performing complex maintenance work on building and building equipment systems
- Performing preventive maintenance inspections of building, building equipment, and building systems
- Maintaining and operating a large automated air conditioning system and a large heating system

QUALIFICATION REQUIREMENTS

Given the nature of the job, you will be required to have at least a basic understanding of several maintenance-related topics, including these:

- Basic mechanics
- Basic electricity
- Basic electronics
- Safety procedures and equipment
- Lubrication materials and procedures
- Cleaning materials and procedures
- National Electrical Code (NEC)
- Refrigeration
- Heating, ventilation, and air conditioning (HVAC)
- Plumbing

Additionally, you'll need to demonstrate the following abilities:

- Ability to perform basic and more complex mathematics
- Ability to apply theoretical knowledge to practical applications
- Ability to detect patterns
- Ability to use written reference materials
- Ability to communicate in writing and orally
- Ability to follow instructions
- Ability to work under pressure
- Ability to work with others
- Ability to work without immediate supervision
- Ability to work from heights
- Ability to use hand tools
- Ability to use portable power tools
- Ability to use shop power equipment
- Ability to use technical drawings
- Ability to use test equipment
- Ability to solder
- Vision of 20/40 (Snellen) in one eye and the ability to read, without strain, printed material the size of typewritten characters (corrective lenses permitted)
- Ability to distinguish basic colors and shades
- Ability to hear the conversational voice in a noisy environment and to identify environmental sounds, such as equipment running or unusual noises (hearing aids permitted)

TESTING REQUIREMENT

Applicants must complete the appropriate written exam.

ADDITIONAL PROVISIONS

Again, given the unique nature of this position, you will need to meet the following additional provisions:

- Complete a prescribed training course (for some positions)
- Be able to operate powered industrial equipment
- Produce a valid state driver's license, and demonstrate and maintain a safe driving record (for driving positions)
- Pass the Postal Service road test to show the ability to safely drive a vehicle of the type used on the job (for driving positions)
- Consent to driving motor vehicles in all kinds of traffic and road conditions

---

Maintenance employees are represented by this organization:

The American Postal Workers Union, AFL-CIO
1300 L St. NW
Washington, D.C. 20005
202-842-4200
www.apwu.org

Electronic Technician

JOB DUTIES

Similar to the maintenance position mentioned previously, the electrical technician may be called upon to possess a specific knowledge base. An electrical technician must independently perform the full range of diagnostic preventive maintenance, alignment, and calibrations, as well as overhaul tasks on both hardware and software on a variety of equipment and systems. These technicians also apply advanced technical knowledge to solve complex problems.

QUALIFICATION REQUIREMENTS

To qualify for this position, you will need to demonstrate the following abilities:

- Familiarity with basic mechanics
- Familiarity with basic electricity
- Familiarity with basic electronics and digital electronics
- Familiarity with safety procedures and equipment
- Familiarity with basic computer concepts
- Ability to perform basic and more complex mathematics
- Ability to apply theoretical knowledge to practical applications
- Ability to detect patterns
- Ability to use written reference materials
- Ability to communicate in writing and orally
- Ability to follow instructions

- Ability to work under pressure
- Ability to work with others
- Ability to work without immediate supervision
- Ability to work from heights
- Ability to use hand tools
- Ability to use portable power tools
- Ability to use technical drawings
- Ability to use test equipment
- Ability to solder
- Vision of 20/40 (Snellen) in one eye and the ability to read, without strain, printed material the size of typewritten characters (corrective lenses permitted)
- Ability to distinguish basic colors and shades
- Ability to hear the conversational voice in a noisy environment and to identify environmental sounds, such as equipment running or unusual noises (hearing aids permitted)

TESTING REQUIREMENT

Applicants must complete the appropriate written exam.

ADDITIONAL PROVISIONS

If you qualify for this position, you may be required to complete a prescribed training course. Additionally, you must be able to operate powered industrial equipment.

For positions requiring driving, you must produce a valid state driver's license and demonstrate and maintain a safe driving record. You also must pass the Postal Service road test to show your ability to safely drive a vehicle of the type used on the job.

Finally, you may be required to drive motor vehicles in all kinds of traffic and road conditions.

Electronic Technicians are represented by this organization:

The American Postal Workers Union, AFL-CIO
1300 L St. NW
Washington, D.C. 20005
202-842-4200
www.apwu.org

Feeling anxious before you take a test is a normal reaction. You've spent many hours studying and preparing for the exam, and you want to get the best score possible. In addition, you probably think (and rightly so) that this test may be just a bit more important than some of those spelling tests you took back in elementary school. This is your career, and you want to prove to yourself and others that you're capable of achieving the highest performance.

Well, you can relax! Although the postal exams are a bit unusual (as compared to other tests), there really is no reason for you to be overly nervous. If you've put in the time studying for the exam, if you use common sense, and if you don't panic, you'll be well on your way to achieving a good score.

This chapter is designed to help alleviate even more of your pre-test anxiety by introducing you to the format of the tests. Then, as you study the rest of this book, you'll have plenty of opportunity to practice the various question types. By test day, you still might be a bit nervous, but you shouldn't encounter any surprises.

This chapter provides you with an introduction to Postal Exams 460 and 470. But you may be asking yourself, "Hey, wait a minute! The last chapters of this book describe five different tests. What about those?"

Although you may encounter different question types if you take an exam other than the 460 or 470 (although nearly all postal employees are required to take the 460/470), the vast majority of questions will be very similar to the ones you encounter—and practice—in this book. So although we may be describing only 460/470 questions, you can be assured that if you master this information, you will be very well prepared, no matter what additional test you may be required to take.

Get to Know the Test

The four-part U.S. Postal Examination is structured as follows:

Question Type	Part Number	Number of Questions	Time Allowed
Address Checking	A	95	6 minutes
Memory for Addresses	B	88	5 minutes*
Number Series	C	24	20 minutes
Following Oral Instructions	D	20–25 (will vary)	25 minutes (approximately)

Does not include the time allowed for memorizing addresses

Test 470 is used by the Postal Service to evaluate job-related skills. However, it is not a true aptitude test of your abilities. Don't fall into the trap of thinking that you must possess certain innate talents to get a high score. On the contrary, preparing for this test will definitely increase your chances for doing well on it. The four question types are extremely coachable and get easier with practice. Use your desire for getting hired as a key motivator throughout the test preparation process.

The remaining chapters of this book, as well as the full-length sample exams, will help you practice the various question types.

Rules and Procedures

You must not underestimate the importance of following all the rules and procedures required at the test center. This includes following all the examiner's test-taking instructions and filling in the answer sheets correctly.

TEST-TAKING INSTRUCTIONS

Instructions read by the examiner are intended to ensure that you and all the other applicants have the same fair and objective opportunity to compete in the examination. All of you are expected to play on a level playing field. Any infraction of the rules is considered cheating. If you cheat, your test paper will not be scored and you will not be eligible for appointment.

- Listen to what the examiner says at all times. Be prepared to immediately act on any exam changes to content, question type, directions, or time limits.
- Follow all instructions the examiner gives you. If you do not understand any of the examiner's instructions, ask questions.
- Don't begin working on any part of the test until told to do so.
- Stop working as soon as the examiner tells you to do so. Remember that your ability to follow instructions is considered in the hiring process.
- If you finish a test part before time is called, review your work for that test part. Although you cannot go on or back to any other part of the test, you have the chance to review answers that you are unsure of or to guess, if guessing is a good strategy for that test part. Use whatever extra time you have wisely.
- Don't work on any other part of the test than the one you are told to work on. Be certain to check that you're working on the right test part immediately. While working in the wrong section could be an inadvertent error on your part, it would not leave a favorable impression and probably could put you out of the running.

FILLING IN ANSWER SHEETS

You will be required to fill in required personal information on the sample answer sheet sent to you by the Postal Service to be admitted to the test center. You cannot take the test without doing this. At the center of the answer sheet, you will be instructed to transfer the personal information you filled in on the sample answer sheet to the actual answer sheet.

HOW TO ENTER YOUR ANSWERS

Test 470 is machine-scored, so you must be careful to fill in your answer sheets clearly and accurately. You will be given instructions in the test kit sent to you by the Postal Service. You also will be given ample opportunity to perfect your skills in the practice material in this book.

You cannot afford to lose precious exam time erasing and re-entering incorrectly entered answers. Therefore, as you answer each question for Parts A–C, look at its number and check that you are marking your answer in the space with the same number. If you cannot do this after each question, then remember to check yourself after every five questions. Either way, plan a strategy and stick to it.

Score Determination and Reporting

When the exam is over, the examiner will collect your test booklet and answer sheet. Your answer sheet will be sent to the National Test Administration Center in Merrifield, Virginia, where a machine will scan your answers and mark them as either right or wrong. Then your raw score will be calculated according to the steps described in the section "Determining Your Raw Score," later in this chapter.

REPORTING OF SCALED SCORES

Your raw score is not your final score:

1. The Postal Service determines your raw scores for each test part.
2. Your part scores are combined according to a certain formula.
3. Your raw score is converted to a scaled score, on a scale of 1 to 100.

The entire process of conversion from raw to scaled score is confidential.

A total scaled score of 70 is a passing score. The names of all persons with 70 or more are placed on an eligibility list (called the register) that remains valid for two years. The register is ordered according to score rankings—the highest scores are at the top of the list. Hiring then takes place from the top of the list as vacancies occur.

Although a total scaled score of 70 is considered passing, it will probably not get you hired. Many candidates prepare rigorously for this test and strive for perfect scores. In fact, most applicants who are hired score between 90 percent and 100 percent.

LEARNING HOW YOU DID

The scoring process may take 6–10 weeks, or even longer. Be patient. The process could take many months, but you remain eligible for employment for two years after taking the test. If you pass the exam, you will receive notice of your scaled score. As the hiring process nears your number, you will be notified to appear for the remaining steps of the hiring process:

1. Drug testing
2. Psychological interview
3. Physical performance tests, according to the requirements of the position
4. Alphanumeric typing test

If you fail the exam, you will not be informed of your score. You will simply be notified that you have failed and will not be considered for postal employment.

> You should know that as many as 50 percent of applicants fail Test 470. Of course, this number will vary per exam administration. Use this number as a reality check for setting a serious study schedule. And while this is a high failure rate, don't let it shake your confidence. Your preparation will give you better odds of getting a higher score than many of the candidates.

General Test-Taking Strategies
KNOW DIRECTIONS FOR EACH QUESTION TYPE

Don't waste time during the test reading directions. You will be given the instructions by the Postal Service in your exam kit; know them inside and out. This book also gives you the most recent directions used on Test 470. Remember, though, to listen to the examiner for an announcement that something has changed.

SKIP QUESTIONS WHEN STUMPED

When you cannot answer a question for Parts A–C, skip the question and come back to it after finishing the other questions in that part of the test. Circle the number of the question in your test booklet to indicate the question skipped, and remember to skip the appropriate space on your answer sheet. A later section discusses whether you should guess.

AVOID PERFECTIONISM

You are not expected to answer every question in Parts A and B. Don't be a perfectionist and waste time on questions you cannot answer. This kind of attitude can restrict the number of questions you attempt to answer, which will lower your score. Come back to the difficult questions if you have extra time to spare.

> Use the practice tests in this book to get used to the quick pace of the test and the stringent time limitations for each test part. Adhere to these time limitations without exception. Use a stopwatch or a kitchen timer for accurate measurement; this will give you a sense of your optimal pace to apply on the actual test. Not doing this will handicap your chances for a higher score.

KNOW HOW MUCH TIME YOU HAVE

To do well on Test 470, you must work quickly within the time limits allowed. The examiner will probably inform you at periodic intervals of how much time you have left. Check your wristwatch as a backup, but don't become obsessed by watching the clock. Your time is better spent answering the questions.

Keeping track of time does not imply that you should rush through a section and answer questions carelessly. You must be in control of the situation to do your best. This means practicing for the test as much as possible, knowing what to expect, and following the strategies provided in this book.

BUILD A TEST-SMART ATTITUDE

By practicing as much as possible for Test 470, you will gain confidence in yourself, which in turn will help you succeed on the actual test. Having a test-smart attitude also will help build your competitive spirit, an essential factor in doing well on this highly competitive examination.

USE THE TEST BOOKLET AS SCRATCH PAPER

You may find it beneficial to make notes or draw lines or arrows in the test booklet to help solve certain test questions. This may focus your thoughts and channel your energy to help solve the question. However, you don't want to spend too much time doing this. If it doesn't help you, just go on to the next question.

ELIMINATE OBVIOUSLY INCORRECT ANSWERS

This common test-taking strategy can be used to different degrees on each test part except Part A, which has only two answer choices. To use this strategy, you must usually read all the answer choices listed to eliminate incorrect answers before choosing the correct answer. This prevents you from picking a red herring (a deliberately misleading answer choice) as the answer.

SCORE HIGHER: ADDRESS-CHECKING STRATEGIES

Address-Checking Strategies

Of all the questions on Test 470, the address-checking questions are probably the easiest. However, you should realize that these questions also carry the highest penalties for guessing. So, you should treat this question type as you would any other question—with the highest degree of speed and accuracy you can muster.

Take a look at the following address-checking quiz, and don't worry about timing yourself. In fact, go through this quiz at your own pace, taking time to become familiar with the question type. When you're done, check your answers against the answer key that follows.

> When you are finished with the quiz, take time to review the questions you missed. If you can spot your errors, you will learn to avoid them in the future.

Practice Quiz

Directions: *For each question, compare the address in the left column with the address in the right column. If the two addresses are ALIKE in every way, write "A" next to the question number. If the two addresses are DIFFERENT in any way, write "D" next to the question number.*

1.	197 Apple Ridge Dr Nw	197 Apple Ridge Dr NW
2.	243 S Calumet Ave	234 S Calumet Ave
3.	4300 Las Pillas Rd	4300 Las Pillas Rd
4.	5551 N Summit Ave	5551 N Summit St
5.	Walden CO 80480	Waldon CO 80480
6.	2200 E Beach St	2200 E Beech St
7.	2700 Helena Way	2700 Helena Way
8.	3968 S Kingsberry Ave	3698 S Kingsbury Ave
9.	14011 Costilla Ave NE	14011 Costilla Ane SE
10.	1899 N Dearborn Dr	1899 N Dearborn Dr
11.	8911 Scranton Way	8911 Scranton Way
12.	3653 Hummingbird St	3563 Hummingbird St
13.	1397 Lewiston Pl	1297 Lewiston Pl
14.	4588 Crystal Way	4588 Crystal Rd
15.	Muscle Shoals AL 35660	Muscle Shoals AL 35660
16.	988 Larkin Johnson Ave SE	988 Larkin Johnson Ave SE
17.	5501 Greenville Blvd NE	5501 Greenview Blvd NE
18.	7133 N Baranmor Pky	7133 N Baranmor Pky
19.	10500 Montana Rd	10500 Montana Rd
20.	4769 E Fox Hollow Dr	4769 E Fox Hollow Cir
21.	Daytona Beach Fla 32016	Daytona Beach FL 32016
22.	2227 W 94th Ave	2272 W 94th Ave
23.	6399 E Ponce De Leon St	6399 E Ponce De Leon Ct
24.	20800 N Rainbow Pl	20800 N Rainbow Pl
25.	Hammond GA 31785	Hammond GA 31785

ANSWER KEY

1.	A	6.	D	11.	A	16.	A	21.	D
2.	D	7.	A	12.	D	17.	D	22.	D
3.	A	8.	D	13.	D	18.	A	23.	D
4.	D	9.	D	14.	D	19.	A	24.	A
5.	D	10.	A	15.	A	20.	D	25.	A

Strategies to Score Higher

How did you do on the quiz? Remember to take time to review the questions you answered incorrectly.

> You face a severe penalty for guessing on this question type. The total number of wrong answers is subtracted from the total number of correct answers. If you start to run out of time, don't panic and start filling in answers at random. Instead, relax and try to remember the tips and guidelines in the rest of this chapter—you may find that you have more time to finish than you thought.

Although everyone will respond to the tests differently, you can use the following tips and guidelines to assist you in answering these questions. In fact, you might read through the following sections and then try the previous quiz again. Does your score improve?

- Read for differences only. Once you spot a difference between the two given addresses, mark your answer sheet with a "D" and go immediately to the next question.
- Vocalize your reading. This doesn't mean simply reading out loud, but rather reading exactly what is listed. For example, if you see "St." don't read it as "Street," but as "ess–t." This will help you to focus on the exact details.

Know Your State and Territory Abbreviations

You should be familiar with conventional abbreviations as well as the two-letter capitalized abbreviations used with ZIP Codes.

Don't worry about memorizing this list. The point of having it included here is to demonstrate how easy it is to mistake one abbreviation for another. If you vocalize what you see, you should (hopefully) hear the differences. And remember: Your task is not to read for meaning, but to spot differences.

Alabama	Ala.	AL	Montana	Mont.	MT
Alaska	n/a	AK	Nebraska	Nebr.	NE
American Samoa	Amer. Samoa	AS	Nevada	Nev.	NV
Arizona	Ariz.	AZ	New Hampshire	N.H.	NH
Arkansas	Ark.	AR	New Jersey	N.J.	NJ
California	Calif.	CA	New Mexico	N. Mex.	NM
Colorado	Colo.	CO	New York	N.Y.	NY
Connecticut	Conn.	CT	North Carolina	N.C.	NC
Delaware	Del.	DE	North Dakota	N.Dak.	ND
District of Columbia	D.C.	DC	Ohio	n/a	OH
Florida	Fla.	FL	Oklahoma	Okla.	OK
Georgia	Ga.	GA	Oregon	Oreg.	OR
Guam	n/a	GU	Pennsylvania	Pa.	PA
Hawaii	n/a	HI	Puerto Rico	P.R.	PR
Idaho	n/a	ID	Rhode Island	R.I.	RI
Illinois	Ill.	IL	South Carolina	S.C.	SC
Indiana	Ind.	IN	South Dakota	S.Dak.	SD
Iowa	n/a	IA	Tennessee	Tenn.	TN
Kansas	Kans.	KS	Texas	Tex.	TX
Kentucky	Ky.	KY	Utah	n/a	UT
Louisiana	La.	LA	Vermont	Vt.	VT
Maine	n/a	ME	Virginia	Va.	VA
Maryland	Md.	MD	Virgin Islands	V.I.	VI
Massachusetts	Mass.	MA	Washington	Wash.	WA
Michigan	Mich.	MI	West Virginia	W.Va.	WV
Minnesota	Minn.	MN	Wisconsin	Wis.	WI
Missouri	Mo.	MO	Wyoming	Wyo.	WY

- Use your hands. Don't be afraid to use your index finger under or alongside the addresses being compared. This will help you to keep your place and to focus on just one line at a time.
- Take the question apart. Try to break the addresses into parts: For example, first compare the street name, then the ZIP Code and so on for each of the two items to be compared. This will help to make the comparison more manageable.
- Read from right to left. This can be very difficult for some people (remember, English-speakers read left to right, so this may take some practice if English—and many other languages—is your natural tongue). However, you might be surprised at how this forces your brain to focus on the details not, for all practical purposes, extraneous information.

- Play the numbers game. You can expect to find many differences in numbers, so keep a close eye on this when you are making your comparison. Questions with two items that are not alike will often have differences in the number of digits as well as differences in the order of digits.
- Watch for differences in abbreviations. Similar to differences in numbers, you'll find many different types of standard abbreviations. You'll also find that it's very easy to misread these, especially when comparing two items.

> Remember you aren't expected to answer all the questions in the time given. Just try to work as quickly and as accurately as possible, and avoid guessing if you start to run out of time.

Practice Exercises

Use the following practice exercises to try out the tips and techniques listed previously for scoring the highest on address-checking questions.

VOCALIZING TECHNIQUES

Try sounding out the following abbreviations and numbers:

NY
CA
OR
VA
AL
HA
MT
MA
IL
TX
68919
828
10001
3694
Ct
Pkw
Cir

INDEX FINGER AS RULER OR POINTER

Try using your index finger or pointer, and compare the following addresses. Are they alike or different?

1.	5115 Colchester Rd	5115 Calchester Rd
2.	4611 N Randall Pl	4611 N Randall Pl
3.	17045 Pascack Cir	17045 Pascack Cir
4.	3349 Palma del Mar Blvd	3346 Palma del Mar Blvd
5.	13211 E 182nd Ave	13211 E 182nd Ave
6.	Francisco WY 82636	Francisco WI 82636
7.	6198 N Albritton Rd	6198 N Albretton Rd
8.	11230 Twinflower Cir	11230 Twintower Cir
9.	6191 MacDonald Station Rd	6191 MacDonald Station Rd
10.	1587 Vanderbilt Dr N	1587 Vanderbilt Dr S

Answers

1.	D	5.	A	9.	A
2.	A	6.	D	10.	D
3.	A	7.	D		
4.	D	8.	D		

BREAK THE ADDRESS INTO PARTS

Try this technique on the following addresses. Are they alike or different?

1.	3993 S Freemont Ter	3993 S Freemount Ter
2.	3654 S Urbane Dr	3564 S Urbane Cir
3.	1408 Oklahoma Ave NE	1408 Oklahoma Ave NE
4.	6201 Meadowland Ln	6201 Meadowlawn Ln
5.	5799 S Rockaway Ln	15799 S Rockaway Ln
6.	3782 SE Verrazanno Bay	37872 SE Verrazanno Bay
7.	2766 N Thunderbird Ct	2766 N Thunderbird Ct
8.	2166 N Elmmorado Ct	2166 N Eldorado Ct
9.	10538 Innsbruck Ln	10538 Innsbruck Ln
10.	888 Powerville Rd	883 Powerville Rd

Answers

1.	A	5.	D	9.	A
2.	D	6.	D	10.	D
3.	A	7.	A		
4.	D	8.	D		

READ FROM RIGHT TO LEFT

Compare the following addresses using this technique:

1.	4202 N Bainbridge Rd	4202 N Bainbridge Rd
2.	300 E Roberta Ave	3000 E Roberta Ave
3.	Quenemo KS 66528	Quenemo KS 66528
4.	13845 Donahoo St	13345 Donahoo St
5.	10466 Gertrude NE	10466 Gertrude NE
6.	2733 N 105th Ave	2773 N 105th Ave
7.	3100 N Wyandotte Cir	3100 N Wyandottte Ave
8.	11796 Summerville Dr	11769 Summerville Dr
9.	Wilburnum Miss 65566	Vilburnum Miss 65566
10.	9334 Kindleberger Rd	9334 Kindleberger Rd

Answers

1.	A	5.	A		9.	D
2.	D	6.	D		10.	A
3.	A	7.	D			
4.	D	8.	D			

DIFFERENCES IN NUMBERS

Answer "A" if the two numbers are exactly alike, and "D" if the two numbers are different in any way.

1.	2003	2003
2.	75864	75864
3.	7300	730
4.	50105	5016
5.	2184	2184
6.	8789	8789
7.	36001	3601
8.	1112	1112
9.	89900	8990
10.	07035	07035

Answers

1.	A	5.	A		9.	D
2.	A	6.	A		10.	A
3.	A	7.	D			
4.	D	8.	A			

The Real Thing: Practice an Exam

Use the following practice exam to try out the techniques you learned in this chapter and to get a good idea of how it will feel on test day to confront this number of address-checking questions. Go through the practice at a steady pace. When you're finished, check your answers.

Directions: For each question, compare the address in the left column with the address in the right column. If the two addresses are ALIKE in every way, write "A" next to the question number. If the two addresses are DIFFERENT in any way, write "D" next to the question number.

1.	...8690 W 134th St	8960 W 134th St
2.	...1912 Berkshire Rd	1912 Berkshire Wy
3.	...5331 W Professor St	5331 W Proffesor St
4.	...Philadelphia PA 19124	Philadelphia PN 19124
5.	...7450 Gaguenay St	7450 Saguenay St
6.	...8650 Christy St	8650 Christey St
7.	...Lumberville PA 18933	Lumberville PA 1998333
8.	...114 Alabama Ave NW	114 Alabama Av NW
9.	...1756 Waterford St	1756 Waterville St
10.	...2214 Wister Wy	2214 Wister Wy
11.	...2974 Repplier Rd	2974 Repplier Dr
12.	...Essex CT 06426	Essex CT 06426
13.	...7676 N Bourbon St	7616 N Bourbon St
14.	...2762 Rosengarten Wy	2762 Rosengarden Wy
15.	...239 Windell Ave	239 Windell Ave
16.	...4667 Edgeworth Rd	4677 Edgeworth Rd
17.	...2661 Kennel St Se	2661 Kennel St Sw
18.	...Alamo TX 78516	Alamo TX 78516
19.	...3709 Columbine St	3709 Columbine St
20.	...9699 W 14th St	9699 W 14th Rd
21.	...2207 Markland Ave	2207 Markham Ave
22.	...Los Angeles CA 90013	Los Angeles CA 90018
23.	...4608 N Warnock St	4806 N Warnock St
24.	...7718 S Summer St	7718 S Sumner St
25.	...New York NY 10016	New York NY 10016
26.	...4514 Ft Hamilton Pk	4514 Ft Hamilton Pk
27.	...5701 Kosciusko St	5701 Koscusko St
28.	...5422 Evergreen St	4522 Evergreen St
29.	...Gainsville FL 43611	Gainsville FL 32611
30.	...5018 Church St	5018 Church Ave
31.	...1079 N Blake St	1097 N Blake St

32.	…8072 W 20th Rd	80702 W 20th Dr
33.	…Onoro ME 04473	Orono ME 04473
34.	…2175 Kimbell Rd	2175 Kimball Rd
35.	…1243 Mermaid St	1243 Mermaid St
36.	…4904 SW 134th St	4904 SW 134th St
37.	…1094 Hancock St	1049 Hancock St
38.	…Des Moines IA 50311	Des Moines IA 50311
39.	…4832 S Rinaldi Rd	48323 S rinaldo Rd
40.	…2015 Dorchester Rd	2015 Dorchester Rd
41.	…5216 Woodbine St	5216 Woodburn St
42.	…Boulder CO 80302	Boulder CA 80302
43.	…4739 N Marion St	479 N Marion St
44.	…3720 Nautilus Wy	3270 Nautilus Way
45.	…3636 Gramercy Pk	3636 Gramercy Pk
46.	…757 Johnson Ave	757 Johnston Ave
47.	…3045 Brighton 12th St	3045 Brighton 12th St
48.	…237 Ovington Ave	237 Ovington Ave
49.	…Kalamazoo MI 49007	Kalamazoo MI 49007
50.	…Lissoula MT 59812	Missoula MS59812
51.	…Stillwater OK 74704	Stillwater OK 47404
52.	…47446 Empire Blvd	4746 Empire Bldg
53.	…6321 St Johns Pl	6321 St Johns Pl
54.	…2242 Vanderbilt Ave	2242 Vanderbilt Ave
55.	…542 Ditmas Blvd	542 Ditmars Blvd
56.	…4603 W Argyle Rd	4603 W Argyle Rd
57.	…653 Knickerbocker Ave NE	653 Knickerbocker Ave NE
58.	…3651 Midwood Terr	3651 Midwood Terr
59.	…Chapel Hill NC 27514	Chaple Hill NC 27514
60.	…3217 Vernon Pl NW	3217 Vernon Dr NW
61.	…1094 Rednor Pkwy	1049 Rednor Pkwy
62.	…986 S Doughty Blvd	986 S Douty Blvd
63.	…Lincoln NE 68508	Lincoln NE 65808
64.	…1517 LaSalle Ave	1517 LaSalle Ave
65.	…3857 S Morris St	3857 S Morriss St
66.	…6104 Saunders Expy	614 Saunders Expy
67.	…2541 Appleton St	2541 Appleton Rd
68.	…Washington DC 20052	Washington DC 20052
69.	…6439 Kessler Blvd S	6439 Kessler Blvd S
70.	…4786 Catalina Dr	4786 Catalana Dr

71.	...132 E Hampton Pkwy	1322 E Hampton Pkwy
72.	...1066 Goethe Sq S	1066 Geothe Sq S
73.	...1118 Jerriman Wy	1218 Jerriman Wy
74.	...5798 Grand Central Pkwy	57998 Grand Central Pkwy
75.	...Delaware OH 43015	Delaware OK 43015
76.	...Corvallis OR 973313	Corvallis OR 97331
77.	...4231 Keating Ave N	4231 Keating Av N
78.	...5689 Central Pk Pl	5869 Central Pk Pl
79.	...1108 Lyndhurst Dr	1108 Lyndhurst Dr
80.	...842 Chambers Ct	842 Chamber Ct
81.	...Athens OH 45701	Athens GA 45701
82.	...Tulsa OK 74171	Tulsa OK 71471
83.	...6892 Beech Grove Ave	6892 Beech Grove Ave
84.	...2939 E Division St	2929 W Division St
85.	...1554 Pitkin Ave	1554 Pitkin Ave
86.	...905 St Edwards Plz	950 St Edwards Plz
87.	...1906 W 152nd St	1906 W 152nd St
88.	...3466 Glenmore Ave	3466 Glenville Ave
89.	...Middlebury VT 05753	Middleberry VT 05753
90.	...Evanston IL 60201	Evanston IN 60201
91.	...9401 W McDonald Ave	9401 W MacDonald Ave
92.	...55527 Albermarle Rd	5527 Albermarle Rd
93.	...9055 Carter Dr	9055 Carter Dr
94.	...Greenvale NY 11548	Greenvale NY 11458
95.	...1149 Cherry Gr S	1149 Cherry Gr S

Answers

1.	D	33.	D	65.	D
2.	A	34.	D	66.	D
3.	D	35.	A	67.	D
4.	D	36.	A	68.	A
5.	A	37.	D	69.	A
6.	D	38.	A	70.	D
7.	D	39.	D	71.	D
8.	D	40.	A	72.	D
9.	D	41.	D	73.	D
10.	A	42.	D	74.	A
11.	D	43.	D	75.	D
12.	A	44.	D	76.	A
13.	D	45.	A	77.	D
14.	D	46.	D	78.	D
15.	A	47.	D	79.	A
16.	D	48.	A	80.	D
17.	D	49.	A	81.	D
18.	A	50.	D	82.	D
19.	A	51.	D	83.	A
20.	D	52.	D	84.	D
21.	D	53.	A	85.	A
22.	D	54.	A	85.	D
23.	D	55.	D	87.	A
24.	D	56.	A	88.	D
25.	A	57.	A	89.	D
26.	A	58.	A	90.	D
27.	D	59.	D	91.	D
28.	D	60.	D	92.	A
29.	A	61.	D	93.	D
30.	D	62.	D	94.	D
31.	D	63.	D	95.	A
32.	D	64.	A		

SCORE HIGHER: MEMORY FOR ADDRESSES

Memory Strategies

Compared to address-checking questions, Memory for Addresses questions are often considered one of the hardest type of questions on the exam. However, as with most exam questions on standardized tests, the questions *look* harder than they really are.

This chapter introduces you to some techniques that will help you score higher on this question type.

To begin, take the following quiz, which consists of an official set of sample questions. Take your time, and become familiar with the question type and what it asks of you.

Practice Quiz

Directions: These five boxes are labeled A, B, C, D, and E. In each box are five addresses: Three are street addresses with number ranges, and two are unnumbered place names. The position of an address within a box is not important. You need only remember the letter of the box in which the address is found. After memorizing the addresses, cover up the boxes and answer the questions. Take as much time as you need to answer the questions.

A	B	C	D	E
4700–5599 Table	6800–6999 Table	5600–6499 Table	6500–6799 Table	4400–4699 Table
Lismore	Kelford	Joel	Tatum	Ruskin
5600–6499 West	6500–6799 West	6800–6999 West	4400–4699 West	4700–5599 West
Hesper	Musella	Sardis	Porter	Nathan
4400–4699 Blake	5600–6499 Blake	6500–6799 Blake	4700–5599 Blake	6800–6999 Blake

55

Directions: *For each of the following addresses, select the letter of the box in which each address is found. Write in the letter next to the question number.*

Questions

1. Sardis
2. 4700–5599 Table
3. 4700–5599 Blake
4. Porter
5. 4400–4699 West
6. Tatum
7. Hesper
8. Musella
9. 6500–6799 West
10. Ruskin

ANSWER KEY

1.	C	5.	E	9.	B
2.	A	6.	D	10.	E
3.	D	7.	A		
4.	D	8.	B		

Tips and Techniques

Did you find this quiz difficult? If you did, don't worry. While some people have great visual memory—that is, they can look at a page and remember what the information said, as well as how it looked—most of us don't have this skill, at least not to a prodigy-like degree.

The actual test requires you to answer up to 88 questions in five minutes without referring back to the original boxes. However, you are given extensive unscored pretest practice with these boxes to help you memorize what's in each box.

While perhaps daunting at first glance, this extensive pretest practice will really pay off for you. Basically, it gives you time to memorize the information you need. If you use the techniques described in this chapter to help you during this practice time, you can turn a very difficult section of the test into one that is perhaps a little more manageable. Read through the tips and techniques listed in this chapter to help you improve your memory techniques.

- Memorize single names first. Take a good look at the five boxes. You should notice that each box contains two single names and three sets of number spans with names. Single names usually are easier to memorize than the name/number combinations, so memorize these single names first.
- Combine name pairs into key words. This is a good way to memorize large chunks of information, as you combine information into one single piece. For example, if one of the boxes contained the names "Tatum" and "Porter"(let's say box C), you could combine this into "TaP." Hopefully, this combination of words would trigger the association to "Tatum" and "Porter" in your mind when you needed to recall the information.
- Use word associations. In the example just used, we combined "Tatum" and "Porter" into "TaP." Don't just leave it at that, though: Go ahead and associate "TaP" with "tap dancing" or "tap water." The point is to make your word combination as useful as possible so that your mind can better associate it with the original information you are attempting to memorize.
- Use the information to make up sentences or phrases. Again drawing on our "Tatum" and "Porter" example, it might be easier for you to simply combine the information to make a sentence. This may prove much more useful if you are struggling with short word combinations. For example, you might make up an associative sentence such as, "Porter found the Tatum Hotel very nice."
- Focus on number spans. If you look again at the five sample lettered boxes used in the practice quiz, you will find five different number spans paired with three street names. In other words, each street name has the same five number spans:

Table	4400–4699, 4700–5599, 5600–6499, 6500–6799, 6800–6999
West	4400–4699, 4700–5599, 5600–6499, 6500–6799, 6800–6999
Blake	4400–4699, 4700–5599, 5600–6499, 6500–6799, 6800–6999

Remember, though, that you have 15 different addresses to remember, not five, because each number span is paired with three difference names in three different locations.

- Shorten the numbers. If you look at the number spans listed, you'll see that they all begin with "00" as the final two digits and end with "99" as the last two digits. So, you can save some precious memory space by not worrying about the "00" and "99," focusing instead on just the beginning two digits.

The Real Thing: Practice an Exam

Directions: Complete the following two practice sets. For Set 1, you can refer back to the boxes. You must answer Set 2 solely from memory. Write your answer next to the question number.

A	B	C	D	E
32 Apple 35 Hills 29 Leaf	10 Apple 22 Hills 32 Leaf	35 Apple 32 Hills 10 Leaf	22 Apple 29 Hills 35 Leaf	29 Apple 10 Hills 22 Leaf

Directions: Now do the two practice sets. For the first practice exercise, you can refer back to the boxes. The second set must be answered solely from memory. Indicate your answers by writing in your answer next to the question number.

Set 1

1. 2200–2899 Hills
2. 3500–3599 Leaf
3. Stewart
4. 3200–3499 Apple
5. 3200–3499 Hills
6. 2200–2899 Apple
7. Inman
8. Gray
9. 3500–3599 Hills
10. 2200–2899 Leaf
11. 2900–3199 Leaf
12. Trace
13. Hard
14. Arden
15. 2200–2899 Hills
16. 1000–2199 Hills
17. 1000–2199 Apple
18. Narrows
19. 3200–3499 Leaf
20. Paris

21. 3500–3599 Leaf
22. 3500–3599 Apple
23. 2200–2899 Apple
24. Fish
25. Book
26. 2900–3199 Apple
27. 2900–3199 Hills
28. 1000–2199 Leaf
29. 2200–2899 Hills
30. 3200–3499 Apple
31. Gray
32. Trace
33. Arden
34. 3200–3499 Hills
35. Narrows
36. Hard
37. 2900–3199 Leaf
38. 2200–2899 Hills
39. 3500–3599 Apple
40. 2900–3199 Hills

41. 2200–2899 Leaf
42. Inman
43. Stewart
44. Paris
45. 3500–3599 Hills
46. 1000–2199 Apple
47. Fish
48. Book
49. 3200–3499 Leaf
50. 2200–2899 Apple
51. 3200–3499 Hills
52. 2900–3199 Apple
53. 2200–2899 Leaf
54. Gray
55. Narrows
56. Hard
57. 3200–3499 Apple
58. 1000–2199 Hills
59. 1000–2199 Leaf
60. Inman

61. Book
62. 3500–3599 Hills
63. 2900–3199 Hills
64. 3500–3599 Apple
65. 3500–3599 Leaf
66. Trace
67. Paris
68. 2200–2899 Apple
69. 2900–3199 Leaf
70. Narrows

71. 2900–3199 Apple
72. 1000–2199 Apple
73. Fish
74. Gray
75. 2200–2899 Leaf
76. 3500–3599 Apple
77. 2200–2899 Hills
78. Stewart
79. Hard
80. 3500–3599 Hills

81. 2200–2899 Apple
82. Paris
83. 3500–3599 Leaf
84. 2900–3199 Leaf
85. Gray
86. 2900–3199 Hills
87. Inman
88. 3500–3599 Apple

Set 2

1. 2200–2899 Leaf
2. Narrows
3. 3200–3499 Hills
4. Fish
5. 3200–3499 Apple
6. 2900–3199 Leaf
7. Trace
8. Stewart
9. 2900–3199 Apple
10. 3500–3599 Apple
11. 1000–2199 Leaf
12. Hard
13. 1000–2199 Hills
14. 3500–3599 Leaf
15. 1000–2199 Apple
16. Gray
17. Arden
18. 2200–2899 Hills
19. 3200–3499 Hills
20. Paris
21. Book

22. 3500–3599 Hills
23. 3500–3599 Apple
24. Inman
25. 2200–2899 Apple
26. 2900–3199 Leaf
27. 2900–3199 Apple
28. 3200–3499 Hills
29. Arden
30. Gray
31. 1000–2199 Apple
32. 3500–3599 Leaf
33. 2200–2899 Leaf
34. 3500–3599 Apple
35. Trace
36. Stewart
37. Inman
38. 3500–3599 Hills
39. 2900–3199 Hills
40. 2200–2899 Hills
41. 2200–2899 Apple
42. Hard

43. Fish
44. 3500–3599 Leaf
45. 3200–3499 Hills
46. 3200–3499 Apple
47. 3200–3499 Leaf
48. Narrows
49. Paris
50. 1000–2199 Apple
51. 2900–3199 Hills
52. 3500–3599 Leaf
53. 2200–2899 Apple
54. Book
55. Stewart
56. 3500–3599 Hills
57. 2900–3199 Leaf
58. 1000–2199 Hills
59. 1000–2199 Leaf
60. Fish
61. Hard
62. 3200–3499 Hills
63. 3200–3499 Leaf

64. 2200–2899 Leaf

65. Arden

66. Inman

67. 2900–3199 Apple

68. 1000–2199 Apple

69. 2900–3199 Hills

70. 3500–3599 Hills

71. 2900–3199 Leaf

72. Paris

73. Book

74. Hard

75. Gray

76. 3200–3499 Leaf

77. 3200–3499 Apple

78. 1000–2199 Hills

79. 2200–2899 Hills

80. Stewart

81. Fish

82. 2200–2899 Apple

83. 2900–3199 Leaf

84. 2900–3199 Hills

85. Book

86. Trace

87. 3500–3599 Leaf

88. 2900–3199 Apple

ANSWERS

Set 1

1.	B	16.	E	31.	A	46.	B	61.	A	76.	C
2.	D	17.	B	32.	B	47.	B	62.	A	77.	B
3.	D	18.	D	33.	C	48.	A	63.	D	78.	D
4.	A	19.	B	34.	C	49.	B	64.	C	79.	E
5.	C	20.	C	35.	D	50.	D	65.	D	80.	A
6.	D	21.	D	36.	E	51.	C	66.	B	81.	D
7.	E	22.	C	37.	A	52.	E	67.	C	82.	C
8.	A	23.	D	38.	B	53.	E	68.	D	83.	D
9.	A	24.	B	39.	C	54.	A	69.	A	84.	A
10.	E	25.	A	40.	D	55.	D	70.	D	85.	A
11.	A	26.	E	41.	E	56.	E	71.	E	86.	D
12.	B	27.	D	42.	E	57.	A	72.	B	87.	E
13.	E	28.	C	43.	D	58.	E	73.	B	88.	C
14.	C	29.	B	44.	C	59.	C	74.	A		
15.	B	30.	A	45.	A	60.	E	75.	E		

Set 2

1.	E	16.	A	31.	B	46.	A	61.	E	76.	B
2.	D	17.	C	32.	D	47.	B	62.	C	77.	A
3.	C	18.	B	33.	E	48.	D	63.	B	78.	E
4.	B	19.	C	34.	C	49.	C	64.	E	79.	B
5.	A	20.	C	35.	B	50.	B	65.	C	80.	D
6.	A	21.	A	36.	D	51.	D	66.	E	81.	B
7.	B	22.	A	37.	E	52.	D	67.	E	82.	D
8.	D	23.	C	38.	A	53.	D	68.	B	83.	A
9.	E	24.	E	39.	D	54.	A	69.	D	84.	D
10.	C	25.	D	40.	B	55.	D	70.	A	85.	A
11.	C	26.	A	41.	D	56.	A	71.	A	86.	B
12.	E	27.	E	42.	E	57.	A	72.	C	87.	D
13.	E	28.	C	43.	B	58.	E	73.	A	88.	E
14.	D	29.	C	44.	D	59.	C	74.	E		
15.	B	30.	A	45.	C	60.	B	75.	A		

SCORE HIGHER: STRATEGIES FOR WORKING WITH NUMBER SERIES

Number Series Strategies

Don't worry too much about these types of questions, especially if you don't have very advanced math skills. You're not going to be asked to do algebra, but rather simple addition, subtraction, multiplication and division. Best of all, you can solve most of these questions quickly, and there is no penalty for guessing.

> Here's a good tip on guessing: If you must guess, make all your guesses the same letter. By the law of averages, this may give you a better chance of hitting the right answer.

Let's get started with the usual practice quiz. The following 10-question test will familiarize you with the question type. The questions are all at varying levels of difficulty, just like on the actual test. Again, take your time with this so that you can get used to the type of question being asked.

Practice Quiz

Directions: For each question, there is at the left a series of numbers that follows some definite order and at the right five sets of two numbers each. You are to look at the numbers in the series at the left and find out what order they follow. Then decide what the next two numbers in the series would be if the same order were continued. Circle the letter of the correct answer.

1.	21 21 19 17 17 15 13 ...	(A) 11 11	(B) 13 11	(C) 11 9	(D) 9 7	(E) 13 13
2.	23 22 20 19 16 15 11 ...	(A) 6 5	(B) 10 9	(C) 6 1	(D) 10 6	(E) 10 5
3.	5 6 8 9 11 12 14	(A) 15 16	(B) 16 17	(C) 15 17	(D) 16 18	(E) 17 19
4.	7 10 8 13 16 8 19	(A) 22 8	(B) 8 22	(C) 20 21	(D) 22 25	(E) 8 25
5.	1 35 2 34 3 33 4	(A) 4 5	(B) 32 31	(C) 32 5	(D) 5 32	(E) 31 6
6.	75 75 72 72 69 69 66 ...	(A) 66 66	(B) 66 68	(C) 63 63	(D) 66 63	(E) 63 60
7.	12 16 21 27 31 36 42 ...	(A) 48 56	(B) 44 48	(C) 48 52	(D) 46 52	(E) 46 51
8.	22 24 12 26 28 12 30 ...	(A) 12 32	(B) 32 34	(C) 32 12	(D) 12 12	(E) 32 36
9.	5 70 10 68 15 66 20	(A) 25 64	(B) 64 25	(C) 24 63	(D) 25 30	(E) 64 62
10.	13 22 32 43 55 68 82 ...	(A) 97 113	(B) 100 115	(C) 96 110	(D) 95 105	(E) 99 112

ANSWER KEY

Remember, take time to review your answers carefully, and spend a little extra time on any that you missed.

1. **(B)** The pattern of this series is: Repeat the number, then subtract 2 and subtract 2 again; repeat the number, then subtract 2 and subtract 2 again, and so on. Following the pattern, the series should continue with B, 13 11, and then go on 9 9 7 5 5 3 1 1.

2. **(E)** The pattern is: −1, −2, −1, −3, −1, −4, −1, −5, and so on. Fitting the pattern to the remaining numbers, it is apparent that E is the answer because 11 − 1 = 10, and 10 − 5 = 5.

3. **(C)** The pattern here is: +1, +2; +1, +2; +1, +2 and so on. The answer is C because 14 + 1 = 15, and 15 + 2 = 17.

4. **(A)** You first must notice that the number 8 is repeated after each two numbers. If you disregard the 8s, you can see that the series is increasing by a factor of +3. With this information, you can choose A as the correct answer because 19 + 3 = 22, and the two numbers, 19 and 22, are then followed by 8.

5. **(C)** This series is actually two alternating series. One series, beginning with 1, increases at the rate of +1. The other series alternates with the first. It begins with 35 and decreases by −1. The answer is C because the next number in the decreasing series is 32, and the next number in the increasing series is 5.

6. **(D)** The pattern established in this series is: Repeat the number, −3; repeat the number, −3; and so on. To continue the series, repeat 66, then subtract 3.

7. **(E)** The pattern is: +4, +5, +6; +4, +5, +6; +4, +5, +6. Continuing the series: 42 + 4 = 46 + 5 = 51.

8. **(C)** In this series, the basic pattern is +2. The series may be read: 22 24 26 28 30 32. After each two numbers of the series, we find the number 12, which serves no function except for repetition. To continue the series, add 2 to 30 to get 32. After 30 and 32, you must put in the number 12.

9. **(B)** In this problem, there are two distinct series alternating with one another. The first series is ascending by a factor of +5. It reads: 10 15 20. The alternating series is descending by a factor of −2. It reads: 70 68 66. At the point where you must continue the series, the next number must be a member of the descending series, so it must be 64. Following that number must come the next number of the ascending series, which is 25.

10. **(A)** The numbers are large, but the progression is simple between each number in the series: +9, +10, +11, +12, +13, +14. Continuing the series: 82 + 15 = 97 + 16 = 113.

Strategies for Working with Number Series Questions

Okay, so you're a bit anxious about working with numbers. Well, put your fears aside. Remember, the test isn't going to ask you to break out the calculus (or a simple calculator, for that matter). As usual, you'll need to work with as much speed and efficiency as you can muster. However, if you try to remember the following tips, you may find that this type of question isn't as frightening as you thought.

- In number series with one pattern, look for the following number arrangements:

    Simple ascending (increasing) or descending (decreasing) numbers, where the same number is added to or subtracted from each number in a series

    Alternating ascending or descending numbers, where two different numbers are alternately added to or subtracted from each number in a series

    Simple or alternating multiplication or division

    Simple repetition, where one or more number in the series is repeated immediately before or after addition or subtraction or other arithmetic operation

    Repetition of a number pattern by itself

    Unusual pattern

- In number series with two or more patterns, look for the following kinds of patterns:

    Random number (not one of the numbers in the series)

    Introduced and repeated number in a one-pattern series

    Two or more alternating series of two or more distinct patterns

    Two or more alternating series of patterns, plus repetitive or random numbers

    Two or more alternating patterns that include simple multiplication and division

    Unusual alternating or combination arrangements

- Solve at a glance. Look for simple number series that jump out at you, such as 1 2 3 1 2 3. Also be on the lookout for patterns that are either adding or subtracting to get the next number, such 20 21 22 23 or 35 34 33 32.
- Vocalize for meaning. With all those numbers flying around, it might be easy for your eye (and, thus, your brain) to get confused, mistakenly reading a number for something else. That's why it sometimes help to vocalize (or, say quietly to yourself) what you are reading. You might be able to hear a pattern more quickly—and more accurately—than if you had just looked at it.
- When you spot a difference, mark it down. By "difference," we mean that you should immediately mark any change in the number series that you find. For example, if you're reading and you notice that the series is increasing by 2 (for example, 2 4 6 8) write down that difference in the numbers of the series (again, in this case, 2). Remember, most series are either ascending, descending, or a combination of the two. If you can't figure it out with addition and subtraction, try multiplication and division. Number series that use multiplication and division are fairly rare. However, you shouldn't discount this possibility entirely—just remember to try addition and subtraction first.
- Know how to spot repeating and random numbers. Repeating and random numbers may not be so obvious. Be sure to mark up the question in your test booklet—this will help you spot these types of numbers more easily than if you simply try to see them in your brain.

Number Series Practice I

You should be able to answer the following questions based on your work so far. Take the quiz at your own pace, using the techniques you've learned in this chapter. When you're finished, check your answers against the answer key and explanations.

Directions: *For each question, there is at the left a series of numbers that follows some definite order and at the right five sets of two numbers each. You are to look at the numbers in the series at the left and find out what order they follow. Then decide what the next two numbers in the series would be if the same order were continued. Circle the letter of the correct answer.*

1. 8 9 10 8 9 10 8 .... (A) 8 9   (B) 9 10   (C) 9 8   (D) 10 8   (E) 8 10
2. 16 16 15 15 14 14 13 ...... (A) 12 13   (B) 14 13   (C) 12 11   (D) 12 10   (E) 13 12
3. 2 6 10 2 7 11 15 .... (A) 12 16   (B) 15 19   (C) 15 16   (D) 12 13   (E) 2 19
4. 30 28 27 25 24 22 21 ...... (A) 21 20   (B) 19 18   (C) 20 19   (D) 20 18   (E) 21 21
5. 25 25 2 22 19 19 16 .... (A) 18 18   (B) 16 16   (C) 16 13   (D) 15 15   (E) 15 13
6. 9 17 24 30 35 39 42 .... (A) 43 44   (B) 44 46   (C) 44 45   (D) 45 49   (E) 46 50
7. 28 31 34 37 40 43 46 ...... (A) 49 52   (B) 47 49   (C) 50 54   (D) 49 53   (E) 51 55
8. 17 17 24 24 31 31 38 ...... (A) 38 39   (B) 38 17   (C) 38 45   (D) 38 44   (E) 39 50
9. 87 83 79 75 71 67 63 ...... (A) 62 61   (B) 63 59   (C) 60 56   (D) 59 55   (E) 59 54
10. 8 9 11 14 18 23 29 .... (A) 35 45   (B) 32 33   (C) 38 48   (D) 34 40   (E) 36 44
11. 4 8 12 16 20 24 .... (A) 26 28   (B) 28 30   (C) 28 30   (D) 28 32   (E) 28 29
12. 3 4 1 3 4 1 3 .... (A) 4 1   (B) 4 5   (C) 4 3   (D) 1 2   (E) 4 4

ANSWER KEY

1.	B	5.	C	9.	D
2.	E	6.	C	10.	E
3.	E	7.	A	11.	D
4.	B	8.	C	12.	A

EXPLANATIONS

1. **(B)** The series is simply a repetition of the sequence 8 9 10.

2. **(E)** This series is a simple descending series combined with repetition. Each number is first repeated and then decreased by 1.

3. **(E)** This pattern is +4, then repeat the number 2.

4. **(B)** This pattern is not as easy to spot as the ones in the previous questions. If you write in the direction and degree of change between each number, you can see that this an alternating descending series with the pattern –2, –1, –2, –1, etc.

5. **(C)** The rule here is: repeat, –3, repeat, –3, repeat, –3.

6. **(C)** The rule here is: +8, +7, +6, +5, +4, +3, +2.

7. **(A)** This is a simple +3 rule.

8. **(C)** Each number repeats itself, then increases by +7.

9. **(D)** Here the rule is: –4.

10. **(E)** The rule here is: +1, +2, +3, +4, +5, +6, +7, +8.

11. **(D)** This is a simple ascending series, where each number increases by 4.

12. **(A)** This is a simple +1 series, with the number 1 repeated after each step of the series.

Number Series Practice II

Answer every question to the best of your ability. Write next to each question which technique you used. After you have finished every question, then check your answers against the answer key and explanations that follow.

Directions: *For each question, there is at the left a series of numbers that follows some definite order and at the right five sets of two numbers each. You are to look at the numbers in the series at the left and find out what order they follow. Then decide what the next two numbers in the series would be if the same order were continued. Circle the letter of the correct answer.*

1. 12 26 15 26 18 26 21 ..... (A) 21 24 (B) 24 26 (C) 21 26 (D) 26 24 (E) 26 25
2. 72 67 69 64 66 61 63 ..... (A) 58 60 (B) 65 62 (C) 60 58 (D) 65 60 (E) 60 65
3. 81 10 29 81 10 29 81 ..... (A) 29 10 (B) 81 29 (C) 10 29 (D) 81 10 (E) 29 81
4. 91 91 90 88 85 81 76 ..... (A) 71 66 (B) 70 64 (C) 75 74 (D) 70 65 (E) 70 63
5. 22 44 29 37 36 30 43 ..... (A) 50 23 (B) 23 50 (C) 53 40 (D) 40 53 (E) 50 57
6. 0 1 1 0 2 2 0 .... (A) 0 0 (B) 0 3 (C) 3 3 (D) 3 4 (E) 2 3
7. 32 34 36 34 36 38 36 ..... (A) 34 32 (B) 36 34 (C) 36 38 (D) 38 40 (E) 38 36
8. 26 36 36 46 46 56 56 ..... (A) 66 66 (B) 56 66 (C) 57 57 (D) 46 56 (E) 26 66
9. 64 63 61 58 57 55 52 ..... (A) 51 50 (B) 52 49 (C) 50 58 (D) 50 47 (E) 51 49
10. 4 6 8 7 6 8 10 9 8 .... (A) 7 9 (B) 11 12 (C) 12 14 (D) 7 10 (E) 10 12
11. 57 57 52 47 47 42 37 ..... (A) 32 32 (B) 37 32 (C) 37 37 (D) 32 27 (E) 27 27
12. 13 26 14 25 16 23 19 ..... (A) 20 21 (B) 20 22 (C) 20 23 (D) 20 24 (E) 22 25
13. 15 27 39 51 63 75 87 ..... (A) 97 112 (B) 99 111 (C) 88 99 (D) 89 99 (E) 90 99
14. 20 22 24 26 28 .... (A) 2 2 (B) 2 8 (C) 2 10 (D) 2 12 (E) 2 16
15. 19 18 18 17 17 17 16 ..... (A) 16 16 (B) 16 15 (C) 15 15 (D) 15 14 (E) 16 17
16. 55 53 44 51 49 44 47 ..... (A) 45 43 (B) 46 45 (C) 46 44 (D) 44 44 (E) 45 44
17. 100 81 64 49 36 25 16 ... (A) 8 4 (B) 8 2 (C) 9 5 (D) 9 4 (E) 9 3
18. 2 2 4 6 8 18 16 .... (A) 32 64 (B) 32 28 (C) 54 32 (D) 32 54 (E) 54 30
19. 47 43 52 48 57 53 62 ..... (A) 58 54 (B) 67 58 (C) 71 67 (D) 58 67 (E) 49 58
20. 38 38 53 48 48 63 58 ..... (A) 58 58 (B) 58 73 (C) 73 73 (D) 58 68 (E) 73 83
21. 12 14 16 13 15 17 14 ..... (A) 17 15 (B) 15 18 (C) 17 19 (D) 15 16 (E) 16 18
22. 30 30 30 37 37 37 30 ..... (A) 30 30 (B) 30 37 (C) 37 37 (D) 37 30 (E) 31 31
23. 75 52 69 56 63 59 57 ..... (A) 58 62 (B) 55 65 (C) 51 61 (D) 61 51 (E) 63 55
24. 176 88 88 44 44 22 22 ... (A) 22 11 (B) 11 11 (C) 11 10 (D) 11 5 (E) 22 10

ANSWER KEY

1.	D	7.	D	13.	B	19.	D
2.	A	8.	A	14.	C	20.	B
3.	C	9.	E	15.	A	21.	E
4.	E	10.	E	16.	E	22.	A
5.	B	11.	B	17.	D	23.	D
6.	C	12.	C	18.	C	24.	B

EXPLANATIONS

1. **(D)** This is an A + 3 series, with the number 26 between terms.

   12 $^{+3}$ ㉖ 15 $^{+3}$ ㉖ 18 $^{+3}$ ㉖ 21 $^{+3}$ ㉖ 24

2. **(A)** You may read this as a –5, +2 series:

   72 $^{-5}$ 67 $^{+2}$ 69 $^{-5}$ 64 $^{+2}$ 66 $^{-5}$ 61 $^{+2}$ 63 $^{-5}$ 58 $^{+2}$ 60

   or as two alternating –3 series.

   $$\overbrace{72\ \underbrace{67\ \ 69}\ \underbrace{64\ \ 66}\ \underbrace{61\ \ 63}\ 58\ \ 60}^{-3\quad -3\quad -3\quad -3}_{\ \ \ \ \ -3\quad\ \ -3\quad\ \ -3}$$

3. **(C)** By inspection or grouping, the sequence 81 10 29 repeats itself.

4. **(E)** Write in the numbers for this one.

   91 $^{-0}$ 91 $^{-1}$ 90 $^{-2}$ 88 $^{-3}$ 85 $^{-4}$ 81 $^{-5}$ 76 $^{-6}$ 70 $^{-7}$ 63

5. **(B)** Here we have two distinct alternating series.

   $$\overbrace{22\ \underbrace{44\ \ 29}\ \underbrace{37\ \ 36}\ \underbrace{30\ \ 43}\ 23\ \ 50}^{+7\quad +7\quad +7\quad +7}_{\ \ \ \ \ -7\quad\ \ -7\quad\ \ -7}$$

6. **(C)** The digit 0 intervenes after each repeating number of a simple +1 and repeat series.

   $$\overbrace{5\ \underbrace{37\ \ 10}\ \underbrace{36\ \ 15}\ \underbrace{35\ \ 20}\ \text{followed by}\ \underbrace{34\ \ 25}\ \underbrace{33\ \ 30}}^{+5\quad +5\quad +5\quad\quad +5\quad\quad +5}_{\ \ \ \ \ -1\quad\ \ -1\quad\quad -1\quad\quad\ \ -1}\ \ldots$$

   ⓪ 1 ^{r} 1 $^{+1}$ ⓪ 2 ^{r} 2 $^{+1}$ ⓪ 3 ^{r} 3

7. **(D)** Group the numbers into threes. Each succeeding group of three begins with a number two higher than the first number of the preceding group of three. Within each group, the pattern is +2, +2.

8. **(A)** The pattern is + 10, repeat the number, +10, repeat the number.

   $26 \overset{+10}{} 36 \ ^r 36 \overset{+10}{} 46 \ ^r 46 \overset{+10}{} 56 \ ^r 56 \overset{+10}{} 66 \ ^r 66$

9. **(E)** The pattern is −1, −2, −3; −1, −2, −3 and so on. If you can't see it, write it in for yourself.

10. **(E)** Here the pattern is +2, +2, −1, −1; +2, +2, −1, −1.

   $4 \overset{+2}{} 6 \overset{+2}{} 8 \overset{-1}{} 7 \overset{-1}{} 6 \overset{+2}{} 8 \overset{+2}{} 10 \overset{-1}{} 9 \overset{-1}{} 8 \overset{+2}{} 10 \overset{+2}{} 12$

   The series that is given to you is a little bit longer than most to better assist you in establishing this extra long pattern.

11. **(B)** This is a −5 pattern with every other term repeated.

   $57 \ ^r 57 \overset{-5}{} 52 \overset{-5}{} 47 \ ^r 47 \overset{-5}{} 42 \overset{-5}{} 37 \ ^r 37 \overset{-5}{} 32$

12. **(C)** This series consists of two alternating series.

   ```
   +1    +2    +3    +4
   13 26 14 25 16 23 19 20 23
      −1    −2    −3
   ```

13. **(B)** This is a simple +12 series.

14. **(C)** Even with the extra length, you may have trouble with this one. You might have to change your approach a couple times to figure it out.

   $2 \overset{\times 2}{} 0; \ 2 \overset{\times 1}{} 2; \ 2 \overset{\times 2}{} 4; \ 2 \overset{\times 3}{} 6; \ 2 \overset{\times 4}{} 8; \ 2 \overset{\times 5}{} 10$

15. **(A)** Each number is repeated one time more than the number before it: 19 appears only once, 18 twice, 17 three times and, if the series were extended beyond the question, 16 would appear four times.

16. **(E)** This is a −2 series, with the number 44 appearing after every two numbers of the series. You probably can see this now without writing it out.

17. **(D)** The series consists of the squares of the numbers from 2 to 10, in descending order.

18. **(C)** This is a tricky alternating series question.

   ```
      ×2  ×2  ×2   ×2
   2 2 4 6 8 18 16 54 32
     ×3  ×3  ×3
   ```

19. **(D)** The progress of this series is –4, +9; –4, +9.

20. **(B)** This series is not really difficult, but you may have to write it out to see it.

   38 ʳ 38 ⁺¹⁵ 53 ⁻⁵ 48 ʳ 48 ⁺¹⁵ 63 ⁻⁵ 58 ʳ 58 ⁺¹⁵ 73

   You may also see this as two alternating +10 series, with the numbers ending in 8 repeated.

21. **(E)** Group into groups of three numbers. Each +2 group begins one step up from the previous group.

22. **(A)** By inspection, you can see that this series is nothing more than the number 30 repeated three times and the number 37 repeated three times. You have no further clues, so you must assume that the series continues with the number 30 repeated three times.

23. **(D)** Here are two alternating series:

$$\begin{array}{c}
\quad\;\overset{-6}{\frown}\quad\overset{-6}{\frown}\quad\overset{-6}{\frown}\quad\overset{-6}{\frown} \\
75\;\;52\;\;69\;\;56\;\;63\;\;59\;\;57\;\;61\;\;51 \\
\underset{+4}{\smile}\;\;\underset{+3}{\smile}\;\;\underset{+2}{\smile}
\end{array}$$

24. **(B)** The pattern is +2 and repeat the number, +2 and repeat the number.

   176 ⁺² 88 ʳ 88 ⁺² 44 ʳ 44 ⁺² 22 ʳ 22 ⁺² 11 ʳ 11

SCORE HIGHER: STRATEGIES FOR FOLLOWING ORAL INSTRUCTIONS

Tips for Oral Instruction Questions

It always pays to be a good listener, and you'll find that oral instruction questions are no exception. Unlike other types of questions you'll encounter, oral instruction questions require you to focus your attention on another individual (or more precisely, the sound of his or her voice) rather than simply the test booklet. However, like all questions on the exam, you'll score your highest if you concentrate, relax, and are well prepared.

The information in this chapter will help you to do just that.

Use the following tips and techniques in tackling the oral instruction questions:

> Due to the nature of these questions, we're going to dismiss with the "warm-up questions" that have been at the opening of each of these strategy chapters, and start with a list of strategies first. Later on in this chapter, you'll have a chance to try out everything you've learned.

- **Pay attention to the instructions!** We've stressed in previous chapters that concentration is important. Well, with oral instruction questions, attention is paramount! Unlike other questions, if you "space out" during this portion of the exam, you can't simply "re-read" the question in your booklet. Try to stay focused!
- **Mark your answer sheet as instructed** Unlike other questions, you will not answer the oral instruction questions in sequential order on your answer sheet. In fact, you will skip around the page, filling in answers in the order specified. (Actually, you will not use all the answer spaces provided to you!)
- **Work from left to right** If the instructions say to mark the "fourth letter," it will be the fourth letter from the left, no exceptions. Of course, if the instructions tell you differently (for example, if they say, "Please put a circle around the fifth letter from the right"), then you'll obviously need to make an exception from reading left to right. Again, listen closely!
- **Don't waste time changing answers** If you are about to enter a choice on your answer sheet, and suddenly realize you've already filled in that choice (i.e., you've made that choice from another question), don't make a change. Wait for the next set of instructions, and move on.

> If you find that you've blackened two answer spaces for the same question, erase one of them only if you have time, and if you won't get distracted and fall behind in the instructions.

Practice with Oral Instructions Questions

For this section, you'll need to find a friend who can read the instructions to you.

As you work through the sample test, try your best to relax, concentrate, and remember the tips listed above. Good luck!

PRACTICE EXAM 1

Answer Sheet

TEAR HERE

1. Ⓐ Ⓑ Ⓒ Ⓓ Ⓔ	23. Ⓐ Ⓑ Ⓒ Ⓓ Ⓔ	45. Ⓐ Ⓑ Ⓒ Ⓓ Ⓔ	67. Ⓐ Ⓑ Ⓒ Ⓓ Ⓔ
2. Ⓐ Ⓑ Ⓒ Ⓓ Ⓔ	24. Ⓐ Ⓑ Ⓒ Ⓓ Ⓔ	46. Ⓐ Ⓑ Ⓒ Ⓓ Ⓔ	68. Ⓐ Ⓑ Ⓒ Ⓓ Ⓔ
3. Ⓐ Ⓑ Ⓒ Ⓓ Ⓔ	25. Ⓐ Ⓑ Ⓒ Ⓓ Ⓔ	47. Ⓐ Ⓑ Ⓒ Ⓓ Ⓔ	69. Ⓐ Ⓑ Ⓒ Ⓓ Ⓔ
4. Ⓐ Ⓑ Ⓒ Ⓓ Ⓔ	26. Ⓐ Ⓑ Ⓒ Ⓓ Ⓔ	48. Ⓐ Ⓑ Ⓒ Ⓓ Ⓔ	70. Ⓐ Ⓑ Ⓒ Ⓓ Ⓔ
5. Ⓐ Ⓑ Ⓒ Ⓓ Ⓔ	27. Ⓐ Ⓑ Ⓒ Ⓓ Ⓔ	49. Ⓐ Ⓑ Ⓒ Ⓓ Ⓔ	71. Ⓐ Ⓑ Ⓒ Ⓓ Ⓔ
6. Ⓐ Ⓑ Ⓒ Ⓓ Ⓔ	28. Ⓐ Ⓑ Ⓒ Ⓓ Ⓔ	50. Ⓐ Ⓑ Ⓒ Ⓓ Ⓔ	72. Ⓐ Ⓑ Ⓒ Ⓓ Ⓔ
7. Ⓐ Ⓑ Ⓒ Ⓓ Ⓔ	29. Ⓐ Ⓑ Ⓒ Ⓓ Ⓔ	51. Ⓐ Ⓑ Ⓒ Ⓓ Ⓔ	73. Ⓐ Ⓑ Ⓒ Ⓓ Ⓔ
8. Ⓐ Ⓑ Ⓒ Ⓓ Ⓔ	30. Ⓐ Ⓑ Ⓒ Ⓓ Ⓔ	52. Ⓐ Ⓑ Ⓒ Ⓓ Ⓔ	74. Ⓐ Ⓑ Ⓒ Ⓓ Ⓔ
9. Ⓐ Ⓑ Ⓒ Ⓓ Ⓔ	31. Ⓐ Ⓑ Ⓒ Ⓓ Ⓔ	53. Ⓐ Ⓑ Ⓒ Ⓓ Ⓔ	75. Ⓐ Ⓑ Ⓒ Ⓓ Ⓔ
10. Ⓐ Ⓑ Ⓒ Ⓓ Ⓔ	32. Ⓐ Ⓑ Ⓒ Ⓓ Ⓔ	54. Ⓐ Ⓑ Ⓒ Ⓓ Ⓔ	76. Ⓐ Ⓑ Ⓒ Ⓓ Ⓔ
11. Ⓐ Ⓑ Ⓒ Ⓓ Ⓔ	33. Ⓐ Ⓑ Ⓒ Ⓓ Ⓔ	55. Ⓐ Ⓑ Ⓒ Ⓓ Ⓔ	77. Ⓐ Ⓑ Ⓒ Ⓓ Ⓔ
12. Ⓐ Ⓑ Ⓒ Ⓓ Ⓔ	34. Ⓐ Ⓑ Ⓒ Ⓓ Ⓔ	56. Ⓐ Ⓑ Ⓒ Ⓓ Ⓔ	78. Ⓐ Ⓑ Ⓒ Ⓓ Ⓔ
13. Ⓐ Ⓑ Ⓒ Ⓓ Ⓔ	35. Ⓐ Ⓑ Ⓒ Ⓓ Ⓔ	57. Ⓐ Ⓑ Ⓒ Ⓓ Ⓔ	79. Ⓐ Ⓑ Ⓒ Ⓓ Ⓔ
14. Ⓐ Ⓑ Ⓒ Ⓓ Ⓔ	36. Ⓐ Ⓑ Ⓒ Ⓓ Ⓔ	58. Ⓐ Ⓑ Ⓒ Ⓓ Ⓔ	80. Ⓐ Ⓑ Ⓒ Ⓓ Ⓔ
15. Ⓐ Ⓑ Ⓒ Ⓓ Ⓔ	37. Ⓐ Ⓑ Ⓒ Ⓓ Ⓔ	59. Ⓐ Ⓑ Ⓒ Ⓓ Ⓔ	81. Ⓐ Ⓑ Ⓒ Ⓓ Ⓔ
16. Ⓐ Ⓑ Ⓒ Ⓓ Ⓔ	38. Ⓐ Ⓑ Ⓒ Ⓓ Ⓔ	60. Ⓐ Ⓑ Ⓒ Ⓓ Ⓔ	82. Ⓐ Ⓑ Ⓒ Ⓓ Ⓔ
17. Ⓐ Ⓑ Ⓒ Ⓓ Ⓔ	39. Ⓐ Ⓑ Ⓒ Ⓓ Ⓔ	61. Ⓐ Ⓑ Ⓒ Ⓓ Ⓔ	83. Ⓐ Ⓑ Ⓒ Ⓓ Ⓔ
18. Ⓐ Ⓑ Ⓒ Ⓓ Ⓔ	40. Ⓐ Ⓑ Ⓒ Ⓓ Ⓔ	62. Ⓐ Ⓑ Ⓒ Ⓓ Ⓔ	84. Ⓐ Ⓑ Ⓒ Ⓓ Ⓔ
19. Ⓐ Ⓑ Ⓒ Ⓓ Ⓔ	41. Ⓐ Ⓑ Ⓒ Ⓓ Ⓔ	63. Ⓐ Ⓑ Ⓒ Ⓓ Ⓔ	85. Ⓐ Ⓑ Ⓒ Ⓓ Ⓔ
20. Ⓐ Ⓑ Ⓒ Ⓓ Ⓔ	42. Ⓐ Ⓑ Ⓒ Ⓓ Ⓔ	64. Ⓐ Ⓑ Ⓒ Ⓓ Ⓔ	86. Ⓐ Ⓑ Ⓒ Ⓓ Ⓔ
21. Ⓐ Ⓑ Ⓒ Ⓓ Ⓔ	43. Ⓐ Ⓑ Ⓒ Ⓓ Ⓔ	65. Ⓐ Ⓑ Ⓒ Ⓓ Ⓔ	87. Ⓐ Ⓑ Ⓒ Ⓓ Ⓔ
22. Ⓐ Ⓑ Ⓒ Ⓓ Ⓔ	44. Ⓐ Ⓑ Ⓒ Ⓓ Ⓔ	66. Ⓐ Ⓑ Ⓒ Ⓓ Ⓔ	88. Ⓐ Ⓑ Ⓒ Ⓓ Ⓔ

Worksheet

Directions: *Listen carefully to the instructions and mark each item on this worksheet as directed. Then complete each question by marking the answer sheet as directed. For each answer, you will darken the answer sheet with a number-letter combination.*

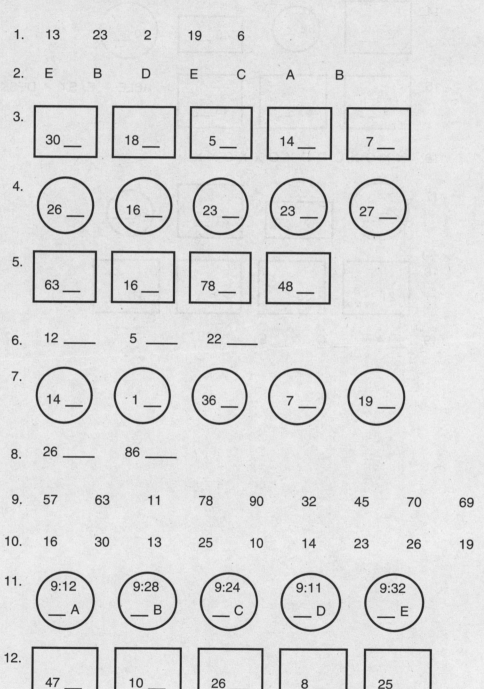

1.   13   23   2   19   6

2.   E   B   D   E   C   A   B

3.   30 __   18 __   5 __   14 __   7 __

4.   26 __   16 __   23 __   23 __   27 __

5.   63 __   16 __   78 __   48 __

6.   12 ___   5 ___   22 ___

7.   14 __   1 __   36 __   7 __   19 __

8.   26 ___   86 ___

9.   57   63   11   78   90   32   45   70   69

10.   16   30   13   25   10   14   23   26   19

11.   9:12 __ A   9:28 __ B   9:24 __ C   9:11 __ D   9:32 __ E

12.   47 __   10 __   26 __   8 __   25 __

TEAR HERE

13.

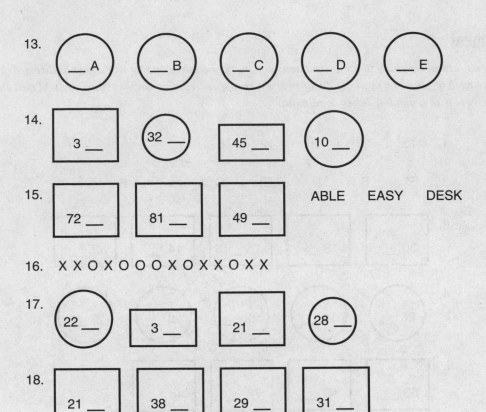

14.

15. ABLE   EASY   DESK

16. X X O X O O O X O X X O X X

17.

18.

19. __A   __C   __E

Oral Instructions

Here are the instructions to be read aloud. Do **not** read aloud the words in parentheses.

On the job you will have to listen to directions and then do what you have been told to do. In this test, I will read instructions to you. Try to understand them as I read them; I cannot repeat them. Once we begin, you may not ask any questions until the end of the test.

On the job you won't have to deal with pictures, numbers, and letters like those in the test, but you will have to listen to instructions and follow them. We are using this test to see how well you can follow instructions.

You are to mark your test booklet according to the instructions that I'll read to you. After each set of instructions, I'll give you time to record your answers on the separate answer sheet.

The actual test begins now.

Look at line 1 on the worksheet. (Pause slightly.) Draw a line under the fourth number in the line. (Pause 2 seconds.) Now, on your answer sheet, find the number under which you just drew the line and darken space A for that number. (Pause 5 seconds.)

Look at the letters in line 2 on the worksheet. (Pause slightly.) Draw a line under the fifth letter in the line. Now, on your answer sheet, find number 59 (pause 2 seconds) and darken the space for the letter under which you drew a line. (Pause 5 seconds.)

Look at the letters in line 2 on the worksheet again. (Pause slightly.) Now draw two lines under the third letter in the line. (Pause 2 seconds.) Now, on your answer sheet, find number 65 (pause 2 seconds) and darken the space for the letter under which you drew two lines. (Pause 5 seconds.)

Look at line 3 on the worksheet. (Pause slightly.) Write an E in the last box. (Pause 2 seconds.) Now, on your answer sheet, find the number in that box and darken space E for that number. (Pause 5 seconds.)

Now look at line 3 again. (Pause slightly.) Write an A in the first box. (Pause 2 seconds.) Now, on your answer sheet, find the number in that box and darken space A for that number. (Pause 5 seconds.)

Look at line 4. The number in each circle is the number of packages in a mail sack. In the circle for the sack holding the largest number of packages, write a B as in baker. (Pause 2 seconds.) Now, on your answer sheet, darken the space for the number-letter combination that is in the circle you just wrote in. (Pause 5 seconds.)

Look at line 4 again. In the circle for the sack holding the smallest number of packages, write an E. (Pause 2 seconds.) Now, on your answer sheet, darken the space for the number-letter combination that is in the circle you just wrote in. (Pause 5 seconds.)

Look at the drawings on line 5 on the worksheet. The four boxes are trucks for carrying mail. (Pause slightly.) The truck with the highest number is to be loaded first. Write B as in baker on the line beside the highest number. (Pause 2 seconds.) Now, on your answer sheet, darken the space for the number-letter combination that is in the box you just wrote in. (Pause 5 seconds.)

Look at line 6 on the worksheet. (Pause slightly.) Next to the middle number write the letter D as in dog. (Pause 2 seconds.) Now, on your answer sheet, find the space for the number beside which you wrote and darken space D as in dog. (Pause 5 seconds.)

Look at the five circles in line 7 on the worksheet. Write B as in baker on the blank in the second circle. (Pause 2 seconds.) Now, on your answer sheet, darken the space for the number-letter combination that is in the circle you just wrote in. (Pause 5 seconds.)

Now take the worksheet again and write C on the blank in the third circle on line 7. (Pause 2 seconds.) Now, on your answer sheet, darken the space for the number-letter combination that is in the circle you just wrote in. (Pause 5 seconds.)

Now look at line 8 on the worksheet. (Pause slightly.) Write an A on the line next to the right-hand number. (Pause 2 seconds.) Now, on your answer sheet, find the space for the number beside which you wrote and darken box A. (Pause 5 seconds.)

Look at line 9 on the worksheet. (Pause slightly.) Draw a line under every number that is more than 60 but less than 70. (Pause 12 seconds.) Now, on your answer sheet, for each number that you drew a line under, darken space C. (Pause 25 seconds.)

Look at line 10 on the worksheet. (Pause slightly.) Draw a line under every number that is more than 5 and less than 15. (Pause 10 seconds.) Now, on your answer sheet, for each number that you drew a line under, darken space D as in dog. (Pause 25 seconds.)

Look at line 11 on the worksheet. (Pause slightly.) In each circle there is a time when the mail must leave. In the circle for the latest time, write on the line the last two figures of the time. (Pause 5 seconds.) Now, on your answer sheet, darken the space for the number-letter combination that is in the circle you just wrote in. (Pause 5 seconds.)

Look at the five boxes in line 12 on your worksheet. (Pause slightly.) If 6 is less than 3, put an E in the fourth box. (Pause slightly.) If 6 is not less than 3, put a B as in baker in the first box. (Pause 10 seconds.) Now, on your answer sheet, darken the space for the number-letter combination that is in the box you just wrote in. (Pause 5 seconds.)

Now look at line 13 on the worksheet. (Pause slightly.) There are five circles. Each circle has a letter. (Pause slightly.) In the second circle, write the answer to this question: Which of the following numbers is smallest: 72, 51, 88, 71, 58? (Pause 10 seconds.) Now, on your answer sheet, darken the space for the number-letter combination that is in the circle you just wrote in. (Pause 5 seconds.) In the third circle on the same line, write 28. (Pause 2 seconds.) Now, on your answer sheet, darken the space for the number-letter combination that is in the circle you just wrote in. (Pause 5 seconds.) In the fourth circle do nothing. In the fifth circle write the answer to this question: How many months are there in a year? (Pause 5 seconds.) Now, on your answer sheet, darken the space for the number-letter combination that is in the circle you just wrote in. (Pause 5 seconds.)

Look at line 14 on your worksheet. (Pause slightly.) There are two circles and two boxes of different sizes with numbers in them. (Pause slightly.) If 2 is smaller than 4 and if 7 is less than 3, write A in the larger circle. (Pause slightly.) Otherwise write B as in baker in the smaller box. (Pause 10 seconds.) Now, on your answer sheet, darken the space for the number-letter combination in the box or circle in which you just wrote. (Pause 5 seconds.)

Look at the boxes and words in line 15 on the worksheet. (Pause slightly.) Write the second letter of the first word in the third box. (Pause 5 seconds.) Write the first letter of the second word in the first box. (Pause 5 seconds.) Write the first letter of the third word in the second box. (Pause 5 seconds.) Now, on your answer sheet, darken the spaces for the number-letter combinations that are in the three boxes you just wrote in. (Pause 15 seconds.)

Look at line 16 on the worksheet. (Pause slightly.) Draw a line under every "0" in the line. (Pause 5 seconds.) Count the number of lines that you have drawn, subtract 2, and write that number at the end of the line. (Pause 5 seconds.) Now, on your answer sheet, find that number and darken space D as in dog for that number. (Pause 5 seconds.)

Look at line 17 on the worksheet. (Pause slightly.) If the number in the left-hand circle is smaller than the number in the right-hand circle, add 2 to the number in the left-hand circle, and change the number in that circle to this number. (Pause 8 seconds.) Then write B as in baker next to the new number. (Pause slightly.) Next, write E beside the number in the smaller box. (Pause 3 seconds.) Then, on your answer sheet, darken the spaces for the number-letter combinations that are in the box and circle you just wrote in. (Pause 5 seconds.)

Look at line 18 on the worksheet. (Pause slightly.) If in a year October comes before September, write A in the box with the smallest number. (Pause slightly.) If it does not, write C in the box with the largest number. (Pause 10 seconds.) Now, on your answer sheet, darken the space for the number-letter combination that is in the box you just wrote in. (Pause 5 seconds.)

Look at line 19 on the worksheet. (Pause slightly.) On the line beside the second letter, write the highest of these numbers: 12, 56, 42, 39, 8. (Pause 2 seconds.) Now, on your answer sheet, darken the space of the number-letter combination you just wrote. (Pause 5 seconds.)

82 POSTAL EXAMS HANDBOOK

ANSWERS TO PRACTICE EXAM I
Correctly Filled Answer Grid

1. A ● C D E
2. A B C D E
3. A B C D ●
4. A B C ● E
5. A B C ● E
6. A B C D E
7. A B C D ●
8. A B C D E
9. A B C D E
10. A B C ● E
11. A B C D E
12. A B C D ●
13. A B C ● E
14. A B C ● E
15. A B C D E
16. A B C D ●
17. A B C D E
18. A B C D E
19. ● B C D E
20. A B C D E
21. A B C D E
22. A B C D E

23. A B C D E
24. A ● C D E
25. A B C D E
26. A B C D E
27. A ● C D E
28. A B ● D E
29. A B C D E
30. ● B C D E
31. A B C D E
32. A B C D ●
33. A B C D E
34. A B C D E
35. A B C D E
36. A B ● D E
37. A B C D E
38. A B ● D E
39. A B C D E
40. A B C D E
41. A B C D E
42. A B C D E
43. A B C D E
44. A B C D E

45. A ● C D E
46. A B C D E
47. A ● C D E
48. A B C D E
49. A ● C D E
50. A B C D E
51. A ● C D E
52. A B C D E
53. A B C D E
54. A B C D E
55. A B C D E
56. A B ● D E
57. A B C D E
58. A B C D E
59. A B ● D E
60. A B C D E
61. A B C D E
62. A B C D E
63. A B ● D E
64. A B C D E
65. A B C ● E
66. A B C D E

67. A B C D E
68. A B C D E
69. A B ● D E
70. A B C D E
71. A B C D E
72. A B C D ●
73. A B C D E
74. A B C D E
75. A B C D E
76. A B C D E
77. A B C D E
78. A ● C D E
79. A B C D E
80. A B C D E
81. A B C ● E
82. A B C D E
83. A B C D E
84. A B C D E
85. A B C D E
86. ● B C D E
87. A B C D E
88. A B C D E

Correctly Filled Worksheet

1. 13   23   2   <u>19</u>   6

2. E   B   <u>D</u>   E   <u>C</u>   A   B

3. [30 <u>A</u>]   [18 __]   [5 __]   [14 __]   [7 <u>E</u>]

4. (26 __)   (16 <u>E</u>)   (23 __)   (23 __)   (27 <u>B</u>)

5. [63 __]   [16 __]   [78 <u>B</u>]   [48 __]

6. 12 ____   5 __d__   22 ____

7. (14 __)   (1 <u>B</u>)   (36 <u>C</u>)   (7 __)   (19 __)

8. 26 ____   86 <u>A</u>

9. 57   <u>63</u>   11   78   90   32   45   70   <u>69</u>

10. 16   30   <u>13</u>   25   <u>10</u>   <u>14</u>   23   26   19

11. (9:12 __ A)   (9:28 __ B)   (9:24 __ C)   (9:11 __ D)   (9:32 <u>32</u> E)

12. [47 <u>B</u>]   [10 __]   [26 __]   [8 __]   [25 __]

13.

(__A)   (5̲1̲ B)   (2̲8̲ C)   (__D)   (1̲2̲ E)

14.

[3 __]   (32 __)   [45 B̲]   (10 __)

15.

[72 E̲]   [81 D̲]   [49 B̲]   ABLE   EASY   DESK

16. X X O̲ X O̲ O̲ O̲ X O̲ X X O̲ X X **4**

17.

(24 2̲2̲ B̲)   [3 E̲]   [21 __]   (28 __)

18.

[21 __]   [38 C̲]   [29 __]   [31 __]

19. __A   5̲6̲ C   __E

PRACTICE EXAM II

How did you do on the first practice exam? Here is another one for you to try.

Answer Sheet

1. Ⓐ Ⓑ Ⓒ Ⓓ Ⓔ	23. Ⓐ Ⓑ Ⓒ Ⓓ Ⓔ	45. Ⓐ Ⓑ Ⓒ Ⓓ Ⓔ	67. Ⓐ Ⓑ Ⓒ Ⓓ Ⓔ
2. Ⓐ Ⓑ Ⓒ Ⓓ Ⓔ	24. Ⓐ Ⓑ Ⓒ Ⓓ Ⓔ	46. Ⓐ Ⓑ Ⓒ Ⓓ Ⓔ	68. Ⓐ Ⓑ Ⓒ Ⓓ Ⓔ
3. Ⓐ Ⓑ Ⓒ Ⓓ Ⓔ	25. Ⓐ Ⓑ Ⓒ Ⓓ Ⓔ	47. Ⓐ Ⓑ Ⓒ Ⓓ Ⓔ	69. Ⓐ Ⓑ Ⓒ Ⓓ Ⓔ
4. Ⓐ Ⓑ Ⓒ Ⓓ Ⓔ	26. Ⓐ Ⓑ Ⓒ Ⓓ Ⓔ	48. Ⓐ Ⓑ Ⓒ Ⓓ Ⓔ	70. Ⓐ Ⓑ Ⓒ Ⓓ Ⓔ
5. Ⓐ Ⓑ Ⓒ Ⓓ Ⓔ	27. Ⓐ Ⓑ Ⓒ Ⓓ Ⓔ	49. Ⓐ Ⓑ Ⓒ Ⓓ Ⓔ	71. Ⓐ Ⓑ Ⓒ Ⓓ Ⓔ
6. Ⓐ Ⓑ Ⓒ Ⓓ Ⓔ	28. Ⓐ Ⓑ Ⓒ Ⓓ Ⓔ	50. Ⓐ Ⓑ Ⓒ Ⓓ Ⓔ	72. Ⓐ Ⓑ Ⓒ Ⓓ Ⓔ
7. Ⓐ Ⓑ Ⓒ Ⓓ Ⓔ	29. Ⓐ Ⓑ Ⓒ Ⓓ Ⓔ	51. Ⓐ Ⓑ Ⓒ Ⓓ Ⓔ	73. Ⓐ Ⓑ Ⓒ Ⓓ Ⓔ
8. Ⓐ Ⓑ Ⓒ Ⓓ Ⓔ	30. Ⓐ Ⓑ Ⓒ Ⓓ Ⓔ	52. Ⓐ Ⓑ Ⓒ Ⓓ Ⓔ	74. Ⓐ Ⓑ Ⓒ Ⓓ Ⓔ
9. Ⓐ Ⓑ Ⓒ Ⓓ Ⓔ	31. Ⓐ Ⓑ Ⓒ Ⓓ Ⓔ	53. Ⓐ Ⓑ Ⓒ Ⓓ Ⓔ	75. Ⓐ Ⓑ Ⓒ Ⓓ Ⓔ
10. Ⓐ Ⓑ Ⓒ Ⓓ Ⓔ	32. Ⓐ Ⓑ Ⓒ Ⓓ Ⓔ	54. Ⓐ Ⓑ Ⓒ Ⓓ Ⓔ	76. Ⓐ Ⓑ Ⓒ Ⓓ Ⓔ
11. Ⓐ Ⓑ Ⓒ Ⓓ Ⓔ	33. Ⓐ Ⓑ Ⓒ Ⓓ Ⓔ	55. Ⓐ Ⓑ Ⓒ Ⓓ Ⓔ	77. Ⓐ Ⓑ Ⓒ Ⓓ Ⓔ
12. Ⓐ Ⓑ Ⓒ Ⓓ Ⓔ	34. Ⓐ Ⓑ Ⓒ Ⓓ Ⓔ	56. Ⓐ Ⓑ Ⓒ Ⓓ Ⓔ	78. Ⓐ Ⓑ Ⓒ Ⓓ Ⓔ
13. Ⓐ Ⓑ Ⓒ Ⓓ Ⓔ	35. Ⓐ Ⓑ Ⓒ Ⓓ Ⓔ	57. Ⓐ Ⓑ Ⓒ Ⓓ Ⓔ	79. Ⓐ Ⓑ Ⓒ Ⓓ Ⓔ
14. Ⓐ Ⓑ Ⓒ Ⓓ Ⓔ	36. Ⓐ Ⓑ Ⓒ Ⓓ Ⓔ	58. Ⓐ Ⓑ Ⓒ Ⓓ Ⓔ	80. Ⓐ Ⓑ Ⓒ Ⓓ Ⓔ
15. Ⓐ Ⓑ Ⓒ Ⓓ Ⓔ	37. Ⓐ Ⓑ Ⓒ Ⓓ Ⓔ	59. Ⓐ Ⓑ Ⓒ Ⓓ Ⓔ	81. Ⓐ Ⓑ Ⓒ Ⓓ Ⓔ
16. Ⓐ Ⓑ Ⓒ Ⓓ Ⓔ	38. Ⓐ Ⓑ Ⓒ Ⓓ Ⓔ	60. Ⓐ Ⓑ Ⓒ Ⓓ Ⓔ	82. Ⓐ Ⓑ Ⓒ Ⓓ Ⓔ
17. Ⓐ Ⓑ Ⓒ Ⓓ Ⓔ	39. Ⓐ Ⓑ Ⓒ Ⓓ Ⓔ	61. Ⓐ Ⓑ Ⓒ Ⓓ Ⓔ	83. Ⓐ Ⓑ Ⓒ Ⓓ Ⓔ
18. Ⓐ Ⓑ Ⓒ Ⓓ Ⓔ	40. Ⓐ Ⓑ Ⓒ Ⓓ Ⓔ	62. Ⓐ Ⓑ Ⓒ Ⓓ Ⓔ	84. Ⓐ Ⓑ Ⓒ Ⓓ Ⓔ
19. Ⓐ Ⓑ Ⓒ Ⓓ Ⓔ	41. Ⓐ Ⓑ Ⓒ Ⓓ Ⓔ	63. Ⓐ Ⓑ Ⓒ Ⓓ Ⓔ	85. Ⓐ Ⓑ Ⓒ Ⓓ Ⓔ
20. Ⓐ Ⓑ Ⓒ Ⓓ Ⓔ	42. Ⓐ Ⓑ Ⓒ Ⓓ Ⓔ	64. Ⓐ Ⓑ Ⓒ Ⓓ Ⓔ	86. Ⓐ Ⓑ Ⓒ Ⓓ Ⓔ
21. Ⓐ Ⓑ Ⓒ Ⓓ Ⓔ	43. Ⓐ Ⓑ Ⓒ Ⓓ Ⓔ	65. Ⓐ Ⓑ Ⓒ Ⓓ Ⓔ	87. Ⓐ Ⓑ Ⓒ Ⓓ Ⓔ
22. Ⓐ Ⓑ Ⓒ Ⓓ Ⓔ	44. Ⓐ Ⓑ Ⓒ Ⓓ Ⓔ	66. Ⓐ Ⓑ Ⓒ Ⓓ Ⓔ	88. Ⓐ Ⓑ Ⓒ Ⓓ Ⓔ

Worksheet

Directions: *Listen carefully to the instructions read to you and mark each item on the following worksheet as directed. Then complete each question by marking the answer sheet on the previous page as directed. For each answer, you will darken the answer sheet for a number-letter combination.*

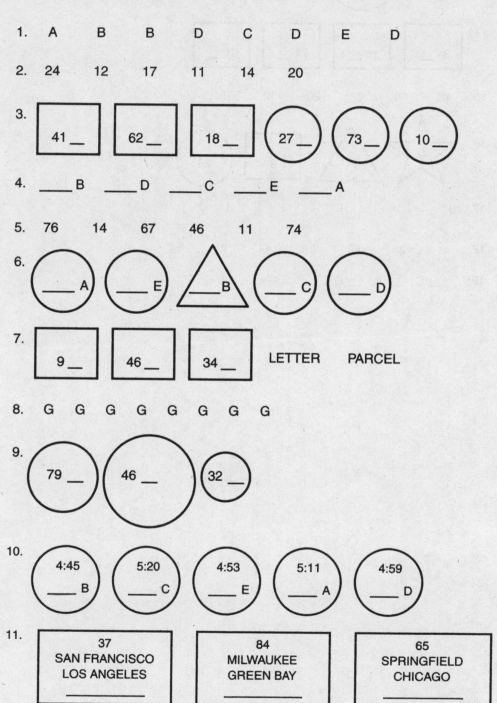

1.   A   B   B   D   C   D   E   D

2.   24   12   17   11   14   20

3.   41__   62__   18__   27__   73__   10__

4.   __B   __D   __C   __E   __A

5.   76   14   67   46   11   74

6.   __A   __E   __B   __C   __D

7.   9__   46__   34__   LETTER   PARCEL

8.   G   G   G   G   G   G   G   G

9.   79__   46__   32__

10.   4:45 __B   5:20 __C   4:53 __E   5:11 __A   4:59 __D

11.

37 SAN FRANCISCO LOS ANGELES _____	84 MILWAUKEE GREEN BAY _____	65 SPRINGFIELD CHICAGO _____

TEAR HERE

12.   E   M   R   B   C   A

13.   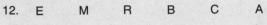 __ C   __ E   __ D   2   51   19

14.   [34 __]   [18 __]   [71 __]   [81 __]

15.   42   68   87   20   12   36

16.   ☆ 8   △ 14   ▭ 6   ◯ 24

17.   J   J   J   L   L   L   J   L   J   J

18.   41   38   62   59   44   40   54

19.   __ C   __ A   __ D

Oral Instructions

Here are the instructions to be read (the words in parentheses should *not* be read aloud).

On the job you will have to listen to instructions and then do what you have been told to do. In this test, I will read instructions to you. Try to understand them as I read them; I cannot repeat them. Once we begin, you may not ask any questions until the end of the test.

On the job you won't have to deal with pictures, numbers and letters like those on the test, but you will have to listen to instructions and follow them. We are using this test to see how well you can follow instructions.

You are to mark your worksheet according to the instruction that I'll read to you. After each set of instructions, I'll give you time to record your answers on the separate answer sheet.

The actual test begins now.

Look at line 1 on your worksheet. (Pause slightly.) Circle the seventh letter on line 1. (Pause 5 seconds.) Now, on your answer sheet, find number 83 and for number 83 darken the space for the letter you just circled. (Pause 5 seconds.)

Look at line 2 on your worksheet. (Pause slightly.) Draw a line under all the odd numbers between 12 and 20. (Pause 5 seconds.) Now, on your answer sheet, darken space B as in baker for all the numbers under which you drew a line. (Pause 5 seconds.)

Look at line 2 again. (Pause slightly.) Find the number that is two times another number on line 2 and circle it. (Pause 5 seconds.) Now, on your answer sheet, darken space A for the number you just circled. (Pause 5 seconds.)

Look at line 3 on your worksheet. (Pause slightly.) Write the letter C in the middle box. (Pause 2 seconds.) Now, on your answer sheet, darken the space for the number-letter combination in the figure you just wrote in. (Pause 5 seconds.)

Look at line 3 again. (Pause slightly.) Write the letter D as in dog in the left-hand circle. (Pause 2 seconds.) Now, on your answer sheet, darken the space for the number-letter combination in the figure you just wrote in. (Pause 5 seconds.)

Look at line 4 on your worksheet. (Pause slightly.) If first class mail costs more than bulk rate mail, write the number 22 on the third line; if not, write the number 19 on the fourth line. (Pause 5 seconds.) Now, on your answer sheet, darken the space for the number-letter combination on the line you just wrote on. (Pause 5 seconds.)

Look at line 4 again. (Pause slightly.) Write the number 31 on the second line from the left. (Pause 2 seconds.) Now, on your answer sheet, darken the space for the number-letter combination on the line on which you just wrote. (Pause 5 seconds.)

Look at line 5 on your worksheet. (Pause slightly.) Find the highest number on line 5 and draw a line under the number. (Pause 2 seconds.) Now, on your answer sheet, find the number under which you just drew a line and darken space E for that number. (Pause 5 seconds.)

Look at line 5 again. (Pause slightly.) Find the lowest number on line 5 and draw two lines under the number. (Pause 2 seconds.) Now, on your answer sheet, find the number under which you just drew two lines and darken space A for that number. (Pause 5 seconds.)

Look at line 6 on your worksheet. (Pause slightly.) Write the number 57 in the figure that does not belong on line 6. (Pause 2 seconds.) Now, on your answer sheet, darken the number-letter combination that is in the figure in which you just wrote. (Pause 5 seconds.)

Look at line 7 on your worksheet. (Pause slightly.) Write the second letter of the second word in the first box. (Pause 5 seconds.) Write the fifth letter of the first word in the third box. (Pause 5 seconds.) Write the fourth letter of the second word in the second box. (Pause 5 seconds.) Now, on your answer sheet, darken the number-letter combinations in all three boxes. (Pause 15 seconds.)

Look at line 8 on your worksheet. (Pause slightly.) Count the number of G's on line 8 and divide the number of G's by 2. Write that number at the end of the line. (Pause 5 seconds.) Now, on your answer sheet, darken space D as in dog for the number you wrote at the end of line 8. (Pause 5 seconds.)

Look at line 9 on your worksheet. (Pause slightly.) Write the letter B as in baker in the middle-sized circle. (Pause 2 seconds.) Now, on your answer sheet, darken the space for the number-letter combination in the circle in which you just wrote. (Pause 5 seconds.)

Look at line 10 on your worksheet. (Pause slightly.) The time in each circle represents the last scheduled pickup of the day from a street letterbox. Find the circle with the earliest pickup time and write the last two figures of that time on the line in the circle. (Pause 10 seconds.) Now, on your answer sheet, darken the space for the number-letter combination in the circle you just wrote in. (Pause 5 seconds.)

Look at line 10 again. (Pause slightly.) Find the circle with the latest pickup time and write the last two figures of that time on the line in the circle. (Pause 10 seconds.) Now, on your answer sheet, darken the space for the number-letter combination in the circle in which you just wrote. (Pause 5 seconds.)

Look at line 11 on your worksheet. (Pause slightly.) Mail directed for San Francisco and Los Angeles is to be placed in box 37; mail for Milwaukee and Green Bay in box 84; mail for Springfield and Chicago in box 65. Find the box for mail being sent to Green Bay and write the letter A in the box. (Pause 2 seconds.) Now, on your answer sheet, darken the number-letter combination for the box you just wrote in. (Pause 5 seconds.)

Look at line 11 again. (Pause slightly.) Mr. Green lives in Springfield. Find the box in which to put Mr. Green's mail and write E on the line. (Pause 2 seconds.) Now, on your answer sheet, darken the space for the number-letter combination in the box in which you just wrote. (Pause 5 seconds.)

Look at line 12 on your worksheet. (Pause slightly.) Find the letter on line 12 that is not in the word CREAM and draw a line under the letter. (Pause 2 seconds.) Now, on your answer sheet, find number 38 and darken the space for the letter under which you just drew a line. (Pause 5 seconds.)

Look at line 13 on your worksheet. (Pause slightly.) Write the smallest number in the largest circle. (Pause 2 seconds.) Write the largest number in the left-hand circle. (Pause 2 seconds.) Now, on your answer sheet, darken the number-letter combinations that are in the circles in which you just wrote. (Pause 10 seconds.)

Look at line 14 on your worksheet. (Pause slightly.) If there are 36 inches in a foot, write B as in baker in the first box; if not, write D as in dog in the third box. (Pause 5 seconds.) Now, on your answer sheet, darken the number-letter combination that is in the box in which you just wrote. (Pause 5 seconds.)

Look at line 14 again. (Pause slightly.) Find the box that contains a number in the teens and write B as in baker in that box. (Pause 2 seconds.) Now, on your answer sheet, darken the number-letter combination that is in the box in which you just wrote. (Pause 5 seconds.)

Look at line 15 on your worksheet. (Pause slightly.) Circle the only number on line 15 that is not divisible by 2. (Pause 2 seconds.) Now, on your answer sheet, darken space A for the number you circled. (Pause 5 seconds.)

Look at line 16 on your worksheet. (Pause slightly.) If the number in the circle is greater than the number in the box, write the letter E in the box; if not, write the letter E in the circle. (Pause 5 seconds.) Now, on your answer sheet, darken the number-letter combination that is in the figure in which you just wrote. (Pause 5 seconds.)

Look at line 16 again. (Pause slightly.) If the number in the triangle is smaller than the number in the figure directly to its left, write the letter A in the triangle; if not, write the letter C in the triangle. (Pause 5 seconds.) Now, on your answer sheet, darken the number-letter combination that is in the figure you just wrote in. (Pause 5 seconds.)

Look at line 17 on your worksheet. (Pause slightly.) Count the number of J's on line 17, multiply the number of J's by 5 and write that number at the end of the line. (Pause 5 seconds.) Now, on your answer sheet, find the number you just wrote at the end of the line and darken space C for that number. (Pause 5 seconds.)

Look at line 18 on your worksheet. (Pause slightly.) Draw one line under the number that is at the middle of line 18. (Pause 5 seconds.) Now, on your answer sheet, darken space B as in baker for the number under which you just drew a line. (Pause 5 seconds.)

Look at line 18 again. (Pause slightly.) Draw two lines under each odd number that falls between 35 and 45. (Pause 10 seconds.) Now, on your answer sheet, darken space D as in dog for each number under which you drew two lines. (Pause 5 seconds.)

Look at line 19 on your worksheet. (Pause slightly.) Next to the last letter on line 19, write the first number you hear: 53, 18, 6, 75. (Pause 2 seconds.) Now, on your answer sheet, darken the space for the number-letter combination you just wrote. (Pause 5 seconds.)

ANSWERS TO PRACTICE EXAM II
Correctly Completed Answer Sheet

1. Ⓐ Ⓑ Ⓒ Ⓓ Ⓔ	23. Ⓐ Ⓑ Ⓒ Ⓓ Ⓔ	45. Ⓐ ● Ⓒ Ⓓ Ⓔ	67. Ⓐ Ⓑ Ⓒ Ⓓ Ⓔ
2. Ⓐ Ⓑ Ⓒ Ⓓ ●	24. ● Ⓑ Ⓒ Ⓓ Ⓔ	46. Ⓐ Ⓑ ● Ⓓ Ⓔ	68. Ⓐ Ⓑ Ⓒ Ⓓ Ⓔ
3. Ⓐ Ⓑ Ⓒ Ⓓ Ⓔ	25. Ⓐ Ⓑ Ⓒ Ⓓ Ⓔ	47. Ⓐ Ⓑ Ⓒ Ⓓ Ⓔ	69. Ⓐ Ⓑ Ⓒ Ⓓ Ⓔ
4. Ⓐ Ⓑ Ⓒ ● Ⓔ	26. Ⓐ Ⓑ Ⓒ Ⓓ Ⓔ	48. Ⓐ Ⓑ Ⓒ Ⓓ Ⓔ	70. Ⓐ Ⓑ Ⓒ Ⓓ Ⓔ
5. Ⓐ Ⓑ Ⓒ Ⓓ Ⓔ	27. Ⓐ Ⓑ Ⓒ ● Ⓔ	49. Ⓐ Ⓑ Ⓒ Ⓓ Ⓔ	71. Ⓐ Ⓑ Ⓒ ● Ⓔ
6. Ⓐ Ⓑ Ⓒ Ⓓ ●	28. Ⓐ Ⓑ Ⓒ Ⓓ Ⓔ	50. Ⓐ Ⓑ Ⓒ Ⓓ Ⓔ	72. Ⓐ Ⓑ Ⓒ Ⓓ Ⓔ
7. Ⓐ Ⓑ Ⓒ Ⓓ Ⓔ	29. Ⓐ Ⓑ Ⓒ Ⓓ Ⓔ	51. Ⓐ Ⓑ ● Ⓓ Ⓔ	73. Ⓐ Ⓑ Ⓒ Ⓓ Ⓔ
8. Ⓐ Ⓑ Ⓒ Ⓓ Ⓔ	30. Ⓐ Ⓑ ● Ⓓ Ⓔ	52. Ⓐ Ⓑ Ⓒ Ⓓ Ⓔ	74. Ⓐ Ⓑ Ⓒ Ⓓ Ⓔ
9. ● Ⓑ Ⓒ Ⓓ Ⓔ	31. Ⓐ Ⓑ Ⓒ ● Ⓔ	53. Ⓐ Ⓑ Ⓒ ● Ⓔ	75. Ⓐ Ⓑ Ⓒ Ⓓ Ⓔ
10. Ⓐ Ⓑ Ⓒ Ⓓ Ⓔ	32. Ⓐ Ⓑ Ⓒ Ⓓ Ⓔ	54. Ⓐ Ⓑ Ⓒ Ⓓ Ⓔ	76. Ⓐ Ⓑ Ⓒ Ⓓ ●
11. ● Ⓑ Ⓒ Ⓓ Ⓔ	33. Ⓐ Ⓑ Ⓒ Ⓓ Ⓔ	55. Ⓐ Ⓑ Ⓒ Ⓓ Ⓔ	77. Ⓐ Ⓑ Ⓒ Ⓓ Ⓔ
12. Ⓐ Ⓑ Ⓒ Ⓓ Ⓔ	34. Ⓐ Ⓑ Ⓒ Ⓓ ●	56. Ⓐ Ⓑ Ⓒ Ⓓ Ⓔ	78. Ⓐ Ⓑ Ⓒ Ⓓ Ⓔ
13. Ⓐ Ⓑ Ⓒ Ⓓ Ⓔ	35. Ⓐ Ⓑ Ⓒ Ⓓ Ⓔ	57. Ⓐ ● Ⓒ Ⓓ Ⓔ	79. Ⓐ ● Ⓒ Ⓓ Ⓔ
14. Ⓐ Ⓑ ● Ⓓ Ⓔ	36. Ⓐ Ⓑ Ⓒ Ⓓ Ⓔ	58. Ⓐ Ⓑ Ⓒ Ⓓ Ⓔ	80. Ⓐ Ⓑ Ⓒ Ⓓ Ⓔ
15. Ⓐ Ⓑ Ⓒ Ⓓ Ⓔ	37. Ⓐ Ⓑ Ⓒ Ⓓ Ⓔ	59. Ⓐ ● Ⓒ Ⓓ Ⓔ	81. Ⓐ Ⓑ Ⓒ Ⓓ Ⓔ
16. Ⓐ Ⓑ Ⓒ Ⓓ Ⓔ	38. Ⓐ ● Ⓒ Ⓓ Ⓔ	60. Ⓐ Ⓑ Ⓒ Ⓓ Ⓔ	82. Ⓐ Ⓑ Ⓒ Ⓓ Ⓔ
17. Ⓐ ● Ⓒ Ⓓ Ⓔ	39. Ⓐ Ⓑ Ⓒ Ⓓ Ⓔ	61. Ⓐ Ⓑ Ⓒ Ⓓ Ⓔ	83. Ⓐ Ⓑ Ⓒ Ⓓ ●
18. Ⓐ ● Ⓒ Ⓓ Ⓔ	40. Ⓐ Ⓑ Ⓒ Ⓓ Ⓔ	62. Ⓐ Ⓑ ● Ⓓ Ⓔ	84. ● Ⓑ Ⓒ Ⓓ Ⓔ
19. Ⓐ Ⓑ Ⓒ Ⓓ Ⓔ	41. Ⓐ Ⓑ Ⓒ ● Ⓔ	63. Ⓐ Ⓑ Ⓒ Ⓓ Ⓔ	85. Ⓐ Ⓑ Ⓒ Ⓓ Ⓔ
20. Ⓐ Ⓑ ● Ⓓ Ⓔ	42. Ⓐ Ⓑ Ⓒ Ⓓ Ⓔ	64. Ⓐ Ⓑ Ⓒ Ⓓ Ⓔ	86. Ⓐ Ⓑ Ⓒ Ⓓ Ⓔ
21. Ⓐ Ⓑ Ⓒ Ⓓ Ⓔ	43. Ⓐ Ⓑ Ⓒ Ⓓ Ⓔ	65. Ⓐ Ⓑ Ⓒ Ⓓ ●	87. ● Ⓑ Ⓒ Ⓓ Ⓔ
22. Ⓐ Ⓑ ● Ⓓ Ⓔ	44. Ⓐ Ⓑ Ⓒ Ⓓ Ⓔ	66. Ⓐ Ⓑ Ⓒ Ⓓ Ⓔ	88. Ⓐ Ⓑ Ⓒ Ⓓ Ⓔ

Correctly Filled Worksheet

1. A   B   B   D   C   D   (E)   D

2. (24)   12   17   11   14   20

3. [41 __]   [62 C]   [18 __]   (27 D)   (73 __)   (10 __)

4. ___ B   31 D   22 C   ___ E   ___ A

5. 76   14   67   46   11   74

6. (___ A)   (___ E)   △ 57 B   (___ C)   (___ D)

7. [9 A]   [46 C]   [34 E]   LETTER   PARCEL

8. G G G G G G G G 4

9. (79 B)   (46 __)   (32 __)

10. (4:45 45 B)   (5:20 20 C)   (4:53 ___ E)   (5:11 ___ A)   (4:59 ___ D)

11.
| 37 SAN FRANCISCO LOS ANGELES ___ | 84 MILWAUKEE GREEN BAY A | 65 SPRINGFIELD CHICAGO E |

12. E   M   M   R   B̲   C   A

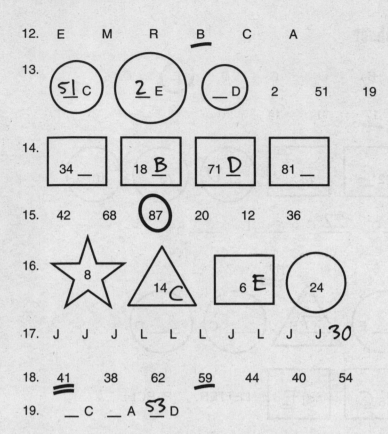

13. (5̲1̲ C)   (2̲ E)   (_ D)   2   51   19

14. [34 _]   [18 B̲]   [71 D̲]   [81 _]

15. 42   68   (87)   20   12   36

16. ☆ 8   △ 14 C   [6 E]   ○ 24

17. J   J   J   L   L   L   J   L   J   J 30

18. 4̲1̲   38   62   5̲9̲   44   40   54

19. _ C   _ A   5̲3̲ D

PART

TWO

Model Examinations

CONTENTS

MODEL EXAMINATION I: EXAM 470 AND EXAM 460

Answer Sheet

Exam 470

Clerk

City Carrier

Distribution Clerk, Machine
(Letter-Sorting Machine Operator)

Flat Sorting Machine Operator

Mail Handler

Mail Processor

Mark-up Clerk, Automated

Exam 460

Rural Carrier

TEAR HERE

Part A—Address Checking

1. Ⓐ Ⓓ	20. Ⓐ Ⓓ	39. Ⓐ Ⓓ	58. Ⓐ Ⓓ	77. Ⓐ Ⓓ
2. Ⓐ Ⓓ	21. Ⓐ Ⓓ	40. Ⓐ Ⓓ	59. Ⓐ Ⓓ	78. Ⓐ Ⓓ
3. Ⓐ Ⓓ	22. Ⓐ Ⓓ	41. Ⓐ Ⓓ	60. Ⓐ Ⓓ	79. Ⓐ Ⓓ
4. Ⓐ Ⓓ	23. Ⓐ Ⓓ	42. Ⓐ Ⓓ	61. Ⓐ Ⓓ	80. Ⓐ Ⓓ
5. Ⓐ Ⓓ	24. Ⓐ Ⓓ	43. Ⓐ Ⓓ	62. Ⓐ Ⓓ	81. Ⓐ Ⓓ
6. Ⓐ Ⓓ	25. Ⓐ Ⓓ	44. Ⓐ Ⓓ	63. Ⓐ Ⓓ	82. Ⓐ Ⓓ
7. Ⓐ Ⓓ	26. Ⓐ Ⓓ	45. Ⓐ Ⓓ	64. Ⓐ Ⓓ	83. Ⓐ Ⓓ
8. Ⓐ Ⓓ	27. Ⓐ Ⓓ	46. Ⓐ Ⓓ	65. Ⓐ Ⓓ	84. Ⓐ Ⓓ
9. Ⓐ Ⓓ	28. Ⓐ Ⓓ	47. Ⓐ Ⓓ	66. Ⓐ Ⓓ	85. Ⓐ Ⓓ
10. Ⓐ Ⓓ	29. Ⓐ Ⓓ	48. Ⓐ Ⓓ	67. Ⓐ Ⓓ	86. Ⓐ Ⓓ
11. Ⓐ Ⓓ	30. Ⓐ Ⓓ	49. Ⓐ Ⓓ	68. Ⓐ Ⓓ	87. Ⓐ Ⓓ
12. Ⓐ Ⓓ	31. Ⓐ Ⓓ	50. Ⓐ Ⓓ	69. Ⓐ Ⓓ	88. Ⓐ Ⓓ
13. Ⓐ Ⓓ	32. Ⓐ Ⓓ	51. Ⓐ Ⓓ	70. Ⓐ Ⓓ	89. Ⓐ Ⓓ
14. Ⓐ Ⓓ	33. Ⓐ Ⓓ	52. Ⓐ Ⓓ	71. Ⓐ Ⓓ	90. Ⓐ Ⓓ
15. Ⓐ Ⓓ	34. Ⓐ Ⓓ	53. Ⓐ Ⓓ	72. Ⓐ Ⓓ	91. Ⓐ Ⓓ
16. Ⓐ Ⓓ	35. Ⓐ Ⓓ	54. Ⓐ Ⓓ	73. Ⓐ Ⓓ	92. Ⓐ Ⓓ
17. Ⓐ Ⓓ	36. Ⓐ Ⓓ	55. Ⓐ Ⓓ	74. Ⓐ Ⓓ	93. Ⓐ Ⓓ
18. Ⓐ Ⓓ	37. Ⓐ Ⓓ	56. Ⓐ Ⓓ	75. Ⓐ Ⓓ	94. Ⓐ Ⓓ
19. Ⓐ Ⓓ	38. Ⓐ Ⓓ	57. Ⓐ Ⓓ	76. Ⓐ Ⓓ	95. Ⓐ Ⓓ

97

Part B—Memory for Addresses

1 Ⓐ Ⓑ Ⓒ Ⓓ Ⓔ 23 Ⓐ Ⓑ Ⓒ Ⓓ Ⓔ 45 Ⓐ Ⓑ Ⓒ Ⓓ Ⓔ 67 Ⓐ Ⓑ Ⓒ Ⓓ Ⓔ
2 Ⓐ Ⓑ Ⓒ Ⓓ Ⓔ 24 Ⓐ Ⓑ Ⓒ Ⓓ Ⓔ 46 Ⓐ Ⓑ Ⓒ Ⓓ Ⓔ 68 Ⓐ Ⓑ Ⓒ Ⓓ Ⓔ
3 Ⓐ Ⓑ Ⓒ Ⓓ Ⓔ 25 Ⓐ Ⓑ Ⓒ Ⓓ Ⓔ 47 Ⓐ Ⓑ Ⓒ Ⓓ Ⓔ 69 Ⓐ Ⓑ Ⓒ Ⓓ Ⓔ
4 Ⓐ Ⓑ Ⓒ Ⓓ Ⓔ 26 Ⓐ Ⓑ Ⓒ Ⓓ Ⓔ 48 Ⓐ Ⓑ Ⓒ Ⓓ Ⓔ 70 Ⓐ Ⓑ Ⓒ Ⓓ Ⓔ
5 Ⓐ Ⓑ Ⓒ Ⓓ Ⓔ 27 Ⓐ Ⓑ Ⓒ Ⓓ Ⓔ 49 Ⓐ Ⓑ Ⓒ Ⓓ Ⓔ 71 Ⓐ Ⓑ Ⓒ Ⓓ Ⓔ
6 Ⓐ Ⓑ Ⓒ Ⓓ Ⓔ 28 Ⓐ Ⓑ Ⓒ Ⓓ Ⓔ 50 Ⓐ Ⓑ Ⓒ Ⓓ Ⓔ 72 Ⓐ Ⓑ Ⓒ Ⓓ Ⓔ
7 Ⓐ Ⓑ Ⓒ Ⓓ Ⓔ 29 Ⓐ Ⓑ Ⓒ Ⓓ Ⓔ 51 Ⓐ Ⓑ Ⓒ Ⓓ Ⓔ 73 Ⓐ Ⓑ Ⓒ Ⓓ Ⓔ
8 Ⓐ Ⓑ Ⓒ Ⓓ Ⓔ 30 Ⓐ Ⓑ Ⓒ Ⓓ Ⓔ 52 Ⓐ Ⓑ Ⓒ Ⓓ Ⓔ 74 Ⓐ Ⓑ Ⓒ Ⓓ Ⓔ
9 Ⓐ Ⓑ Ⓒ Ⓓ Ⓔ 31 Ⓐ Ⓑ Ⓒ Ⓓ Ⓔ 53 Ⓐ Ⓑ Ⓒ Ⓓ Ⓔ 75 Ⓐ Ⓑ Ⓒ Ⓓ Ⓔ
10 Ⓐ Ⓑ Ⓒ Ⓓ Ⓔ 32 Ⓐ Ⓑ Ⓒ Ⓓ Ⓔ 54 Ⓐ Ⓑ Ⓒ Ⓓ Ⓔ 76 Ⓐ Ⓑ Ⓒ Ⓓ Ⓔ
11 Ⓐ Ⓑ Ⓒ Ⓓ Ⓔ 33 Ⓐ Ⓑ Ⓒ Ⓓ Ⓔ 55 Ⓐ Ⓑ Ⓒ Ⓓ Ⓔ 77 Ⓐ Ⓑ Ⓒ Ⓓ Ⓔ
12 Ⓐ Ⓑ Ⓒ Ⓓ Ⓔ 34 Ⓐ Ⓑ Ⓒ Ⓓ Ⓔ 56 Ⓐ Ⓑ Ⓒ Ⓓ Ⓔ 78 Ⓐ Ⓑ Ⓒ Ⓓ Ⓔ
13 Ⓐ Ⓑ Ⓒ Ⓓ Ⓔ 35 Ⓐ Ⓑ Ⓒ Ⓓ Ⓔ 57 Ⓐ Ⓑ Ⓒ Ⓓ Ⓔ 79 Ⓐ Ⓑ Ⓒ Ⓓ Ⓔ
14 Ⓐ Ⓑ Ⓒ Ⓓ Ⓔ 36 Ⓐ Ⓑ Ⓒ Ⓓ Ⓔ 58 Ⓐ Ⓑ Ⓒ Ⓓ Ⓔ 80 Ⓐ Ⓑ Ⓒ Ⓓ Ⓔ
15 Ⓐ Ⓑ Ⓒ Ⓓ Ⓔ 37 Ⓐ Ⓑ Ⓒ Ⓓ Ⓔ 59 Ⓐ Ⓑ Ⓒ Ⓓ Ⓔ 81 Ⓐ Ⓑ Ⓒ Ⓓ Ⓔ
16 Ⓐ Ⓑ Ⓒ Ⓓ Ⓔ 38 Ⓐ Ⓑ Ⓒ Ⓓ Ⓔ 60 Ⓐ Ⓑ Ⓒ Ⓓ Ⓔ 82 Ⓐ Ⓑ Ⓒ Ⓓ Ⓔ
17 Ⓐ Ⓑ Ⓒ Ⓓ Ⓔ 39 Ⓐ Ⓑ Ⓒ Ⓓ Ⓔ 61 Ⓐ Ⓑ Ⓒ Ⓓ Ⓔ 83 Ⓐ Ⓑ Ⓒ Ⓓ Ⓔ
18 Ⓐ Ⓑ Ⓒ Ⓓ Ⓔ 40 Ⓐ Ⓑ Ⓒ Ⓓ Ⓔ 62 Ⓐ Ⓑ Ⓒ Ⓓ Ⓔ 84 Ⓐ Ⓑ Ⓒ Ⓓ Ⓔ
19 Ⓐ Ⓑ Ⓒ Ⓓ Ⓔ 41 Ⓐ Ⓑ Ⓒ Ⓓ Ⓔ 63 Ⓐ Ⓑ Ⓒ Ⓓ Ⓔ 85 Ⓐ Ⓑ Ⓒ Ⓓ Ⓔ
20 Ⓐ Ⓑ Ⓒ Ⓓ Ⓔ 42 Ⓐ Ⓑ Ⓒ Ⓓ Ⓔ 64 Ⓐ Ⓑ Ⓒ Ⓓ Ⓔ 86 Ⓐ Ⓑ Ⓒ Ⓓ Ⓔ
21 Ⓐ Ⓑ Ⓒ Ⓓ Ⓔ 43 Ⓐ Ⓑ Ⓒ Ⓓ Ⓔ 65 Ⓐ Ⓑ Ⓒ Ⓓ Ⓔ 87 Ⓐ Ⓑ Ⓒ Ⓓ Ⓔ
22 Ⓐ Ⓑ Ⓒ Ⓓ Ⓔ 44 Ⓐ Ⓑ Ⓒ Ⓓ Ⓔ 66 Ⓐ Ⓑ Ⓒ Ⓓ Ⓔ 88 Ⓐ Ⓑ Ⓒ Ⓓ Ⓔ

TEAR HERE

Part C—Number Series

1. Ⓐ Ⓑ Ⓒ Ⓓ Ⓔ 7. Ⓐ Ⓑ Ⓒ Ⓓ Ⓔ 13. Ⓐ Ⓑ Ⓒ Ⓓ Ⓔ 19. Ⓐ Ⓑ Ⓒ Ⓓ Ⓔ
2. Ⓐ Ⓑ Ⓒ Ⓓ Ⓔ 8. Ⓐ Ⓑ Ⓒ Ⓓ Ⓔ 14. Ⓐ Ⓑ Ⓒ Ⓓ Ⓔ 20. Ⓐ Ⓑ Ⓒ Ⓓ Ⓔ
3. Ⓐ Ⓑ Ⓒ Ⓓ Ⓔ 9. Ⓐ Ⓑ Ⓒ Ⓓ Ⓔ 15. Ⓐ Ⓑ Ⓒ Ⓓ Ⓔ 21. Ⓐ Ⓑ Ⓒ Ⓓ Ⓔ
4. Ⓐ Ⓑ Ⓒ Ⓓ Ⓔ 10. Ⓐ Ⓑ Ⓒ Ⓓ Ⓔ 16. Ⓐ Ⓑ Ⓒ Ⓓ Ⓔ 22. Ⓐ Ⓑ Ⓒ Ⓓ Ⓔ
5. Ⓐ Ⓑ Ⓒ Ⓓ Ⓔ 11. Ⓐ Ⓑ Ⓒ Ⓓ Ⓔ 17. Ⓐ Ⓑ Ⓒ Ⓓ Ⓔ 23. Ⓐ Ⓑ Ⓒ Ⓓ Ⓔ
6. Ⓐ Ⓑ Ⓒ Ⓓ Ⓔ 12. Ⓐ Ⓑ Ⓒ Ⓓ Ⓔ 18. Ⓐ Ⓑ Ⓒ Ⓓ Ⓔ 24. Ⓐ Ⓑ Ⓒ Ⓓ Ⓔ

Part D—Following Oral Instructions

1 Ⓐ Ⓑ Ⓒ Ⓓ Ⓔ 23 Ⓐ Ⓑ Ⓒ Ⓓ Ⓔ 45 Ⓐ Ⓑ Ⓒ Ⓓ Ⓔ 67 Ⓐ Ⓑ Ⓒ Ⓓ Ⓔ
2 Ⓐ Ⓑ Ⓒ Ⓓ Ⓔ 24 Ⓐ Ⓑ Ⓒ Ⓓ Ⓔ 46 Ⓐ Ⓑ Ⓒ Ⓓ Ⓔ 68 Ⓐ Ⓑ Ⓒ Ⓓ Ⓔ
3 Ⓐ Ⓑ Ⓒ Ⓓ Ⓔ 25 Ⓐ Ⓑ Ⓒ Ⓓ Ⓔ 47 Ⓐ Ⓑ Ⓒ Ⓓ Ⓔ 69 Ⓐ Ⓑ Ⓒ Ⓓ Ⓔ
4 Ⓐ Ⓑ Ⓒ Ⓓ Ⓔ 26 Ⓐ Ⓑ Ⓒ Ⓓ Ⓔ 48 Ⓐ Ⓑ Ⓒ Ⓓ Ⓔ 70 Ⓐ Ⓑ Ⓒ Ⓓ Ⓔ
5 Ⓐ Ⓑ Ⓒ Ⓓ Ⓔ 27 Ⓐ Ⓑ Ⓒ Ⓓ Ⓔ 49 Ⓐ Ⓑ Ⓒ Ⓓ Ⓔ 71 Ⓐ Ⓑ Ⓒ Ⓓ Ⓔ
6 Ⓐ Ⓑ Ⓒ Ⓓ Ⓔ 28 Ⓐ Ⓑ Ⓒ Ⓓ Ⓔ 50 Ⓐ Ⓑ Ⓒ Ⓓ Ⓔ 72 Ⓐ Ⓑ Ⓒ Ⓓ Ⓔ
7 Ⓐ Ⓑ Ⓒ Ⓓ Ⓔ 29 Ⓐ Ⓑ Ⓒ Ⓓ Ⓔ 51 Ⓐ Ⓑ Ⓒ Ⓓ Ⓔ 73 Ⓐ Ⓑ Ⓒ Ⓓ Ⓔ
8 Ⓐ Ⓑ Ⓒ Ⓓ Ⓔ 30 Ⓐ Ⓑ Ⓒ Ⓓ Ⓔ 52 Ⓐ Ⓑ Ⓒ Ⓓ Ⓔ 74 Ⓐ Ⓑ Ⓒ Ⓓ Ⓔ
9 Ⓐ Ⓑ Ⓒ Ⓓ Ⓔ 31 Ⓐ Ⓑ Ⓒ Ⓓ Ⓔ 53 Ⓐ Ⓑ Ⓒ Ⓓ Ⓔ 75 Ⓐ Ⓑ Ⓒ Ⓓ Ⓔ
10 Ⓐ Ⓑ Ⓒ Ⓓ Ⓔ 32 Ⓐ Ⓑ Ⓒ Ⓓ Ⓔ 54 Ⓐ Ⓑ Ⓒ Ⓓ Ⓔ 76 Ⓐ Ⓑ Ⓒ Ⓓ Ⓔ
11 Ⓐ Ⓑ Ⓒ Ⓓ Ⓔ 33 Ⓐ Ⓑ Ⓒ Ⓓ Ⓔ 55 Ⓐ Ⓑ Ⓒ Ⓓ Ⓔ 77 Ⓐ Ⓑ Ⓒ Ⓓ Ⓔ
12 Ⓐ Ⓑ Ⓒ Ⓓ Ⓔ 34 Ⓐ Ⓑ Ⓒ Ⓓ Ⓔ 56 Ⓐ Ⓑ Ⓒ Ⓓ Ⓔ 78 Ⓐ Ⓑ Ⓒ Ⓓ Ⓔ
13 Ⓐ Ⓑ Ⓒ Ⓓ Ⓔ 35 Ⓐ Ⓑ Ⓒ Ⓓ Ⓔ 57 Ⓐ Ⓑ Ⓒ Ⓓ Ⓔ 79 Ⓐ Ⓑ Ⓒ Ⓓ Ⓔ
14 Ⓐ Ⓑ Ⓒ Ⓓ Ⓔ 36 Ⓐ Ⓑ Ⓒ Ⓓ Ⓔ 58 Ⓐ Ⓑ Ⓒ Ⓓ Ⓔ 80 Ⓐ Ⓑ Ⓒ Ⓓ Ⓔ
15 Ⓐ Ⓑ Ⓒ Ⓓ Ⓔ 37 Ⓐ Ⓑ Ⓒ Ⓓ Ⓔ 59 Ⓐ Ⓑ Ⓒ Ⓓ Ⓔ 81 Ⓐ Ⓑ Ⓒ Ⓓ Ⓔ
16 Ⓐ Ⓑ Ⓒ Ⓓ Ⓔ 38 Ⓐ Ⓑ Ⓒ Ⓓ Ⓔ 60 Ⓐ Ⓑ Ⓒ Ⓓ Ⓔ 82 Ⓐ Ⓑ Ⓒ Ⓓ Ⓔ
17 Ⓐ Ⓑ Ⓒ Ⓓ Ⓔ 39 Ⓐ Ⓑ Ⓒ Ⓓ Ⓔ 61 Ⓐ Ⓑ Ⓒ Ⓓ Ⓔ 83 Ⓐ Ⓑ Ⓒ Ⓓ Ⓔ
18 Ⓐ Ⓑ Ⓒ Ⓓ Ⓔ 40 Ⓐ Ⓑ Ⓒ Ⓓ Ⓔ 62 Ⓐ Ⓑ Ⓒ Ⓓ Ⓔ 84 Ⓐ Ⓑ Ⓒ Ⓓ Ⓔ
19 Ⓐ Ⓑ Ⓒ Ⓓ Ⓔ 41 Ⓐ Ⓑ Ⓒ Ⓓ Ⓔ 63 Ⓐ Ⓑ Ⓒ Ⓓ Ⓔ 85 Ⓐ Ⓑ Ⓒ Ⓓ Ⓔ
20 Ⓐ Ⓑ Ⓒ Ⓓ Ⓔ 42 Ⓐ Ⓑ Ⓒ Ⓓ Ⓔ 64 Ⓐ Ⓑ Ⓒ Ⓓ Ⓔ 86 Ⓐ Ⓑ Ⓒ Ⓓ Ⓔ
21 Ⓐ Ⓑ Ⓒ Ⓓ Ⓔ 43 Ⓐ Ⓑ Ⓒ Ⓓ Ⓔ 65 Ⓐ Ⓑ Ⓒ Ⓓ Ⓔ 87 Ⓐ Ⓑ Ⓒ Ⓓ Ⓔ
22 Ⓐ Ⓑ Ⓒ Ⓓ Ⓔ 44 Ⓐ Ⓑ Ⓒ Ⓓ Ⓔ 66 Ⓐ Ⓑ Ⓒ Ⓓ Ⓔ 88 Ⓐ Ⓑ Ⓒ Ⓓ Ⓔ

PART A—ADDRESS CHECKING

Sample Questions

You will be allowed three minutes to read the directions and answer the five sample questions that follow. On the actual test, however, you will have only six minutes to answer 95 questions, so see how quickly you can compare addresses and still get the correct answer.

Directions: *Each question consists of two addresses. If the two addresses are alike in EVERY way, mark A on your answer sheet. If the two addresses are different in ANY way, mark D on your answer sheet.*

1. ...... 4836 Mineola Blvd   4386 Mineola Blvd
2. ...... 3062 W 197th St   3062 W 197th Rd
3. ...... Columbus OH 43210   Columbus OH 43210
4. ...... 9413 Alcan Hwy So   9413 Alcan Hwy So
5. ...... 4186 Carrier Ln   4186 Carreer Ln

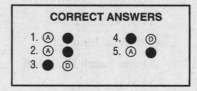

ADDRESS CHECKING

Time: 6 Minutes. 95 Questions.

Directions: For each question, compare the address in the left column with the address in the right column. If the two addresses are ALIKE IN EVERY WAY, blacken space A on your answer sheet. If the two addresses are DIFFERENT IN ANY WAY, blacken space D on your answer sheet. Correct answers for this test are on page 129.

1.	......	462 Midland Ave	462 Midland Ave
2.	......	2319 Sherry Dr	3219 Sherry Dr
3.	......	1015 Kimball Ave	1015 Kimball Av
4.	......	Wappinger Falls NY 12590	Wappinger Falls NY 12590
5.	......	1255 North Ave	1225 North Ave
6.	......	1826 Tibbets Rd	1826 Tibetts Rd
7.	......	603 N Division St	603 N Division St
8.	......	2304 Manhattan Ave	2034 Manhattan Ave
9.	......	Worcester MA 01610	Worcester ME 01610
10.	......	1186 Vernon Drive	1186 Vernon Drive
11.	......	209 Peter Bont Rd	209 Peter Bent Rd
12.	......	Miami Beach FL 33139	Miami Beach FL 33193
13.	......	1100 West Ave	1100 East Ave
14.	......	2063 Winyah Ter	2036 Winyah Ter
15.	......	3483 Suncrest Ave	3483 Suncrest Dr
16.	......	234 Rochambeau Rd	234 Roshambeau Rd
17.	......	306 N Terrace Blvd	306 N Terrace Blvd
18.	......	1632 Paine St	1632 Pain St
19.	......	Palm Springs CA 92262	Palm Spring CA 92262
20.	......	286 Marietta Ave	286 Marrietta Ave
21.	......	2445 Pigott Rd	2445 Pigott Rd
22.	......	2204 PineBrook Blvd	2204 Pinebrook Blvd
23.	......	Buffalo NY 42113	Buffulo NY 42113
24.	......	487 Warburton Ave	487 Warburton Ave
25.	......	9386 North St	9386 North Ave
26.	......	2272 Glandale Rd	2772 Glandale Rd
27.	......	9236 Puritan Dr	9236 Puritan Pl
28.	......	Watertown MA 02172	Watertown MA 02172
29.	......	7803 Kimball Ave	7803 Kimbal Ave
30.	......	1362 Colonial Pkwy	1362 Colonial Pkwy
31.	......	115 Rolling Hills Rd	115 Rolling Hills Rd
32.	......	218 Rockledge Rd	2181 Rockledge Rd
33.	......	8346 N Broadway	8346 W Broadway

MODEL EXAMINATION I **103**

34.	......	West Chester PA 19380	West Chester PA 19830
35.	......	9224 Highland Way	9244 Highland Way
36.	......	8383 Mamaroneck Ave	8383 Mamaroneck Ave
37.	......	276 Furnace Dock Rd	276 Furnace Dock Rd
38.	......	4137 Loockerman St	4137 Lockerman St
39.	......	532 Broadhollow Rd	532 Broadhollow Rd
40.	......	Sunrise FL 33313	Sunrise FL 33133
41.	......	148 Cortlandt Rd	148 Cortland Rd
42.	......	5951 W Hartsdale Rd	5951 W Hartsdale Ave
43.	......	5231 Alta Vista Cir	5321 Alta Vista Cir
44.	......	6459 Chippewa Rd	6459 Chippewa Rd
45.	......	1171 S Highland Rd	1771 S Highland Rd
46.	......	Dover DE 19901	Dover DL 19901
47.	......	2363 Old Farm Ln	2363 Old Farm Ln
48.	......	1001 Hemingway Dr	1001 Hemmingway Dr
49.	......	1555 Morningside Ave	1555 Morningslide Ave
50.	......	Purchase NY 10577	Purchase NY 10577
51.	......	1189 E 9th St	1189 E 9th St
52.	......	168 Old Lyme Rd	186 Old Lyme Rd
53.	......	106 Notingham Rd	106 Nottingham Rd
54.	......	1428 Midland Ave	1428 Midland Ave
55.	......	Elmhurst NY 11373	Elmherst NY 11373
56.	......	1450 West Chester Pike	1450 West Chester Pike
57.	......	3357 NW Main St	3357 NE Main St
58.	......	5062 Marietta Ave	5062 Marrietta Ave
59.	......	1890 NE 3rd Ct	1980 NE 3rd Ct
60.	......	Wilmington DE 19810	Wilmington DE 19810
61.	......	1075 Central Park Av	1075 Central Park W
62.	......	672 Bacon Hill Rd	672 Beacon Hill Rd
63.	......	1725 W 17th St	1725 W 17th St
64.	......	Bronxville NY 10708	Bronxville NJ 10708
65.	......	2066 Old Wilmot Rd	2066 Old Wilmont Rd
66.	......	3333 S State St	3333 S State St
67.	......	1483 Meritoria Dr	1438 Meritoria Dr
68.	......	2327 E 23rd St	2327 E 27th St
69.	......	Baltimore MD 21215	Baltimore MD 21215
70.	......	137 Clarence Rd	137 Claremont Rd
71.	......	3516 N Ely Ave	3516 N Ely Ave
72.	......	111 Beechwood St	1111 Beechwood St

73. ……	143 N Highland Ave	143 N Highland Ave
74. ……	Miami Beach FL 33179	Miami FL 33179
75. ……	6430 Spring Mill Rd	6340 Spring Mill Rd
76. ……	1416 87th Ave	1416 78th Ave
77. ……	4204 S Lexington Ave	4204 Lexington Ave
78. ……	3601 Clarks Lane	3601 Clark Lane
79. ……	Indianapolis IN 46260	Indianapolis IN 46260
80. ……	4256 Fairfield Ave	4256 Fairfield Ave
81. ……	Jamaica NY 11435	Jamiaca NY 11435
82. ……	1809 83rd St	1809 83rd St
83. ……	3288 Page Ct	3288 Paige Ct
84. ……	2436 S Broadway	2436 S Broadway
85. ……	6309 The Green	6309 The Green
86. ……	Kew Gardens NY 11415	Kew Garden NY 11415
87. ……	4370 W 158th St	4370 W 158th St
88. ……	4263 3rd Ave	4623 3rd Ave
89. ……	1737 Fisher Ave	1737 Fischer Ave
90. ……	Bronx NY 10475	Bronx NY 10475
91. ……	5148 West End Ave	5184 West End Ave
92. ……	1011 Ocean Ave	1011 Ocean Ave
93. ……	1593 Webster Dr	1593 Webster Dr
94. ……	Darien CT 06820	Darien CT 06820
95. ……	1626 E 115th St	1662 E 115th St

END OF ADDRESS CHECKING

PART B—MEMORY FOR ADDRESSES

Sample Questions

The sample questions for this part are based on the addresses in the five boxes below. Your task is to mark on your answer sheet the letter of the box in which each address belongs. You will have five minutes now to study the locations of the addresses. Then cover the boxes and try to mark the location of the sample questions. You may look back at the boxes if you cannot yet mark the address locations from memory.

The exam itself provides three practice sessions before the question set that really counts. Practice I and Practice III supply you with the boxes and permit you to refer to them if necessary. Practice II and the Memory for Addresses Test itself do not permit you to look at the boxes. The test itself is based on memory.

A	B	C	D	E
4100–4199 Plum	1000–1399 Plum	4200–4599 Plum	1400–4099 Plum	4600–5299 Plum
Bardack	Greenhouse	Flynn	Pepper	Cedar
4200–4599 Ash	4600–5299 Ash	1400–4099 Ash	1000–1399 Ash	4100–4199 Ash
Lemon	Dalby	Race	Clown	Hawk
1000–1399 Neff	4100–4199 Neff	4600–5299 Neff	4200–4599 Neff	1400–4099 Neff

1. 1400–4099 Plum

2. 1000–1399 Neff

3. Lemon

4. Flynn

5. 4200–4599 Ash

6. 4600–5299 Ash

7. Cedar

8. Pepper

9. 4100–4199 Plum

10. 4600–5299 Neff

11. 1000–1399 Plum

12. Clown

13. Greenhouse

14. 4100–4199 Ash

SAMPLE ANSWER SHEET

1. Ⓐ Ⓑ Ⓒ Ⓓ Ⓔ   8. Ⓐ Ⓑ Ⓒ Ⓓ Ⓔ
2. Ⓐ Ⓑ Ⓒ Ⓓ Ⓔ   9. Ⓐ Ⓑ Ⓒ Ⓓ Ⓔ
3. Ⓐ Ⓑ Ⓒ Ⓓ Ⓔ   10. Ⓐ Ⓑ Ⓒ Ⓓ Ⓔ
4. Ⓐ Ⓑ Ⓒ Ⓓ Ⓔ   11. Ⓐ Ⓑ Ⓒ Ⓓ Ⓔ
5. Ⓐ Ⓑ Ⓒ Ⓓ Ⓔ   12. Ⓐ Ⓑ Ⓒ Ⓓ Ⓔ
6. Ⓐ Ⓑ Ⓒ Ⓓ Ⓔ   13. Ⓐ Ⓑ Ⓒ Ⓓ Ⓔ
7. Ⓐ Ⓑ Ⓒ Ⓓ Ⓔ   14. Ⓐ Ⓑ Ⓒ Ⓓ Ⓔ

CORRECT ANSWERS

1. Ⓐ Ⓑ Ⓒ ● Ⓔ   8. Ⓐ Ⓑ Ⓒ ● Ⓔ
2. ● Ⓑ Ⓒ Ⓓ Ⓔ   9. ● Ⓑ Ⓒ Ⓓ Ⓔ
3. ● Ⓑ Ⓒ Ⓓ Ⓔ   10. Ⓐ Ⓑ ● Ⓓ Ⓔ
4. Ⓐ Ⓑ ● Ⓓ Ⓔ   11. Ⓐ ● Ⓒ Ⓓ Ⓔ
5. ● Ⓑ Ⓒ Ⓓ Ⓔ   12. Ⓐ Ⓑ Ⓒ ● Ⓔ
6. Ⓐ ● Ⓒ Ⓓ Ⓔ   13. Ⓐ ● Ⓒ Ⓓ Ⓔ
7. Ⓐ Ⓑ Ⓒ Ⓓ ●   14. Ⓐ Ⓑ Ⓒ Ⓓ ●

PRACTICE FOR MEMORY FOR ADDRESSES

Directions: The five boxes below are labeled A, B, C, D, and E. In each box are three sets of number spans with names and two names that are not associated with numbers. In the next THREE MINUTES, you must try to memorize the box location of each name and number span. The position of a name or number span within its box is not important. You need only remember the letter of the box in which the item is to be found. You will use these names and numbers to answer three sets of practice questions that are NOT scored and one actual test that is scored. Correct answers are on pages 130 and 131.

A	B	C	D	E
4100–4199 Plum	1000–1399 Plum	4200–4599 Plum	1400–4099 Plum	4600–5299 Plum
Bardack	Greenhouse	Flynn	Pepper	Cedar
4200–4599 Ash	4600–5299 Ash	1400–4099 Ash	1000–1399 Ash	4100–4199 Ash
Lemon	Dalby	Race	Clown	Hawk
1000–1399 Neff	4100–4199 Neff	4600–5299 Neff	4200–4599 Neff	1400–4099 Neff

Practice 1

Directions: Use the next THREE MINUTES to mark on your answer sheet the letter of the box in which each item that follows is to be found. Try to mark each item without looking back at the boxes. If, however, you get stuck, you may refer to the boxes during this practice exercise. If you find that you must look at the boxes, try to memorize as you do so. This test is for practice only. It will not be scored.

1. 4600–5299 Ash
2. 4600–5299 Neff
3. 1400–4099 Plum
4. Cedar
5. Bardack
6. 1400–4099 Neff
7. 1400–4099 Ash
8. 1000–1399 Plum
9. Greenhouse
10. Lemon
11. 4600–5299 Plum
12. 4200–4599 Ash
13. 4600–5299 Neff

14. Dalby
15. Hawk
16. 4100–4199 Plum
17. 4200–4599 Plum
18. 4600–5299 Ash
19. 4200–4599 Neff
20. Race
21. Pepper
22. 4100–4199 Ash
23. 1000–1399 Neff
24. 1000–1399 Plum
25. Cedar
26. Dalby

27. 4600–5299 Plum
28. 1400–4099 Plum
29. Bardack
30. 4200–4599 Ash
31. 1400–4099 Neff
32. 4600–5299 Neff
33. 1400–4099 Ash
34. Flynn
35. Lemon
36. Clown
37. 4100–4199 Plum
38. 1000–1399 Ash
39. 4100–4199 Neff

40. Greenhouse

41. Hawk

42. 4600–5299 Plum

43. 1000–1399 Neff

44. 1400–4099 Ash

45. 4600–5299 Ash

46. Cedar

47. Greenhouse

48. 1400–4099 Plum

49. 4200–4599 Neff

50. 1000–1399 Ash

51. Race

52. Flynn

53. 4600–5299 Ash

54. 4600–5299 Plum

55. 4600–5299 Neff

56. Pepper

57. Lemon

58. 1000–1399 Plum

59. 4100–4199 Plum

60. 1000–1399 Neff

61. 4100–4199 Ash

62. Bardack

63. Dalby

64. Clown

65. 4200–4599 Ash

66. 1400–4099 Ash

67. 4200–4599 Plum

68. Hawk

69. 4100–4199 Neff

70. 1400–4099 Neff

71. 1000–1399 Plum

72. Pepper

73. 1000–1399 Neff

74. 4100–4199 Ash

75. Dalby

76. Cedar

77. 4100–4199 Plum

78. 1400–4099 Ash

79. 1400–4099 Plum

80. 1400–4099 Neff

81. Pepper

82. Hawk

83. 4600–5299 Ash

84. 4600–5299 Plum

85. 1000–1399 Ash

86. 1000–1399 Neff

87. Cedar

88. Greenhouse

Practice 1 Answer Sheet

1 Ⓐ Ⓑ Ⓒ Ⓓ Ⓔ	23 Ⓐ Ⓑ Ⓒ Ⓓ Ⓔ	45 Ⓐ Ⓑ Ⓒ Ⓓ Ⓔ	67 Ⓐ Ⓑ Ⓒ Ⓓ Ⓔ
2 Ⓐ Ⓑ Ⓒ Ⓓ Ⓔ	24 Ⓐ Ⓑ Ⓒ Ⓓ Ⓔ	46 Ⓐ Ⓑ Ⓒ Ⓓ Ⓔ	68 Ⓐ Ⓑ Ⓒ Ⓓ Ⓔ
3 Ⓐ Ⓑ Ⓒ Ⓓ Ⓔ	25 Ⓐ Ⓑ Ⓒ Ⓓ Ⓔ	47 Ⓐ Ⓑ Ⓒ Ⓓ Ⓔ	69 Ⓐ Ⓑ Ⓒ Ⓓ Ⓔ
4 Ⓐ Ⓑ Ⓒ Ⓓ Ⓔ	26 Ⓐ Ⓑ Ⓒ Ⓓ Ⓔ	48 Ⓐ Ⓑ Ⓒ Ⓓ Ⓔ	70 Ⓐ Ⓑ Ⓒ Ⓓ Ⓔ
5 Ⓐ Ⓑ Ⓒ Ⓓ Ⓔ	27 Ⓐ Ⓑ Ⓒ Ⓓ Ⓔ	49 Ⓐ Ⓑ Ⓒ Ⓓ Ⓔ	71 Ⓐ Ⓑ Ⓒ Ⓓ Ⓔ
6 Ⓐ Ⓑ Ⓒ Ⓓ Ⓔ	28 Ⓐ Ⓑ Ⓒ Ⓓ Ⓔ	50 Ⓐ Ⓑ Ⓒ Ⓓ Ⓔ	72 Ⓐ Ⓑ Ⓒ Ⓓ Ⓔ
7 Ⓐ Ⓑ Ⓒ Ⓓ Ⓔ	29 Ⓐ Ⓑ Ⓒ Ⓓ Ⓔ	51 Ⓐ Ⓑ Ⓒ Ⓓ Ⓔ	73 Ⓐ Ⓑ Ⓒ Ⓓ Ⓔ
8 Ⓐ Ⓑ Ⓒ Ⓓ Ⓔ	30 Ⓐ Ⓑ Ⓒ Ⓓ Ⓔ	52 Ⓐ Ⓑ Ⓒ Ⓓ Ⓔ	74 Ⓐ Ⓑ Ⓒ Ⓓ Ⓔ
9 Ⓐ Ⓑ Ⓒ Ⓓ Ⓔ	31 Ⓐ Ⓑ Ⓒ Ⓓ Ⓔ	53 Ⓐ Ⓑ Ⓒ Ⓓ Ⓔ	75 Ⓐ Ⓑ Ⓒ Ⓓ Ⓔ
10 Ⓐ Ⓑ Ⓒ Ⓓ Ⓔ	32 Ⓐ Ⓑ Ⓒ Ⓓ Ⓔ	54 Ⓐ Ⓑ Ⓒ Ⓓ Ⓔ	76 Ⓐ Ⓑ Ⓒ Ⓓ Ⓔ
11 Ⓐ Ⓑ Ⓒ Ⓓ Ⓔ	33 Ⓐ Ⓑ Ⓒ Ⓓ Ⓔ	55 Ⓐ Ⓑ Ⓒ Ⓓ Ⓔ	77 Ⓐ Ⓑ Ⓒ Ⓓ Ⓔ
12 Ⓐ Ⓑ Ⓒ Ⓓ Ⓔ	34 Ⓐ Ⓑ Ⓒ Ⓓ Ⓔ	56 Ⓐ Ⓑ Ⓒ Ⓓ Ⓔ	78 Ⓐ Ⓑ Ⓒ Ⓓ Ⓔ
13 Ⓐ Ⓑ Ⓒ Ⓓ Ⓔ	35 Ⓐ Ⓑ Ⓒ Ⓓ Ⓔ	57 Ⓐ Ⓑ Ⓒ Ⓓ Ⓔ	79 Ⓐ Ⓑ Ⓒ Ⓓ Ⓔ
14 Ⓐ Ⓑ Ⓒ Ⓓ Ⓔ	36 Ⓐ Ⓑ Ⓒ Ⓓ Ⓔ	58 Ⓐ Ⓑ Ⓒ Ⓓ Ⓔ	80 Ⓐ Ⓑ Ⓒ Ⓓ Ⓔ
15 Ⓐ Ⓑ Ⓒ Ⓓ Ⓔ	37 Ⓐ Ⓑ Ⓒ Ⓓ Ⓔ	59 Ⓐ Ⓑ Ⓒ Ⓓ Ⓔ	81 Ⓐ Ⓑ Ⓒ Ⓓ Ⓔ
16 Ⓐ Ⓑ Ⓒ Ⓓ Ⓔ	38 Ⓐ Ⓑ Ⓒ Ⓓ Ⓔ	60 Ⓐ Ⓑ Ⓒ Ⓓ Ⓔ	82 Ⓐ Ⓑ Ⓒ Ⓓ Ⓔ
17 Ⓐ Ⓑ Ⓒ Ⓓ Ⓔ	39 Ⓐ Ⓑ Ⓒ Ⓓ Ⓔ	61 Ⓐ Ⓑ Ⓒ Ⓓ Ⓔ	83 Ⓐ Ⓑ Ⓒ Ⓓ Ⓔ
18 Ⓐ Ⓑ Ⓒ Ⓓ Ⓔ	40 Ⓐ Ⓑ Ⓒ Ⓓ Ⓔ	62 Ⓐ Ⓑ Ⓒ Ⓓ Ⓔ	84 Ⓐ Ⓑ Ⓒ Ⓓ Ⓔ
19 Ⓐ Ⓑ Ⓒ Ⓓ Ⓔ	41 Ⓐ Ⓑ Ⓒ Ⓓ Ⓔ	63 Ⓐ Ⓑ Ⓒ Ⓓ Ⓔ	85 Ⓐ Ⓑ Ⓒ Ⓓ Ⓔ
20 Ⓐ Ⓑ Ⓒ Ⓓ Ⓔ	42 Ⓐ Ⓑ Ⓒ Ⓓ Ⓔ	64 Ⓐ Ⓑ Ⓒ Ⓓ Ⓔ	86 Ⓐ Ⓑ Ⓒ Ⓓ Ⓔ
21 Ⓐ Ⓑ Ⓒ Ⓓ Ⓔ	43 Ⓐ Ⓑ Ⓒ Ⓓ Ⓔ	65 Ⓐ Ⓑ Ⓒ Ⓓ Ⓔ	87 Ⓐ Ⓑ Ⓒ Ⓓ Ⓔ
22 Ⓐ Ⓑ Ⓒ Ⓓ Ⓔ	44 Ⓐ Ⓑ Ⓒ Ⓓ Ⓔ	66 Ⓐ Ⓑ Ⓒ Ⓓ Ⓔ	88 Ⓐ Ⓑ Ⓒ Ⓓ Ⓔ

Practice II

Directions: The next 88 questions constitute another practice exercise. Again, you should mark your answers on your answer sheet. Again, the time limit is THREE MINUTES. This time, however, you must NOT look at the boxes while answering the questions. You must rely on your memory in marking the box location of each item. This practice test will not be scored.

1. 4100–4199 Plum
2. 1400–4099 Neff
3. 1400–4099 Ash
4. Clown
5. Greenhouse
6. 4100–4199 Neff
7. 1000–1399 Ash
8. 4100–4199 Ash
9. Race
10. Flynn
11. 4600–5299 Plum
12. 1000–1399 Neff
13. 4200–4599 Ash
14. 1000–1399 Plum
15. Cedar
16. Dalby
17. Pepper
18. 4600–5299 Neff
19. 4200–4599 Neff
20. 1400–4099 Plum
21. Bardack

22. Lemon
23. Hawk
24. 4200–4599 Plum
25. 4600–5299 Ash
26. 4200–4599 Plum
27. 4600–5299 Neff
28. 1400–4099 Ash
29. Lemon
30. Pepper
31. 4100–4199 Neff
32. 1400–4099 Plum
33. 4200–4599 Neff
34. Dalby
35. Flynn
36. 4200–4599 Ash
37. 4600–5299 Plum
38. 4100–4199 Plum
39. Bardack
40. Hawk
41. 1000–1399 Plum
42. 1000–1399 Neff

43. 1000–1399 Ash
44. Greenhouse
45. Clown
46. 4600–5299 Ash
47. 4100–4199 Ash
48. 1400–4099 Neff
49. Race
50. Cedar
51. Flynn
52. Hawk
53. 4100–4199 Neff
54. 1000–1399 Ash
55. 4100–4199 Plum
56. 1400–4099 Plum
57. 4200–4599 Plum
58. Bardack
59. 4600–5299 Neff
60. 4200–4599 Neff
61. 4200–4599 Ash
62. Pepper
63. Clown

64. 4600–5299 Ash

65. 1000–1399 Neff

66. 1000–1399 Plum

67. Race

68. Dalby

69. 1400–4099 Ash

70. 4100–4199 Ash

71. 4600–5299 Plum

72. 4600–5299 Neff

73. Cedar

74. 1400–4099 Neff

75. Greenhouse

76. 4100–4199 Plum

77. 4200–4599 Neff

78. 4200–4599 Ash

79. Clown

80. Dalby

81. 4200–4599 Plum

82. 1400–4099 Ash

83. 1000–1399 Neff

84. Pepper

85. Bardack

86. 4100–4199 Plum

87. 1400–4099 Neff

88. 4100–4199 Ash

Practice II Answer Sheet

1 Ⓐ Ⓑ Ⓒ Ⓓ Ⓔ	23 Ⓐ Ⓑ Ⓒ Ⓓ Ⓔ	45 Ⓐ Ⓑ Ⓒ Ⓓ Ⓔ	67 Ⓐ Ⓑ Ⓒ Ⓓ Ⓔ
2 Ⓐ Ⓑ Ⓒ Ⓓ Ⓔ	24 Ⓐ Ⓑ Ⓒ Ⓓ Ⓔ	46 Ⓐ Ⓑ Ⓒ Ⓓ Ⓔ	68 Ⓐ Ⓑ Ⓒ Ⓓ Ⓔ
3 Ⓐ Ⓑ Ⓒ Ⓓ Ⓔ	25 Ⓐ Ⓑ Ⓒ Ⓓ Ⓔ	47 Ⓐ Ⓑ Ⓒ Ⓓ Ⓔ	69 Ⓐ Ⓑ Ⓒ Ⓓ Ⓔ
4 Ⓐ Ⓑ Ⓒ Ⓓ Ⓔ	26 Ⓐ Ⓑ Ⓒ Ⓓ Ⓔ	48 Ⓐ Ⓑ Ⓒ Ⓓ Ⓔ	70 Ⓐ Ⓑ Ⓒ Ⓓ Ⓔ
5 Ⓐ Ⓑ Ⓒ Ⓓ Ⓔ	27 Ⓐ Ⓑ Ⓒ Ⓓ Ⓔ	49 Ⓐ Ⓑ Ⓒ Ⓓ Ⓔ	71 Ⓐ Ⓑ Ⓒ Ⓓ Ⓔ
6 Ⓐ Ⓑ Ⓒ Ⓓ Ⓔ	28 Ⓐ Ⓑ Ⓒ Ⓓ Ⓔ	50 Ⓐ Ⓑ Ⓒ Ⓓ Ⓔ	72 Ⓐ Ⓑ Ⓒ Ⓓ Ⓔ
7 Ⓐ Ⓑ Ⓒ Ⓓ Ⓔ	29 Ⓐ Ⓑ Ⓒ Ⓓ Ⓔ	51 Ⓐ Ⓑ Ⓒ Ⓓ Ⓔ	73 Ⓐ Ⓑ Ⓒ Ⓓ Ⓔ
8 Ⓐ Ⓑ Ⓒ Ⓓ Ⓔ	30 Ⓐ Ⓑ Ⓒ Ⓓ Ⓔ	52 Ⓐ Ⓑ Ⓒ Ⓓ Ⓔ	74 Ⓐ Ⓑ Ⓒ Ⓓ Ⓔ
9 Ⓐ Ⓑ Ⓒ Ⓓ Ⓔ	31 Ⓐ Ⓑ Ⓒ Ⓓ Ⓔ	53 Ⓐ Ⓑ Ⓒ Ⓓ Ⓔ	75 Ⓐ Ⓑ Ⓒ Ⓓ Ⓔ
10 Ⓐ Ⓑ Ⓒ Ⓓ Ⓔ	32 Ⓐ Ⓑ Ⓒ Ⓓ Ⓔ	54 Ⓐ Ⓑ Ⓒ Ⓓ Ⓔ	76 Ⓐ Ⓑ Ⓒ Ⓓ Ⓔ
11 Ⓐ Ⓑ Ⓒ Ⓓ Ⓔ	33 Ⓐ Ⓑ Ⓒ Ⓓ Ⓔ	55 Ⓐ Ⓑ Ⓒ Ⓓ Ⓔ	77 Ⓐ Ⓑ Ⓒ Ⓓ Ⓔ
12 Ⓐ Ⓑ Ⓒ Ⓓ Ⓔ	34 Ⓐ Ⓑ Ⓒ Ⓓ Ⓔ	56 Ⓐ Ⓑ Ⓒ Ⓓ Ⓔ	78 Ⓐ Ⓑ Ⓒ Ⓓ Ⓔ
13 Ⓐ Ⓑ Ⓒ Ⓓ Ⓔ	35 Ⓐ Ⓑ Ⓒ Ⓓ Ⓔ	57 Ⓐ Ⓑ Ⓒ Ⓓ Ⓔ	79 Ⓐ Ⓑ Ⓒ Ⓓ Ⓔ
14 Ⓐ Ⓑ Ⓒ Ⓓ Ⓔ	36 Ⓐ Ⓑ Ⓒ Ⓓ Ⓔ	58 Ⓐ Ⓑ Ⓒ Ⓓ Ⓔ	80 Ⓐ Ⓑ Ⓒ Ⓓ Ⓔ
15 Ⓐ Ⓑ Ⓒ Ⓓ Ⓔ	37 Ⓐ Ⓑ Ⓒ Ⓓ Ⓔ	59 Ⓐ Ⓑ Ⓒ Ⓓ Ⓔ	81 Ⓐ Ⓑ Ⓒ Ⓓ Ⓔ
16 Ⓐ Ⓑ Ⓒ Ⓓ Ⓔ	38 Ⓐ Ⓑ Ⓒ Ⓓ Ⓔ	60 Ⓐ Ⓑ Ⓒ Ⓓ Ⓔ	82 Ⓐ Ⓑ Ⓒ Ⓓ Ⓔ
17 Ⓐ Ⓑ Ⓒ Ⓓ Ⓔ	39 Ⓐ Ⓑ Ⓒ Ⓓ Ⓔ	61 Ⓐ Ⓑ Ⓒ Ⓓ Ⓔ	83 Ⓐ Ⓑ Ⓒ Ⓓ Ⓔ
18 Ⓐ Ⓑ Ⓒ Ⓓ Ⓔ	40 Ⓐ Ⓑ Ⓒ Ⓓ Ⓔ	62 Ⓐ Ⓑ Ⓒ Ⓓ Ⓔ	84 Ⓐ Ⓑ Ⓒ Ⓓ Ⓔ
19 Ⓐ Ⓑ Ⓒ Ⓓ Ⓔ	41 Ⓐ Ⓑ Ⓒ Ⓓ Ⓔ	63 Ⓐ Ⓑ Ⓒ Ⓓ Ⓔ	85 Ⓐ Ⓑ Ⓒ Ⓓ Ⓔ
20 Ⓐ Ⓑ Ⓒ Ⓓ Ⓔ	42 Ⓐ Ⓑ Ⓒ Ⓓ Ⓔ	64 Ⓐ Ⓑ Ⓒ Ⓓ Ⓔ	86 Ⓐ Ⓑ Ⓒ Ⓓ Ⓔ
21 Ⓐ Ⓑ Ⓒ Ⓓ Ⓔ	43 Ⓐ Ⓑ Ⓒ Ⓓ Ⓔ	65 Ⓐ Ⓑ Ⓒ Ⓓ Ⓔ	87 Ⓐ Ⓑ Ⓒ Ⓓ Ⓔ
22 Ⓐ Ⓑ Ⓒ Ⓓ Ⓔ	44 Ⓐ Ⓑ Ⓒ Ⓓ Ⓔ	66 Ⓐ Ⓑ Ⓒ Ⓓ Ⓔ	88 Ⓐ Ⓑ Ⓒ Ⓓ Ⓔ

Practice III

Directions: The names and address are repeated for you in the boxes below. Each name and each number span is in the same box in which you found it in the original set. You will now be allowed FIVE MINUTES to study the locations again. Do your best to memorize the letter of the box in which each item is located. This is your last chance to see the boxes.

A	B	C	D	E
4100–4199 Plum	1000–1399 Plum	4200–4599 Plum	1400–4099 Plum	4600–5299 Plum
Bardack	Greenhouse	Flynn	Pepper	Cedar
4200–4599 Ash	4600–5299 Ash	1400–4099 Ash	1000–1399 Ash	4100–4199 Ash
Lemon	Dalby	Race	Clown	Hawk
1000–1399 Neff	4100–4199 Neff	4600–5299 Neff	4200–4599 Neff	1400–4099 Neff

Directions: This is your last practice test. Mark the location of each of the 88 items on your answer sheet. You will have FIVE MINUTES to answer these questions. Do NOT look back at the boxes. This practice test will not be scored.

1. 1400–4099 Ash
2. 4600–5299 Plum
3. 1000–1399 Neff
4. Pepper
5. Greenhouse
6. 4100–4199 Plum
7. 1400–4099 Neff
8. 4600–5299 Ash
9. 1000–1399 Ash
10. Bardack
11. Lemon
12. Hawk
13. 1000–1399 Plum
14. 4200–4599 Neff
15. 4200–4599 Ash

16. 4100–4199 Neff
17. 1400–4099 Plum
18. 4100–4199 Ash
19. Clown
20. Flynn
21. 4600–5299 Ash
22. 1000–1399 Plum
23. 4200–4599 Ash
24. Lemon
25. Race
26. 4600–5299 Neff
27. 4600–5299 Plum
28. Dalby
29. Cedar
30. 4200–4599 Neff

31. 1000–1399 Plum
32. 1400–4099 Ash
33. 4200–4599 Neff
34. 1400–4099 Plum
35. 4100–4199 Neff
36. Ceda
37. Clown
38. Dalby
39. 4200–4599 Ash
40. 4100–4199 Ash
41. 4600–5299 Plum
42. 1000–1399 Neff
43. Greenhouse
44. Pepper
45. 4100–4199 Plum

46. 1400–4099 Neff

47. 4600–5299 Ash

48. 1000–1399 Ash

49. Clown

50. Bardack

51. Lemon

52. 4200–4599 Plum

53. 4600–5299 Neff

54. Hawk

55. Flynn

56. Race

57. 1400–4099 Plum

58. 1000–1399 Neff

59. 4100–4199 Ash

60. 1400–4099 Ash

61. 1400–4099 Plum

62. 4100–4199 Neff

63. 1400–4099 Neff

64. Hawk

65. Lemon

66. 1000–1399 Plum

67. 4100–4199 Neff

68. 4600–5299 Ash

69. Pepper

70. Dalby

71. 1000–1399 Neff

72. 4600–5299 Plum

73. 4100–4199 Ash

74. Greenhouse

75. Race

76. 4200–4599 Neff

77. 1000–1399 Ash

78. 4200–4599 Plum

79. Bardack

80. Cedar

81. 4200–4599 Ash

82. 4100–4199 Plum

83. 4600–5299 Neff

84. Flynn

85. Clown

86. 1400–4099 Ash

87. 4600–5299 Plum

88. 4100–4199 Plum

Practice III Answer Sheet

1 Ⓐ Ⓑ Ⓒ Ⓓ Ⓔ	23 Ⓐ Ⓑ Ⓒ Ⓓ Ⓔ	45 Ⓐ Ⓑ Ⓒ Ⓓ Ⓔ	67 Ⓐ Ⓑ Ⓒ Ⓓ Ⓔ
2 Ⓐ Ⓑ Ⓒ Ⓓ Ⓔ	24 Ⓐ Ⓑ Ⓒ Ⓓ Ⓔ	46 Ⓐ Ⓑ Ⓒ Ⓓ Ⓔ	68 Ⓐ Ⓑ Ⓒ Ⓓ Ⓔ
3 Ⓐ Ⓑ Ⓒ Ⓓ Ⓔ	25 Ⓐ Ⓑ Ⓒ Ⓓ Ⓔ	47 Ⓐ Ⓑ Ⓒ Ⓓ Ⓔ	69 Ⓐ Ⓑ Ⓒ Ⓓ Ⓔ
4 Ⓐ Ⓑ Ⓒ Ⓓ Ⓔ	26 Ⓐ Ⓑ Ⓒ Ⓓ Ⓔ	48 Ⓐ Ⓑ Ⓒ Ⓓ Ⓔ	70 Ⓐ Ⓑ Ⓒ Ⓓ Ⓔ
5 Ⓐ Ⓑ Ⓒ Ⓓ Ⓔ	27 Ⓐ Ⓑ Ⓒ Ⓓ Ⓔ	49 Ⓐ Ⓑ Ⓒ Ⓓ Ⓔ	71 Ⓐ Ⓑ Ⓒ Ⓓ Ⓔ
6 Ⓐ Ⓑ Ⓒ Ⓓ Ⓔ	28 Ⓐ Ⓑ Ⓒ Ⓓ Ⓔ	50 Ⓐ Ⓑ Ⓒ Ⓓ Ⓔ	72 Ⓐ Ⓑ Ⓒ Ⓓ Ⓔ
7 Ⓐ Ⓑ Ⓒ Ⓓ Ⓔ	29 Ⓐ Ⓑ Ⓒ Ⓓ Ⓔ	51 Ⓐ Ⓑ Ⓒ Ⓓ Ⓔ	73 Ⓐ Ⓑ Ⓒ Ⓓ Ⓔ
8 Ⓐ Ⓑ Ⓒ Ⓓ Ⓔ	30 Ⓐ Ⓑ Ⓒ Ⓓ Ⓔ	52 Ⓐ Ⓑ Ⓒ Ⓓ Ⓔ	74 Ⓐ Ⓑ Ⓒ Ⓓ Ⓔ
9 Ⓐ Ⓑ Ⓒ Ⓓ Ⓔ	31 Ⓐ Ⓑ Ⓒ Ⓓ Ⓔ	53 Ⓐ Ⓑ Ⓒ Ⓓ Ⓔ	75 Ⓐ Ⓑ Ⓒ Ⓓ Ⓔ
10 Ⓐ Ⓑ Ⓒ Ⓓ Ⓔ	32 Ⓐ Ⓑ Ⓒ Ⓓ Ⓔ	54 Ⓐ Ⓑ Ⓒ Ⓓ Ⓔ	76 Ⓐ Ⓑ Ⓒ Ⓓ Ⓔ
11 Ⓐ Ⓑ Ⓒ Ⓓ Ⓔ	33 Ⓐ Ⓑ Ⓒ Ⓓ Ⓔ	55 Ⓐ Ⓑ Ⓒ Ⓓ Ⓔ	77 Ⓐ Ⓑ Ⓒ Ⓓ Ⓔ
12 Ⓐ Ⓑ Ⓒ Ⓓ Ⓔ	34 Ⓐ Ⓑ Ⓒ Ⓓ Ⓔ	56 Ⓐ Ⓑ Ⓒ Ⓓ Ⓔ	78 Ⓐ Ⓑ Ⓒ Ⓓ Ⓔ
13 Ⓐ Ⓑ Ⓒ Ⓓ Ⓔ	35 Ⓐ Ⓑ Ⓒ Ⓓ Ⓔ	57 Ⓐ Ⓑ Ⓒ Ⓓ Ⓔ	79 Ⓐ Ⓑ Ⓒ Ⓓ Ⓔ
14 Ⓐ Ⓑ Ⓒ Ⓓ Ⓔ	36 Ⓐ Ⓑ Ⓒ Ⓓ Ⓔ	58 Ⓐ Ⓑ Ⓒ Ⓓ Ⓔ	80 Ⓐ Ⓑ Ⓒ Ⓓ Ⓔ
15 Ⓐ Ⓑ Ⓒ Ⓓ Ⓔ	37 Ⓐ Ⓑ Ⓒ Ⓓ Ⓔ	59 Ⓐ Ⓑ Ⓒ Ⓓ Ⓔ	81 Ⓐ Ⓑ Ⓒ Ⓓ Ⓔ
16 Ⓐ Ⓑ Ⓒ Ⓓ Ⓔ	38 Ⓐ Ⓑ Ⓒ Ⓓ Ⓔ	60 Ⓐ Ⓑ Ⓒ Ⓓ Ⓔ	82 Ⓐ Ⓑ Ⓒ Ⓓ Ⓔ
17 Ⓐ Ⓑ Ⓒ Ⓓ Ⓔ	39 Ⓐ Ⓑ Ⓒ Ⓓ Ⓔ	61 Ⓐ Ⓑ Ⓒ Ⓓ Ⓔ	83 Ⓐ Ⓑ Ⓒ Ⓓ Ⓔ
18 Ⓐ Ⓑ Ⓒ Ⓓ Ⓔ	40 Ⓐ Ⓑ Ⓒ Ⓓ Ⓔ	62 Ⓐ Ⓑ Ⓒ Ⓓ Ⓔ	84 Ⓐ Ⓑ Ⓒ Ⓓ Ⓔ
19 Ⓐ Ⓑ Ⓒ Ⓓ Ⓔ	41 Ⓐ Ⓑ Ⓒ Ⓓ Ⓔ	63 Ⓐ Ⓑ Ⓒ Ⓓ Ⓔ	85 Ⓐ Ⓑ Ⓒ Ⓓ Ⓔ
20 Ⓐ Ⓑ Ⓒ Ⓓ Ⓔ	42 Ⓐ Ⓑ Ⓒ Ⓓ Ⓔ	64 Ⓐ Ⓑ Ⓒ Ⓓ Ⓔ	86 Ⓐ Ⓑ Ⓒ Ⓓ Ⓔ
21 Ⓐ Ⓑ Ⓒ Ⓓ Ⓔ	43 Ⓐ Ⓑ Ⓒ Ⓓ Ⓔ	65 Ⓐ Ⓑ Ⓒ Ⓓ Ⓔ	87 Ⓐ Ⓑ Ⓒ Ⓓ Ⓔ
22 Ⓐ Ⓑ Ⓒ Ⓓ Ⓔ	44 Ⓐ Ⓑ Ⓒ Ⓓ Ⓔ	66 Ⓐ Ⓑ Ⓒ Ⓓ Ⓔ	88 Ⓐ Ⓑ Ⓒ Ⓓ Ⓔ

MEMORY FOR ADDRESSES

Time: 5 Minutes. 88 Questions.

Directions: *Mark your answers on the answer sheet in the section headed "MEMORY FOR AD-DRESSES." This test will be scored. You are NOT permitted to look at the boxes. Work from memory, as quickly and as accurately as you can. Correct answers are on page 131.*

1. 1400–4099 Neff
2. 4100–4199 Plum
3. 1400–4099 Ash
4. Pepper
5. Dalby
6. 4200–4599 Plum
7. 4600–5299 Neff
8. 4100–4199 Ash
9. 4200–4599 Ash
10. Bardack
11. Hawk
12. 4600–5299 Plum
13. 1000–1399 Neff
14. 1000–1399 Ash
15. Clown
16. Flynn
17. 4600–5299 Ash
18. 1400–4099 Plum
19. 1000–1399 Plum
20. Cedar
21. Race

22. Lemon
23. 4100–4199 Neff
24. Greenhouse
25. 4200–4599 Neff
26. 1000–1399 Plum
27. 1400–4099 Neff
28. 4200–4599 Ash
29. Hawk
30. Flynn
31. 4100–4199 Plum
32. 4200–4599 Neff
33. 1400–4099 Ash
34. Clown
35. Dalby
36. 4100–4199 Ash
37. 4100–4199 Neff
38. 1400–4099 Plum
39. Cedar
40. Bardack
41. 1000–1399 Plum
42. 4600–5299 Neff

43. 1400–4099 Plum
44. Lemon
45. Cedar
46. 4200–4599 Ash
47. 4100–4199 Ash
48. 4100–4199 Plum
49. 1000–1399 Neff
50. 4100–4199 Neff
51. Hawk
52. Greenhouse
53. Dalby
54. 1400–4099 Ash
55. 4600–5299 Ash
56. 4200–4599 Plum
57. Clown
58. Race
59. 1000–1399 Ash
60. 4600–5299 Plum
61. Bardack
62. 4200–4599 Neff
63. Flynn

64. Pepper

65. 1400–4099 Neff

66. 4100–4199 Ash

67. 4600–5299 Neff

68. 1000–1399 Plum

69. 4100–4199 Plum

70. 4600–5299 Ash

71. 4600–5299 Neff

72. Lemon

73. Pepper

74. Cedar

75. 1400–4099 Ash

76. 1400–4099 Neff

77. 4100–4199 Ash

78. 4600–5299 Plum

79. Greenhouse

80. Dalby

81. 1000–1399 Plum

82. 1000–1399 Ash

83. 4100–4199 Neff

84. 4200–4599 Plum

85. Flynn

86. Clown

87. 4200–4599 Ash

88. 4100–4199 Ash

END OF MEMORY FOR ADDRESSES

PART C—NUMBER SERIES

Sample Questions

The following sample questions show you the type of question that will be used in Part C. You will have three minutes to answer the sample questions below and to study the explanations.

Directions: Each number series question consists of a series of numbers that follows some definite order. The numbers progress from left to right according to some rule. One pair of numbers to the right of the series comprises the next two numbers in the series. Study each series to try to find a pattern to the series and to figure out the rule that governs the progression. Choose the answer pair that continues the series according to the pattern established and mark its letter on your answer sheet.

1. 23 25·27 29 31 33 35 ....(A) 35 36   (B) 35 37   (C) 36 37   (D) 37 38   (E) 37 39

The answer (**E**) should be easy to see. This series progresses by adding 2. 35 + 2 = 37 + 2 = 39.

2. 3 3 6 6 12 12 24 ....(A) 24 36   (B) 36 36   (C) 24 24   (D) 24 48   (E) 48 48

The answer is (**D**) because the series requires you to repeat a number, then multiply it by 2.

3. 11 13 16 20 25 31 38 ....(A) 46 55   (B) 45 55   (C) 40 42   (D) 47 58   (E) 42 46

The easiest way to solve this problem is to write the degree and direction of change between the numbers. By doing this, you see that the pattern is +2, +3, +4, +5, +6, +7. Continue the series by continuing the pattern: 38 + 8 = 46 + 9 = 55. The answer is (**A**).

4. 76 72 72 68 64 64 60 ....(A) 60 56   (B) 60 60   (C) 56 56   (D) 56 52   (E) 56 54

Here the pattern is: –4, repeat the number, –4; –4, repeat the number, –4. To find that (**C**) is the answer you must realize that you are at the beginning of the pattern. 60 – 4 = 56, then repeat the number 56.

5. 92 94 96 92 94 96 92 ....(A) 92 94   (B) 94 96   (C) 96 92   (D) 96 94   (E) 96 98

The series consists of the sequence 92 94 96 repeated over and over again. (**B**) is the answer because 94 96 continues the sequence after 92.

<table>
<tr><td>

SAMPLE ANSWER SHEET

1. Ⓐ Ⓑ Ⓒ Ⓓ Ⓔ
2. Ⓐ Ⓑ Ⓒ Ⓓ Ⓔ
3. Ⓐ Ⓑ Ⓒ Ⓓ Ⓔ
4. Ⓐ Ⓑ Ⓒ Ⓓ Ⓔ
5. Ⓐ Ⓑ Ⓒ Ⓓ Ⓔ

</td><td>

CORRECT ANSWERS

1. Ⓐ Ⓑ Ⓒ Ⓓ ●
2. Ⓐ Ⓑ Ⓒ ● Ⓔ
3. ● Ⓑ Ⓒ Ⓓ Ⓔ
4. Ⓐ Ⓑ ● Ⓓ Ⓔ
5. Ⓐ ● Ⓒ Ⓓ Ⓔ

</td></tr>
</table>

NUMBER SERIES

Time: 20 Minutes. 24 Questions.

Directions: *Each number series question consists of a series of numbers that follows some definite order. The numbers progress from left to right according to some rule. One lettered pair of numbers comprises the next two numbers in the series. Study each series to try to find a pattern to the series and to figure out the rule that governs the progression. Choose the answer pair that continues the series according to the pattern established and mark its letter on your answer sheet. Correct answers are on page 132.*

1. 8 9 9 8 10 10 8 ....(A) 11 8   (B) 8 13   (C) 8 11   (D) 11 11   (E) 8 8
2. 10 10 11 11 12 12 13 ....(A) 15 15   (B) 13 13   (C) 14 14   (D) 13 14   (E) 14 15
3. 6 6 10 6 6 12 6 ....(A) 6 14   (B) 13 6   (C) 14 6   (D) 6 13   (E) 6 6
4. 17 11 5 16 10 4 15 ....(A) 13 9   (B) 13 11   (C) 8 5   (D) 9 5   (E) 9 3
5. 1 3 2 4 3 5 4 ....(A) 6 8   (B) 5 6   (C) 6 5   (D) 3 4   (E) 3 5
6. 11 11 10 12 12 11 13 ....(A) 12 14   (B) 14 12   (C) 14 14   (D) 13 14   (E) 13 12
7. 18 5 6 18 7 8 18 ....(A) 9 9   (B) 9 10   (C) 18 9   (D) 8 9   (E) 18 7
8. 8 1 9 3 10 5 11 ....(A) 7 12   (B) 6 12   (C) 12 6   (D) 7 8   (E) 6 7
9. 14 12 10 20 18 16 32 30 ...(A) 60 18   (B) 32 64   (C) 30 28   (D) 28 56   (E) 28 28
10. 67 59 52 44 37 29 22 ....(A) 15 7   (B) 14 8   (C) 14 7   (D) 15 8   (E) 16 11
11. 17 79 20 74 23 69 26 ....(A) 64 29   (B) 65 30   (C) 29 64   (D) 23 75   (E) 26 64
12. 3 5 10 8 4 6 12 10 5 ....(A) 8 16   (B) 7 14   (C) 10 20   (D) 10 5   (E) 7 9
13. 58 52 52 46 46 40 40 ....(A) 34 28   (B) 28 28   (C) 40 34   (D) 35 35   (E) 34 34
14. 32 37 33 33 38 34 34 ....(A) 38 43   (B) 34 39   (C) 39 35   (D) 39 39   (E) 34 40
15. 15 17 19 16 18 20 17 ....(A) 14 16   (B) 19 21   (C) 17 19   (D) 16 18   (E) 19 16
16. 5 15 7 21 13 39 31 ....(A) 93 85   (B) 62 69   (C) 39 117 (D) 93 87   (E) 31 93
17. 84 76 70 62 56 48 42 ....(A) 42 36   (B) 34 26   (C) 36 28   (D) 36 24   (E) 34 28
18. 47 23 43 27 39 31 35 ....(A) 31 27   (B) 39 43   (C) 39 35   (D) 35 31   (E) 31 35
19. 14 23 31 38 44 49 53 ....(A) 55 57   (B) 57 61   (C) 56 58   (D) 57 59   (E) 58 62
20. 5 6 8 8 9 11 11 12 ....(A) 12 13   (B) 14 14   (C) 14 15   (D) 14 16   (E) 12 14
21. 9 18 41 41 36 72 41 ....(A) 108 108   (B) 41 108 (C) 41 144 (D) 144 144 (E) 72 41
22. 13 15 17 13 15 17 13 ....(A) 17 15   (B) 13 15   (C) 17 13   (D) 15 13   (E) 15 17
23. 13 92 17 89 21 86 25 ....(A) 83 29   (B) 24 89   (C) 29 83   (D) 25 83   (E) 89 21
24. 10 20 23 13 26 29 19 ....(A) 9 12   (B) 38 41   (C) 22 44   (D) 44 33   (E) 36 39

END OF NUMBER SERIES

PART D—FOLLOWING ORAL INSTRUCTIONS

Directions and Sample Questions

Listening to Instructions: When you are ready to try these sample questions, give the following instructions to a friend and have the friend read them aloud to you at the rate of 80 words per minute. Do not read them to yourself. Your friend will need a watch with a second hand. Listen carefully and do exactly what your friend tells you to do with the worksheet and answer sheet. Your friend will tell you some things to do with each item on the worksheet. After each set of instructions, your friend will give you time to mark your answer by darkening a circle on the sample answer sheet. Since B and D sound very much alike, your friend will say "B as in baker" when he or she means B and "D as in dog" when he or she means D.

Before proceeding further, tear out the worksheet on page 121. Then hand this book to your friend.

To the Person Who Is to Read the Instructions: The instructions are to be read at the rate of 80 words per minute. Do not read aloud the material that is in parentheses. Do not repeat any instructions.

Read Aloud to the Candidate

Look at line 1 on your worksheet. (Pause slightly.) Draw two lines under the middle number on line 1. (Pause 2 seconds.) Now, on your answer sheet, find the number under which you just drew two lines and darken space D as in dog for that number. (Pause 5 seconds.)

Look at line 2 on your worksheet. (Pause slightly.) Write the letter A in the left-hand circle. (Pause 2 seconds.) Now, on your answer sheet, darken the space for the number-letter combination in the circle in which you just wrote. (Pause 5 seconds.)

Look at line 3 on your worksheet. (Pause slightly.) Count the number of times the letter E appears on line 3 and write the number at the end of the line. (Pause 2 seconds.) Now, on your answer sheet, darken space C for the number you just wrote. (Pause 5 seconds.)

Look at line 4 on your worksheet. (Pause slightly.) If an hour is longer than a day, write the letter B as in baker on the line next to the first number on line 4; if not, write the letter E on the line next to the third number. (Pause 5 seconds.) Now, on your answer sheet, darken the space for the number-letter combination you just wrote. (Pause 5 seconds.)

Look at line 4 again. (Pause slightly.) Write the second letter of the alphabet on the line next to the middle number. (Pause 2 seconds.) Now, on your answer sheet, darken the space for the number-letter combination you just wrote. (Pause 5 seconds.)

Sample Worksheet

Directions: *Listening carefully to each set of instructions, mark each item on this worksheet as directed. Then complete each question by marking the sample answer sheet below as directed. For each answer you will darken the answer for a number-letter combination. Should you fall behind and miss an instruction, don't become excited. Let that one go and listen for the next one. If, when you start to darken a space for a number, you find that you have already darkened another space for that number, either erase the first mark and darken the space for the new combination or let the first mark stay and do not darken a space for the new combination. Write with a pencil that has a clean eraser. When you finish, you should have no more than one space darkened for each number.*

1.   9   7   12   14   1

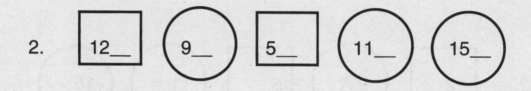

2.   12__   9__   5__   11__   15__

3.   WARNING. BEWARE OF DOG. __

4.   4___   13___   6___

SAMPLE ANSWER SHEET

1. Ⓐ Ⓑ Ⓒ Ⓓ Ⓔ	6. Ⓐ Ⓑ Ⓒ Ⓓ Ⓔ	11. Ⓐ Ⓑ Ⓒ Ⓓ Ⓔ
2. Ⓐ Ⓑ Ⓒ Ⓓ Ⓔ	7. Ⓐ Ⓑ Ⓒ Ⓓ Ⓔ	12. Ⓐ Ⓑ Ⓒ Ⓓ Ⓔ
3. Ⓐ Ⓑ Ⓒ Ⓓ Ⓔ	8. Ⓐ Ⓑ Ⓒ Ⓓ Ⓔ	13. Ⓐ Ⓑ Ⓒ Ⓓ Ⓔ
4. Ⓐ Ⓑ Ⓒ Ⓓ Ⓔ	9. Ⓐ Ⓑ Ⓒ Ⓓ Ⓔ	14. Ⓐ Ⓑ Ⓒ Ⓓ Ⓔ
5. Ⓐ Ⓑ Ⓒ Ⓓ Ⓔ	10. Ⓐ Ⓑ Ⓒ Ⓓ Ⓔ	15. Ⓐ Ⓑ Ⓒ Ⓓ Ⓔ

TEAR HERE

CORRECT ANSWERS TO SAMPLE QUESTIONS

1. Ⓐ Ⓑ Ⓒ Ⓓ Ⓔ   6. Ⓐ Ⓑ Ⓒ Ⓓ ●   11. Ⓐ Ⓑ Ⓒ Ⓓ Ⓔ
2. Ⓐ Ⓑ ● Ⓓ Ⓔ   7. Ⓐ Ⓑ Ⓒ Ⓓ Ⓔ   12. Ⓐ Ⓑ Ⓒ ● Ⓔ
3. Ⓐ Ⓑ Ⓒ Ⓓ Ⓔ   8. Ⓐ Ⓑ Ⓒ Ⓓ Ⓔ   13. Ⓐ ● Ⓒ Ⓓ Ⓔ
4. Ⓐ Ⓑ Ⓒ Ⓓ Ⓔ   9. ● Ⓑ Ⓒ Ⓓ Ⓔ   14. Ⓐ Ⓑ Ⓒ Ⓓ Ⓔ
5. Ⓐ Ⓑ Ⓒ Ⓓ Ⓔ   10. Ⓐ Ⓑ Ⓒ Ⓓ Ⓔ   15. Ⓐ Ⓑ Ⓒ Ⓓ Ⓔ

Correctly Filled Worksheet

1.   9   7   <u>12</u>   14   1

2.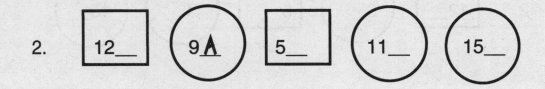

3.   WARNING. BEWARE OF DOG. <u>2</u>

4.   4___   13 <u>B</u>   6 <u>E</u>

FOLLOWING ORAL INSTRUCTIONS

Time: 25 Minutes.

Listening to Instructions

Directions: *When you are ready to try this test of the Model Exam, give the following instructions to a friend and have the friend read them aloud to you at the rate of 80 words per minute. Do NOT read them to yourself. Your friend will need a watch with a second hand. Listen carefully and do exactly what your friend tells you to do with the worksheet and with the answer sheet. Your friend will tell you some things to do with each item on the worksheet. After each set of instructions, you friend will give you time to mark your answer by darkening a circle on the answer sheet. Since B and D sound very much alike, your friend will say "B as in baker" when he or she means B and "D as in dog" when he or she means D.*

> Before proceeding further, tear out the worksheet on page 127. Then hand this book to your friend.

To the Person Who Is to Read the Instructions: *The instructions are to be read at the rate of 80 words per minute. Do not read aloud the material that is in parentheses. Once you have begun the test itself do not repeat any instructions. The next three paragraphs consist of approximately 120 words. Read these three paragraphs aloud to the candidate in about one and one-half minutes. You may reread these paragraphs as often as necessary to establish an 80 words-per-minute reading speed.*

Read Aloud to the Candidate

On the job you will have to listen to directions and then do what you have been told to do. In this test, I will read instructions to you. Try to understand them as I read them; I cannot repeat them. Once we begin, you may not ask any questions until the end of the test.

On the job you won't have to deal with pictures, numbers, and letters like those in the test, but you will have to listen to instructions and follow them. We are using this test to see how well you can follow instructions.

You are to mark your test booklet according to the instructions that I'll read to you. After each set of instructions, I'll give you time to record your answers on the separate answer sheet.

The actual test begins now.

Look at line 1 on your worksheet. (Pause slightly.) Draw one line under the first number on line 1. (Pause 2 seconds.) Now, on your answer sheet, darken space E for the number under which you just drew one line. (Pause 5 seconds.)

Look at line 1 again. (Pause slightly.) Draw two lines under the lowest number on line 1. (Pause 2 seconds.) Now, on your answer sheet, darken space B as in baker for the number under which you just drew two lines. (Pause 5 seconds.)

Look at line 2 on your worksheet. (Pause slightly.) Write the number 38 in front of the letter that comes second in the alphabet. (Pause 2 seconds.) Now, on your answer sheet, darken the space for the number-letter combination you just wrote. (Pause 5 seconds.)

Look at line 3 on your worksheet. The numbers represent afternoon pickup times at corner mailboxes. (Pause slightly.) Draw a line under the latest pickup time. (Pause 2 seconds.) Now, on your answer sheet, darken the letter A for the last two digits, the minutes, of the time under which you just drew a line. (Pause 5 seconds.)

Look at line 3 again. (Pause slightly.) Find the earliest pickup time and add together all the digits of that time. Write the sum of the digits on the line at the end of line 3. (Pause 8 seconds.) Now, on your answer sheet, darken letter D as in dog for the number you just wrote. (Pause 5 seconds.)

Look at line 4 on your worksheet. (Pause slightly.) In the first circle, write the answer to this question: How many hours are there in a day? (Pause 2 seconds.) In the third circle, write the answer to this question: How many working hours are there in a 5-day, 8-hours-per-day workweek? (Pause 5 seconds.) Now, on your answer sheet, darken the number-letter combinations that appear in both circles that you wrote in. (Pause 10 seconds.)

Look at line 5 on your worksheet. (Pause slightly.) If a yard is longer than ten inches, write the letter C in the triangle. If not, write E. (Pause 2 seconds.) Now, on your answer sheet, darken the space for the number-letter combination in the triangle. (Pause 5 seconds.)

Look at line 5 again. (Pause slightly.) If you are older than 36 months, write the letter A in the rectangle. If not, write the letter B as in baker in the square. (Pause 5 seconds.) Now, on your answer sheet, darken the space for the number-letter combination in the figure you just wrote in. (Pause 5 seconds.)

Look at line 6 on your worksheet. (Pause slightly.) Write the letter E beside the number that is second from the last on line 6. (Pause 2 seconds.) Now, on your answer sheet, darken the space for the number-letter combination you just wrote. (Pause 5 seconds.)

Look at line 7 on your worksheet. The numbers on line 7 represent a bar code. (Pause slightly.) Draw a line under each 0 in the bar code. (Pause 5 seconds.) Count the number of lines you have drawn, add 50, and write that number at the end of line 7. (Pause 5 seconds.) Now, on your answer sheet, darken space E for the number you just wrote. (Pause 5 seconds.)

Look at line 8 on your worksheet. The numbers in the mailsacks represent the weight of the mailsacks in pounds. (Pause slightly.) Write the letter D as in dog in the heaviest mailsack. (Pause 2 seconds.) Now, on your answer sheet, darken the space for the number-letter combination in the mailsack you just wrote in. (Pause 5 seconds.)

Look at line 9 on your worksheet. (Pause slightly.) Mark an X through the second number on line 9 and an X through every other number thereafter on line 9. (Pause 5 seconds.) Now, on your answer sheet, darken space A for the first number you drew an X through. (Pause 5 seconds.)

Look at line 9 again. (Pause slightly.) For all other numbers through which you drew an X, mark C on your answer sheet. (Pause 15 seconds.)

Look at line 10 on your worksheet. (Pause slightly.) Write the number 1 in the second figure in line 10. (Pause 2 seconds.) Now, on your answer sheet, darken the space for the number-letter combination in the figure you just wrote in. (Pause 5 seconds.)

Look at line 10 again. (Pause slightly.) Write the number 12 in the first circle on line 10. (Pause 2 seconds.) Now, on your answer sheet, darken the space for the number-letter combination in the figure you just wrote in. (Pause 5 seconds.)

Look at line 11 on your worksheet. (Pause slightly.) Write the letter A in the figure with fewer sides. (Pause 2 seconds.) Now, on your answer sheet, darken the space for the number-letter combination in the figure you just wrote in. (Pause 5 seconds.)

Look at line 12 on your worksheet. (Pause slightly.) If 3 is less than 5 and 10 is more than 2, write the number 79 in the first box. (Pause 5 seconds.) If not, write the number 76 in the second box. (Pause 5 seconds.) Now, on your answer sheet, darken the space for the number-letter combination in the box you just wrote in. (Pause 5 seconds.)

Look at line 13 on your worksheet. (Pause slightly.) Write the first letter of the third word in the second box. (Pause 5 seconds.) Write the third letter of the second word in the first box. (Pause 5 seconds.) Write the second letter of the first word in the third box. (Pause 5 seconds.) Now, on your answer sheet, darken the spaces for the number-letter combinations in the three boxes. (Pause 15 seconds.)

Look at line 14 on your worksheet. (Pause slightly.) If it is possible to purchase two 29¢ stamps for 55¢, write the number 72 on the second line. (Pause 5 seconds.) If not, write the number 19 on the first line. (Pause 5 seconds.) Now, on your answer sheet, darken the space for the number-letter combination you just wrote. (Pause 5 seconds.)

Look at line 15 on your worksheet. (Pause slightly.) Write the larger of these two numbers, 65 and 46, in the smaller box. (Pause 2 seconds.) Now, on your answer sheet, darken the space for the number-letter combination in the figure you just wrote in. (Pause 5 seconds.)

Look at line 15 again. (Pause slightly.) Write the sum of 10 plus 20 in the first box. (Pause 2 seconds.) Now, on your answer sheet, darken the space for the number-letter combination in the figure you just wrote in. (Pause 5 seconds.)

Look at line 16 on your worksheet. (Pause slightly.) Circle the fourth number on line 16. (Pause 2 seconds.) Now, on your answer sheet, darken the space for letter C for the number you just circled. (Pause 5 seconds.)

Look at line 17 on your worksheet. (Pause slightly.) If the number in the oval is greater than the number in the square, write the letter A in the circle. (Pause 5 seconds.) If not, write the letter B as in baker in the square. (Pause 5 seconds.) Now, on your answer sheet, darken the space for the number-letter combination in the figure you just wrote in. (Pause 5 seconds.)

Look at line 17 again. (Pause slightly.) If the number in the triangle is less than 25, write the letter D as in dog in the triangle. (Pause 2 seconds.) If not, write the letter C in the oval. (Pause 2 seconds.) Now, on your answer sheet, darken the space for the number-letter combination in the figure you just wrote in. (Pause 5 seconds.)

Look at line 18 on your worksheet. (Pause slightly.) Find the letter on line 18 that does not appear in the word GRADE and circle that letter. (Pause 2 seconds.) Now, on your answer sheet, find the number 44 and darken the space for the letter you just circled. (Pause 5 seconds.)

Look at line 19 on your worksheet. (Pause slightly.) Listen to the following numbers and write the smallest number beside the second letter: 59, 62, 49, 54, 87. (Pause 5 seconds.) Now, on your answer sheet, darken the number-letter combination you just wrote. (Pause 5 seconds.)

FOLLOWING ORAL INSTRUCTIONS

Worksheet

Directions: *Listening carefully to each set of instructions, mark each item on this worksheet as directed. Then complete each question by marking the answer sheet as directed. For each answer you will darken the answer for a number-letter combination. Should you fall behind and miss an instruction, don't become excited. Let that one go and listen for the next one. If when you start to darken a space for a number, you find that you have already darkened another space for that number, either erase the first mark and darken the space for the new combination or let the first mark stay and do not darken a space for the new combination. Write with a pencil that has a clean eraser. When you finish, you should have no more than one space darkened for each number. Correct answers are on pages 134–136.*

TEAR HERE

1. 75   14   9   27   54   12

2. ___ B   ___ D   ___ C   ___ A   ___ E

3. 5:43   4:32   3:58   6:27

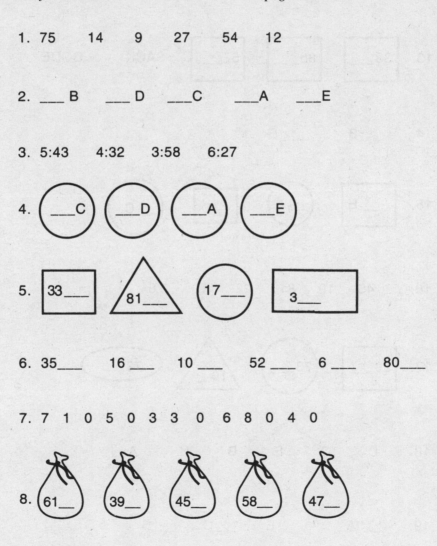

4. ___ C   ___ D   ___ A   ___ E

5. 33___   81___   17___   3___

6. 35___   16 ___   10 ___   52 ___   6 ___   80___

7. 7 1 0 5 0 3 3 0 6 8 0 4 0

8. 61__   39__   45__   58__   47__

9. 17   51   37   46   76   87   12   5

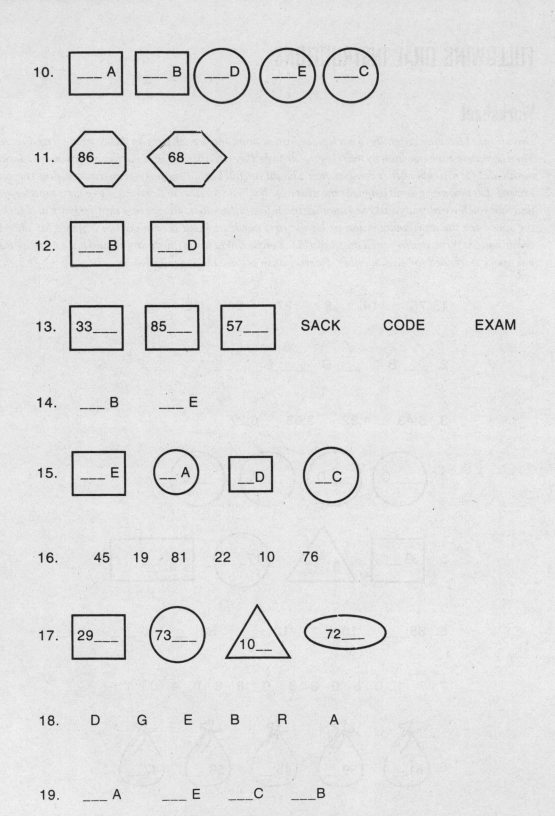

10. ___ A   ___ B   ___ D   ___ E   ___ C

11. 86___   68___

12. ___ B   ___ D

13. 33___   85___   57___   SACK   CODE   EXAM

14. ___ B   ___ E

15. ___ E   __ A   __ D   __ C

16. 45   19   81   22   10   76

17. 29___   73___   10__   72___

18. D   G   E   B   R   A

19. ___ A   ___ E   ___ C   ___ B

END OF EXAMINATION

CORRECT ANSWERS FOR MODEL EXAMINATION I

PART A—ADDRESS CHECKING

1.	A	13.	D	25.	D	37.	A	49.	D	61.	D	73.	A	85.	A
2.	D	14.	D	26.	D	38.	D	50.	A	62.	D	74.	D	86.	D
3.	D	15.	D	27.	D	39.	A	51.	A	63.	A	75.	D	87.	A
4.	A	16.	D	28.	A	40.	D	52.	D	64.	D	76.	D	88.	D
5.	D	17.	A	29.	D	41.	D	53.	D	65.	D	77.	D	89.	D
6.	D	18.	D	30.	A	42.	D	54.	A	66.	A	78.	D	90.	A
7.	A	19.	D	31.	A	43.	D	55.	D	67.	D	79.	A	91.	D
8.	D	20.	D	32.	D	44.	A	56.	A	68.	D	80.	A	92.	A
9.	D	21.	A	33.	D	45.	D	57.	D	69.	A	81.	D	93.	A
10.	A	22.	D	34.	D	46.	D	58.	D	70.	D	82.	A	94.	A
11.	D	23.	D	35.	D	47.	A	59.	D	71.	A	83.	D	95.	D
12.	D	24.	A	36.	A	48.	D	60.	A	72.	D	84.	A		

Analyzing Your Errors

This Address Checking Test contains 35 addresses that are exactly alike and 60 addresses that are different. The chart below shows what kind of difference occurs in each of the addresses that contains a difference. Check your answers against this chart to see which kind of difference you missed most often. Note also the questions in which you thought you saw a difference but in which there really was none. Becoming aware of your errors will help you to eliminate those errors on the actual exam.

Type of Difference	Question Numbers	Number of Questions You Missed
Difference in NUMBERS	2, 5, 8, 12, 14, 26, 32, 34, 35, 40, 43, 45, 52, 59, 67, 68, 72, 75, 76, 88, 91, 95	
Difference in ABBREVIATIONS	3, 9, 15, 25, 27, 33, 42, 46, 57, 61, 64, 77	
Difference in NAMES	6, 11, 13, 16, 18, 19, 20, 22, 23, 29, 38, 41, 48, 49, 53, 55, 58, 62, 65, 70, 74, 78, 81, 83, 86, 89	
No Difference	1, 4, 7, 10, 17, 21, 24, 28, 30, 31, 36, 37, 39, 44, 47, 50, 51, 54, 56, 60, 63, 66, 69, 71, 73, 79, 80, 82, 84, 85, 87, 90, 92, 93, 94	

PART B—MEMORY FOR ADDRESSES

Practice I

1.	B	12.	A	23.	A	34.	C	45.	B	56.	D	67.	C	78.	C
2.	C	13.	C	24.	B	35.	A	46.	E	57.	A	68.	E	79.	D
3.	D	14.	B	25.	E	36.	D	47.	B	58.	B	69.	B	80.	E
4.	E	15.	E	26.	B	37.	A	48.	D	59.	A	70.	E	81.	D
5.	A	16.	A	27.	E	38.	D	49.	D	60.	A	71.	B	82.	E
6.	E	17.	C	28.	D	39.	B	50.	D	61.	E	72.	D	83.	B
7.	C	18.	B	29.	A	40.	B	51.	C	62.	A	73.	A	84.	E
8.	B	19.	D	30.	A	41.	E	52.	C	63.	B	74.	E	85.	D
9.	B	20.	C	31.	E	42.	E	53.	B	64.	D	75.	B	86.	A
10.	A	21.	D	32.	C	43.	A	54.	E	65.	A	76.	E	87.	E
11.	E	22.	E	33.	C	44.	C	55.	C	66.	C	77.	A	88.	B

Practice II

1.	A	12.	A	23.	E	34.	B	45.	D	56.	D	67.	C	78.	A
2.	E	13.	A	24.	C	35.	C	46.	B	57.	C	68.	B	79.	D
3.	C	14.	B	25.	B	36.	A	47.	E	58.	A	69.	C	80.	B
4.	D	15.	E	26.	C	37.	E	48.	E	59.	C	70.	E	81.	C
5.	B	16.	B	27.	C	38.	A	49.	C	60.	D	71.	E	82.	C
6.	B	17.	D	28.	C	39.	A	50.	E	61.	A	72.	C	83.	A
7.	D	18.	C	29.	A	40.	E	51.	C	62.	D	73.	E	84.	D
8.	E	19.	D	30.	D	41.	B	52.	E	63.	D	74.	E	85.	A
9.	C	20.	D	31.	B	42.	A	53.	B	64.	B	75.	B	86.	A
10.	C	21.	A	32.	D	43.	D	54.	D	65.	A	76.	A	87.	E
11.	E	22.	A	33.	D	44.	B	55.	A	66.	B	77.	D	88.	E

Practice III

1.	C	12.	E	23.	A	34.	D	45.	A	56.	C	67.	B	78.	C
2.	E	13.	B	24.	A	35.	B	46.	E	57.	D	68.	B	79.	A
3.	A	14.	D	25.	C	36.	E	47.	B	58.	A	69.	D	80.	E
4.	D	15.	A	26.	C	37.	D	48.	D	59.	E	70.	B	81.	A
5.	B	16.	B	27.	E	38.	B	49.	D	60.	C	71.	A	82.	A
6.	A	17.	D	28.	B	39.	A	50.	A	61.	D	72.	E	83.	C
7.	E	18.	E	29.	E	40.	E	51.	A	62.	B	73.	E	84.	C
8.	B	19.	D	30.	D	41.	E	52.	C	63.	E	74.	B	85.	D
9.	D	20.	C	31.	B	42.	A	53.	C	64.	E	75.	C	86.	C
10.	A	21.	B	32.	C	43.	B	54.	E	65.	A	76.	D	87.	E
11.	A	22.	B	33.	D	44.	D	55.	C	66.	B	77.	D	88.	A

Memory for Addresses

1.	E	12.	E	23.	B	34.	D	45.	E	56.	C	67.	C	78.	E
2.	A	13.	A	24.	B	35.	B	46.	A	57.	D	68.	B	79.	B
3.	C	14.	D	25.	D	36.	E	47.	E	58.	C	69.	A	80.	B
4.	D	15.	D	26.	B	37.	B	48.	A	59.	D	70.	B	81.	B
5.	B	16.	C	27.	E	38.	D	49.	A	60.	E	71.	C	82.	D
6.	C	17.	B	28.	A	39.	E	50.	B	61.	A	72.	A	83.	B
7.	C	18.	D	29.	E	40.	A	51.	E	62.	D	73.	D	84.	C
8.	E	19.	B	30.	C	41.	B	52.	B	63.	C	74.	E	85.	C
9.	A	20.	E	31.	A	42.	C	53.	B	64.	D	75.	C	86.	D
10.	A	21.	C	32.	D	43.	D	54.	C	65.	E	76.	E	87.	A
11.	E	22.	A	33.	C	44.	A	55.	B	66.	E	77.	E	88.	E

PART C—NUMBER SERIES

1.	D	4.	E	7.	B	10.	C	13.	E	16.	A	19.	C	22.	E
2.	D	5.	C	8.	A	11.	A	14.	C	17.	E	20.	B	23.	A
3.	A	6.	E	9.	D	12.	B	15.	B	18.	D	21.	C	24.	B

Explanations

1. **(D)** The series really begins with <u>9</u> and consists of repeated numbers moving upward in order. The number <u>8</u> is inserted between each pair of repeated numbers in the series.

2. **(D)** The numbers repeat themselves and move up in order.

3. **(A)** <u>6 6</u> is a repetitive theme. Between each set of 6s, the numbers move up by +2.

4. **(E)** The full sequence is a number of sets of mini-series. Each mini-series consists of three numbers decreasing by –6. Each succeeding mini-series begins with a number one lower than the previous mini-series.

5. **(C)** Two alternating series each increase by +1. The first series starts at <u>1</u> and the second series starts at <u>3</u>.

6. **(E)** Two series alternate. The first series consists of repeating numbers that move up by +1. The alternating series consists of numbers that move up by +1 without repeating.

7. **(B)** The series proceeds 5 6 7 8 9 10, with the number <u>18</u> appearing between each two numbers.

8. **(A)** The first series ascends one number at a time starting from <u>8</u>. The alternating series ascends by +2 starting from <u>1</u>.

9. **(D)** The pattern is: –2, –2, ×2; –2, –2, ×2….

10. **(C)** The pattern is: –8, –7; –8, –7; –8, –7….

11. **(A)** Two series alternate. The first series ascends by +3; the alternating series descends by –5.

12. **(B)** This is a tough one. The pattern is +2, ×2, –2, ÷ 2; +2, ×2, –2, ÷ 2….

13. **(E)** The pattern is: –6, repeat the number; –6, repeat the number….

14. **(C)** The pattern is: +5, –4, repeat the number; +5, –4, repeat the number….

15. **(B)** The pattern is: +2, +2, –3; +2, +2, –3….

16. **(A)** The pattern is: ×3, –8; ×3, –8; ×3, –8….

17. **(E)** The pattern is: –8, –6; –8, –6; –8, –6….

18. **(D)** There are two alternating series. The first series descends by –4 starting from <u>47</u>; the alternating series ascends by +4, starting from <u>23</u>.

19. **(C)** The pattern is: +9, +8, +7, +6, +5, +4, +3, +2, +1.

20. **(B)** The pattern is: +1, +2, repeat the number; +1, +2, repeat the number....

21. **(C)** This is really a times 2 series with the number 41 appearing twice after each two numbers in the series. Thus: $9 \overset{\times 2}{} 18 \overset{\times 2}{} 36 \overset{\times 2}{} 72 \overset{\times 2}{} 144$.

22. **(E)** The sequence 13 15 17 repeats itself over and over.

23. **(A)** Two series alternate. The first series ascends by +4; the alternating series descends by −3.

24. **(B)** The pattern is: ×2, +3, −10; ×2, +3, −10; ×2, +3, −10....

PART D—FOLLOWING ORAL INSTRUCTIONS

Correctly Filled Answer Grid

1. (A) ● (C) (D) (E)
2. (A) (B) (C) (D) (E)
3. ● (B) (C) (D) (E)
4. (A) (B) (C) (D) (E)
5. (A) (B) ● (D) (E)
6. (A) (B) (C) (D) ●
7. (A) (B) (C) (D) (E)
8. (A) (B) (C) (D) (E)
9. (A) ● (C) (D) (E)
10. (A) (B) (C) ● (E)
11. (A) (B) (C) (D) (E)
12. (A) (B) (C) ● (E)
13. (A) (B) (C) (D) (E)
14. (A) (B) (C) (D) (E)
15. (A) (B) (C) (D) (E)
16. (A) (B) (C) ● (E)
17. (A) (B) (C) (D) (E)
18. (A) (B) (C) (D) (E)
19. (A) ● (C) (D) (E)
20. (A) (B) (C) (D) (E)
21. (A) (B) (C) (D) (E)
22. (A) (B) ● (D) (E)

23. (A) (B) (C) (D) (E)
24. (A) (B) ● (D) (E)
25. (A) (B) (C) (D) (E)
26. (A) (B) (C) (D) (E)
27. ● (B) (C) (D) (E)
28. (A) (B) (C) (D) (E)
29. (A) (B) (C) (D) (E)
30. (A) (B) (C) (D) ●
31. (A) (B) (C) (D) (E)
32. (A) (B) (C) (D) (E)
33. (A) (B) (C) ● (E)
34. (A) (B) (C) (D) (E)
35. (A) (B) (C) (D) (E)
36. (A) (B) (C) (D) (E)
37. (A) (B) (C) (D) (E)
38. (A) ● (C) (D) (E)
39. (A) (B) (C) (D) (E)
40. ● (B) (C) (D) (E)
41. (A) (B) (C) (D) (E)
42. (A) (B) (C) (D) (E)
43. (A) (B) (C) (D) (E)
44. (A) ● (C) (D) (E)

45. (A) (B) (C) (D) (E)
46. (A) (B) ● (D) (E)
47. (A) (B) (C) (D) (E)
48. (A) (B) (C) (D) (E)
49. (A) (B) (C) (D) ●
50. (A) (B) (C) (D) (E)
51. ● (B) (C) (D) (E)
52. (A) (B) (C) (D) (E)
53. (A) (B) (C) (D) (E)
54. (A) (B) (C) (D) (E)
55. (A) (B) (C) (D) ●
56. (A) (B) (C) (D) (E)
57. ● (B) (C) (D) (E)
58. (A) (B) (C) (D) (E)
59. (A) (B) (C) (D) (E)
60. (A) (B) (C) (D) (E)
61. (A) (B) (C) ● (E)
62. (A) (B) (C) (D) (E)
63. (A) (B) (C) (D) (E)
64. (A) (B) (C) (D) (E)
65. (A) (B) (C) ● (E)
66. (A) (B) (C) (D) (E)

67. (A) (B) (C) (D) (E)
68. ● (B) (C) (D) (E)
69. (A) (B) (C) (D) (E)
70. (A) (B) (C) (D) (E)
71. (A) (B) (C) (D) (E)
72. (A) (B) (C) (D) (E)
73. ● (B) (C) (D) (E)
74. (A) (B) (C) (D) (E)
75. (A) (B) (C) (D) ●
76. (A) (B) (C) (D) (E)
77. (A) (B) (C) (D) (E)
78. (A) (B) (C) (D) (E)
79. (A) ● (C) (D) (E)
80. (A) (B) (C) (D) (E)
81. (A) (B) ● (D) (E)
82. (A) (B) (C) (D) (E)
83. (A) (B) (C) (D) (E)
84. (A) (B) (C) (D) (E)
85. (A) (B) (C) (D) ●
86. (A) (B) (C) (D) (E)
87. (A) (B) ● (D) (E)
88. (A) (B) (C) (D) (E)

Correctly Filled Worksheet

1. <u>75</u>   14 <u><u>9</u></u>   27   54   12

2. <u>*38*</u> B   ___ D   ___ C   ___ A   ___ E

3. 5:43   4:32   3:58   <u>6:27</u>   <u>*16*</u>

4. (<u>*24*</u> C)   (___ D)   (<u>*40*</u> A)   (___ E)

5. [33 ___]   △ 81 <u>*C*</u>   (17 ___)   [3 <u>*A*</u>]

6. 35 ___   16 ___   10 ___   52 ___   6 <u>*E*</u>   80 ___

7. 7 1 <u>0</u> 5 <u>0</u> 3 3 <u>0</u> 6 8 <u>0</u> 4 <u>0</u>   <u>*55*</u>

8. (61 <u>*D*</u>)   (39 ___)   (45 ___)   (58 ___)   (47 ___)

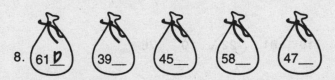

9. 17   ✗   37   ✗   76   ✗   12   ✗

10. ___A | I B | (12 D) | (___E) | (___C)

11. 86___ (octagon) | 68 A (hexagon)

12. 79 B | ___ D

13. 33 D | 85 E | 57 A | SACK | CODE | EXAM

14. 19 B | ___E

15. 30 E | (__A) | 65 D | (__C)

16. 45 19 81 (22) 10 76

17. 29___ | (73 A) | (10 D triangle) | (72___ oval)

18. D G E (B) R A

19. ___A | 49 E | ___C | ___B

SCORE SHEET

ADDRESS CHECKING: Your score on the Address Checking part is based upon the number of questions you answered correctly minus the number of questions you answered incorrectly. To determine your score, subtract the number of wrong answers from the number of correct answers.

Number Right   –   Number Wrong   =   Raw Score

_____   –   _____   =   _____

MEMORY FOR ADDRESSES: Your score on the Memory for Addresses part is based upon the number of questions you answered correctly minus one-fourth of the questions you answered incorrectly (number wrong divided by 4). Calculate this now: Number Wrong ÷ 4 = __.

Number Right   –   Number Wrong ÷ 4   =   Raw Score

_____   –   _____   =   _____

NUMBER SERIES: Your score on the Number Series part is based only on the number of questions you answered correctly. Wrong answers do not count against you.

Number Right   =   Raw Score

_____   =   _____

FOLLOWING ORAL INSTRUCTIONS: Your score on the Following Oral Instructions part is based only upon the number of questions you marked correctly on the answer sheet. The worksheet is not scored, and wrong answers on the answer sheet do not count against you.

Number Right   =   Raw Score

_____   =   _____

TOTAL SCORE: To find your total raw score, add together the raw scores for each section of the exam.

Address Checking Score   _____

+

Memory for Addresses Score   _____

+

Number Series Score   _____

+

Following Oral Instructions Score   _____

=   _____

Total Raw Score   _____

Self Evaluation Chart

Calculate your raw score for each test as shown above. Then check to see where your score falls on the scale from Poor to Excellent. Lightly shade in the boxes in which your scores fall.

Part	Excellent	Good	Average	Fair	Poor
Address Checking	80–95	65–79	50–64	35–49	1–34
Memory for Addresses	75–88	60–74	45–59	30–44	1–29
Number Series	21–24	18–20	14–17	11–13	1–10
Following Oral Instructions	27–32	23–26	19–22	14–18	1–13

For step-by-step instruction on how to prepare for and do well on Exam 470 and Exam 460, and for lots of practice with six additional full-length model exams, purchase Arco's Postal Clerk and Carrier.

MODEL EXAMINATION II: EXAM 710 (PARTS A & B) AND EXAM 711 (PART C)

Answer Sheet

Exam 710 (Parts A & B)

Clerk-Typist
Clerk-Stenographer
Data Conversion Operator

Exam 711 (Part C)

Clerk-Stenographer only

Part A

1. Ⓐ Ⓑ Ⓒ Ⓓ Ⓔ	23. Ⓐ Ⓑ Ⓒ Ⓓ Ⓔ	44. Ⓐ Ⓑ Ⓒ Ⓓ Ⓔ	65. Ⓐ Ⓑ Ⓒ Ⓓ Ⓔ
2. Ⓐ Ⓑ Ⓒ Ⓓ Ⓔ	24. Ⓐ Ⓑ Ⓒ Ⓓ Ⓔ	45. Ⓐ Ⓑ Ⓒ Ⓓ Ⓔ	66. Ⓐ Ⓑ Ⓒ Ⓓ Ⓔ
3. Ⓐ Ⓑ Ⓒ Ⓓ Ⓔ	25. Ⓐ Ⓑ Ⓒ Ⓓ Ⓔ	46. Ⓐ Ⓑ Ⓒ Ⓓ Ⓔ	67. Ⓐ Ⓑ Ⓒ Ⓓ Ⓔ
4. Ⓐ Ⓑ Ⓒ Ⓓ Ⓔ	26. Ⓐ Ⓑ Ⓒ Ⓓ Ⓔ	47. Ⓐ Ⓑ Ⓒ Ⓓ Ⓔ	68. Ⓐ Ⓑ Ⓒ Ⓓ Ⓔ
5. Ⓐ Ⓑ Ⓒ Ⓓ Ⓔ	27. Ⓐ Ⓑ Ⓒ Ⓓ Ⓔ	48. Ⓐ Ⓑ Ⓒ Ⓓ Ⓔ	69. Ⓐ Ⓑ Ⓒ Ⓓ Ⓔ
6. Ⓐ Ⓑ Ⓒ Ⓓ Ⓔ	28. Ⓐ Ⓑ Ⓒ Ⓓ Ⓔ	49. Ⓐ Ⓑ Ⓒ Ⓓ Ⓔ	70. Ⓐ Ⓑ Ⓒ Ⓓ Ⓔ
7. Ⓐ Ⓑ Ⓒ Ⓓ Ⓔ	29. Ⓐ Ⓑ Ⓒ Ⓓ Ⓔ	50. Ⓐ Ⓑ Ⓒ Ⓓ Ⓔ	71. Ⓐ Ⓑ Ⓒ Ⓓ Ⓔ
8. Ⓐ Ⓑ Ⓒ Ⓓ Ⓔ	30. Ⓐ Ⓑ Ⓒ Ⓓ Ⓔ	51. Ⓐ Ⓑ Ⓒ Ⓓ Ⓔ	72. Ⓐ Ⓑ Ⓒ Ⓓ Ⓔ
9. Ⓐ Ⓑ Ⓒ Ⓓ Ⓔ	31. Ⓐ Ⓑ Ⓒ Ⓓ Ⓔ	52. Ⓐ Ⓑ Ⓒ Ⓓ Ⓔ	73. Ⓐ Ⓑ Ⓒ Ⓓ Ⓔ
10. Ⓐ Ⓑ Ⓒ Ⓓ Ⓔ	32. Ⓐ Ⓑ Ⓒ Ⓓ Ⓔ	53. Ⓐ Ⓑ Ⓒ Ⓓ Ⓔ	74. Ⓐ Ⓑ Ⓒ Ⓓ Ⓔ
11. Ⓐ Ⓑ Ⓒ Ⓓ Ⓔ	33. Ⓐ Ⓑ Ⓒ Ⓓ Ⓔ	54. Ⓐ Ⓑ Ⓒ Ⓓ Ⓔ	75. Ⓐ Ⓑ Ⓒ Ⓓ Ⓔ
12. Ⓐ Ⓑ Ⓒ Ⓓ Ⓔ	34. Ⓐ Ⓑ Ⓒ Ⓓ Ⓔ	55. Ⓐ Ⓑ Ⓒ Ⓓ Ⓔ	76. Ⓐ Ⓑ Ⓒ Ⓓ Ⓔ
13. Ⓐ Ⓑ Ⓒ Ⓓ Ⓔ	35. Ⓐ Ⓑ Ⓒ Ⓓ Ⓔ	56. Ⓐ Ⓑ Ⓒ Ⓓ Ⓔ	77. Ⓐ Ⓑ Ⓒ Ⓓ Ⓔ
14. Ⓐ Ⓑ Ⓒ Ⓓ Ⓔ	36. Ⓐ Ⓑ Ⓒ Ⓓ Ⓔ	57. Ⓐ Ⓑ Ⓒ Ⓓ Ⓔ	78. Ⓐ Ⓑ Ⓒ Ⓓ Ⓔ
15. Ⓐ Ⓑ Ⓒ Ⓓ Ⓔ	37. Ⓐ Ⓑ Ⓒ Ⓓ Ⓔ	58. Ⓐ Ⓑ Ⓒ Ⓓ Ⓔ	79. Ⓐ Ⓑ Ⓒ Ⓓ Ⓔ
16. Ⓐ Ⓑ Ⓒ Ⓓ Ⓔ	38. Ⓐ Ⓑ Ⓒ Ⓓ Ⓔ	59. Ⓐ Ⓑ Ⓒ Ⓓ Ⓔ	80. Ⓐ Ⓑ Ⓒ Ⓓ Ⓔ
17. Ⓐ Ⓑ Ⓒ Ⓓ Ⓔ	39. Ⓐ Ⓑ Ⓒ Ⓓ Ⓔ	60. Ⓐ Ⓑ Ⓒ Ⓓ Ⓔ	81. Ⓐ Ⓑ Ⓒ Ⓓ Ⓔ
18. Ⓐ Ⓑ Ⓒ Ⓓ Ⓔ	40. Ⓐ Ⓑ Ⓒ Ⓓ Ⓔ	61. Ⓐ Ⓑ Ⓒ Ⓓ Ⓔ	82. Ⓐ Ⓑ Ⓒ Ⓓ Ⓔ
19. Ⓐ Ⓑ Ⓒ Ⓓ Ⓔ	41. Ⓐ Ⓑ Ⓒ Ⓓ Ⓔ	62. Ⓐ Ⓑ Ⓒ Ⓓ Ⓔ	83. Ⓐ Ⓑ Ⓒ Ⓓ Ⓔ
20. Ⓐ Ⓑ Ⓒ Ⓓ Ⓔ	42. Ⓐ Ⓑ Ⓒ Ⓓ Ⓔ	63. Ⓐ Ⓑ Ⓒ Ⓓ Ⓔ	84. Ⓐ Ⓑ Ⓒ Ⓓ Ⓔ
21. Ⓐ Ⓑ Ⓒ Ⓓ Ⓔ	43. Ⓐ Ⓑ Ⓒ Ⓓ Ⓔ	64. Ⓐ Ⓑ Ⓒ Ⓓ Ⓔ	85. Ⓐ Ⓑ Ⓒ Ⓓ Ⓔ
22. Ⓐ Ⓑ Ⓒ Ⓓ Ⓔ			

TEAR HERE

Part B

1. Ⓐ Ⓑ Ⓒ Ⓓ Ⓔ	33. Ⓐ Ⓑ Ⓒ Ⓓ Ⓔ	65. Ⓐ Ⓑ Ⓒ Ⓓ Ⓔ	97. Ⓐ Ⓑ Ⓒ Ⓓ Ⓔ
2. Ⓐ Ⓑ Ⓒ Ⓓ Ⓔ	34. Ⓐ Ⓑ Ⓒ Ⓓ Ⓔ	66. Ⓐ Ⓑ Ⓒ Ⓓ Ⓔ	98. Ⓐ Ⓑ Ⓒ Ⓓ Ⓔ
3. Ⓐ Ⓑ Ⓒ Ⓓ Ⓔ	35. Ⓐ Ⓑ Ⓒ Ⓓ Ⓔ	67. Ⓐ Ⓑ Ⓒ Ⓓ Ⓔ	99. Ⓐ Ⓑ Ⓒ Ⓓ Ⓔ
4. Ⓐ Ⓑ Ⓒ Ⓓ Ⓔ	36. Ⓐ Ⓑ Ⓒ Ⓓ Ⓔ	68. Ⓐ Ⓑ Ⓒ Ⓓ Ⓔ	100. Ⓐ Ⓑ Ⓒ Ⓓ Ⓔ
5. Ⓐ Ⓑ Ⓒ Ⓓ Ⓔ	37. Ⓐ Ⓑ Ⓒ Ⓓ Ⓔ	69. Ⓐ Ⓑ Ⓒ Ⓓ Ⓔ	101. Ⓐ Ⓑ Ⓒ Ⓓ Ⓔ
6. Ⓐ Ⓑ Ⓒ Ⓓ Ⓔ	38. Ⓐ Ⓑ Ⓒ Ⓓ Ⓔ	70. Ⓐ Ⓑ Ⓒ Ⓓ Ⓔ	102. Ⓐ Ⓑ Ⓒ Ⓓ Ⓔ
7. Ⓐ Ⓑ Ⓒ Ⓓ Ⓔ	39. Ⓐ Ⓑ Ⓒ Ⓓ Ⓔ	71. Ⓐ Ⓑ Ⓒ Ⓓ Ⓔ	103. Ⓐ Ⓑ Ⓒ Ⓓ Ⓔ
8. Ⓐ Ⓑ Ⓒ Ⓓ Ⓔ	40. Ⓐ Ⓑ Ⓒ Ⓓ Ⓔ	72. Ⓐ Ⓑ Ⓒ Ⓓ Ⓔ	104. Ⓐ Ⓑ Ⓒ Ⓓ Ⓔ
9. Ⓐ Ⓑ Ⓒ Ⓓ Ⓔ	41. Ⓐ Ⓑ Ⓒ Ⓓ Ⓔ	73. Ⓐ Ⓑ Ⓒ Ⓓ Ⓔ	105. Ⓐ Ⓑ Ⓒ Ⓓ Ⓔ
10. Ⓐ Ⓑ Ⓒ Ⓓ Ⓔ	42. Ⓐ Ⓑ Ⓒ Ⓓ Ⓔ	74. Ⓐ Ⓑ Ⓒ Ⓓ Ⓔ	106. Ⓐ Ⓑ Ⓒ Ⓓ Ⓔ
11. Ⓐ Ⓑ Ⓒ Ⓓ Ⓔ	43. Ⓐ Ⓑ Ⓒ Ⓓ Ⓔ	75. Ⓐ Ⓑ Ⓒ Ⓓ Ⓔ	107. Ⓐ Ⓑ Ⓒ Ⓓ Ⓔ
12. Ⓐ Ⓑ Ⓒ Ⓓ Ⓔ	44. Ⓐ Ⓑ Ⓒ Ⓓ Ⓔ	76. Ⓐ Ⓑ Ⓒ Ⓓ Ⓔ	108. Ⓐ Ⓑ Ⓒ Ⓓ Ⓔ
13. Ⓐ Ⓑ Ⓒ Ⓓ Ⓔ	45. Ⓐ Ⓑ Ⓒ Ⓓ Ⓔ	77. Ⓐ Ⓑ Ⓒ Ⓓ Ⓔ	109. Ⓐ Ⓑ Ⓒ Ⓓ Ⓔ
14. Ⓐ Ⓑ Ⓒ Ⓓ Ⓔ	46. Ⓐ Ⓑ Ⓒ Ⓓ Ⓔ	78. Ⓐ Ⓑ Ⓒ Ⓓ Ⓔ	110. Ⓐ Ⓑ Ⓒ Ⓓ Ⓔ
15. Ⓐ Ⓑ Ⓒ Ⓓ Ⓔ	47. Ⓐ Ⓑ Ⓒ Ⓓ Ⓔ	79. Ⓐ Ⓑ Ⓒ Ⓓ Ⓔ	111. Ⓐ Ⓑ Ⓒ Ⓓ Ⓔ
16. Ⓐ Ⓑ Ⓒ Ⓓ Ⓔ	48. Ⓐ Ⓑ Ⓒ Ⓓ Ⓔ	80. Ⓐ Ⓑ Ⓒ Ⓓ Ⓔ	112. Ⓐ Ⓑ Ⓒ Ⓓ Ⓔ
17. Ⓐ Ⓑ Ⓒ Ⓓ Ⓔ	49. Ⓐ Ⓑ Ⓒ Ⓓ Ⓔ	81. Ⓐ Ⓑ Ⓒ Ⓓ Ⓔ	113. Ⓐ Ⓑ Ⓒ Ⓓ Ⓔ
18. Ⓐ Ⓑ Ⓒ Ⓓ Ⓔ	50. Ⓐ Ⓑ Ⓒ Ⓓ Ⓔ	82. Ⓐ Ⓑ Ⓒ Ⓓ Ⓔ	114. Ⓐ Ⓑ Ⓒ Ⓓ Ⓔ
19. Ⓐ Ⓑ Ⓒ Ⓓ Ⓔ	51. Ⓐ Ⓑ Ⓒ Ⓓ Ⓔ	83. Ⓐ Ⓑ Ⓒ Ⓓ Ⓔ	115. Ⓐ Ⓑ Ⓒ Ⓓ Ⓔ
20. Ⓐ Ⓑ Ⓒ Ⓓ Ⓔ	52. Ⓐ Ⓑ Ⓒ Ⓓ Ⓔ	84. Ⓐ Ⓑ Ⓒ Ⓓ Ⓔ	116. Ⓐ Ⓑ Ⓒ Ⓓ Ⓔ
21. Ⓐ Ⓑ Ⓒ Ⓓ Ⓔ	53. Ⓐ Ⓑ Ⓒ Ⓓ Ⓔ	85. Ⓐ Ⓑ Ⓒ Ⓓ Ⓔ	117. Ⓐ Ⓑ Ⓒ Ⓓ Ⓔ
22. Ⓐ Ⓑ Ⓒ Ⓓ Ⓔ	54. Ⓐ Ⓑ Ⓒ Ⓓ Ⓔ	86. Ⓐ Ⓑ Ⓒ Ⓓ Ⓔ	118. Ⓐ Ⓑ Ⓒ Ⓓ Ⓔ
23. Ⓐ Ⓑ Ⓒ Ⓓ Ⓔ	55. Ⓐ Ⓑ Ⓒ Ⓓ Ⓔ	87. Ⓐ Ⓑ Ⓒ Ⓓ Ⓔ	119. Ⓐ Ⓑ Ⓒ Ⓓ Ⓔ
24. Ⓐ Ⓑ Ⓒ Ⓓ Ⓔ	56. Ⓐ Ⓑ Ⓒ Ⓓ Ⓔ	88. Ⓐ Ⓑ Ⓒ Ⓓ Ⓔ	120. Ⓐ Ⓑ Ⓒ Ⓓ Ⓔ
25. Ⓐ Ⓑ Ⓒ Ⓓ Ⓔ	57. Ⓐ Ⓑ Ⓒ Ⓓ Ⓔ	89. Ⓐ Ⓑ Ⓒ Ⓓ Ⓔ	121. Ⓐ Ⓑ Ⓒ Ⓓ Ⓔ
26. Ⓐ Ⓑ Ⓒ Ⓓ Ⓔ	58. Ⓐ Ⓑ Ⓒ Ⓓ Ⓔ	90. Ⓐ Ⓑ Ⓒ Ⓓ Ⓔ	122. Ⓐ Ⓑ Ⓒ Ⓓ Ⓔ
27. Ⓐ Ⓑ Ⓒ Ⓓ Ⓔ	59. Ⓐ Ⓑ Ⓒ Ⓓ Ⓔ	91. Ⓐ Ⓑ Ⓒ Ⓓ Ⓔ	123. Ⓐ Ⓑ Ⓒ Ⓓ Ⓔ
28. Ⓐ Ⓑ Ⓒ Ⓓ Ⓔ	60. Ⓐ Ⓑ Ⓒ Ⓓ Ⓔ	92. Ⓐ Ⓑ Ⓒ Ⓓ Ⓔ	124. Ⓐ Ⓑ Ⓒ Ⓓ Ⓔ
29. Ⓐ Ⓑ Ⓒ Ⓓ Ⓔ	61. Ⓐ Ⓑ Ⓒ Ⓓ Ⓔ	93. Ⓐ Ⓑ Ⓒ Ⓓ Ⓔ	125. Ⓐ Ⓑ Ⓒ Ⓓ Ⓔ
30. Ⓐ Ⓑ Ⓒ Ⓓ Ⓔ	62. Ⓐ Ⓑ Ⓒ Ⓓ Ⓔ	94. Ⓐ Ⓑ Ⓒ Ⓓ Ⓔ	
31. Ⓐ Ⓑ Ⓒ Ⓓ Ⓔ	63. Ⓐ Ⓑ Ⓒ Ⓓ Ⓔ	95. Ⓐ Ⓑ Ⓒ Ⓓ Ⓔ	
32. Ⓐ Ⓑ Ⓒ Ⓓ Ⓔ	64. Ⓐ Ⓑ Ⓒ Ⓓ Ⓔ	96. Ⓐ Ⓑ Ⓒ Ⓓ Ⓔ	

Part C

1. Ⓐ Ⓑ Ⓒ Ⓓ Ⓔ	15. Ⓐ Ⓑ Ⓒ Ⓓ Ⓔ	29. Ⓐ Ⓑ Ⓒ Ⓓ Ⓔ	43. Ⓐ Ⓑ Ⓒ Ⓓ Ⓔ
2. Ⓐ Ⓑ Ⓒ Ⓓ Ⓔ	16. Ⓐ Ⓑ Ⓒ Ⓓ Ⓔ	30. Ⓐ Ⓑ Ⓒ Ⓓ Ⓔ	44. Ⓐ Ⓑ Ⓒ Ⓓ Ⓔ
3. Ⓐ Ⓑ Ⓒ Ⓓ Ⓔ	17. Ⓐ Ⓑ Ⓒ Ⓓ Ⓔ	31. Ⓐ Ⓑ Ⓒ Ⓓ Ⓔ	45. Ⓐ Ⓑ Ⓒ Ⓓ Ⓔ
4. Ⓐ Ⓑ Ⓒ Ⓓ Ⓔ	18. Ⓐ Ⓑ Ⓒ Ⓓ Ⓔ	32. Ⓐ Ⓑ Ⓒ Ⓓ Ⓔ	46. Ⓐ Ⓑ Ⓒ Ⓓ Ⓔ
5. Ⓐ Ⓑ Ⓒ Ⓓ Ⓔ	19. Ⓐ Ⓑ Ⓒ Ⓓ Ⓔ	33. Ⓐ Ⓑ Ⓒ Ⓓ Ⓔ	47. Ⓐ Ⓑ Ⓒ Ⓓ Ⓔ
6. Ⓐ Ⓑ Ⓒ Ⓓ Ⓔ	20. Ⓐ Ⓑ Ⓒ Ⓓ Ⓔ	34. Ⓐ Ⓑ Ⓒ Ⓓ Ⓔ	48. Ⓐ Ⓑ Ⓒ Ⓓ Ⓔ
7. Ⓐ Ⓑ Ⓒ Ⓓ Ⓔ	21. Ⓐ Ⓑ Ⓒ Ⓓ Ⓔ	35. Ⓐ Ⓑ Ⓒ Ⓓ Ⓔ	49. Ⓐ Ⓑ Ⓒ Ⓓ Ⓔ
8. Ⓐ Ⓑ Ⓒ Ⓓ Ⓔ	22. Ⓐ Ⓑ Ⓒ Ⓓ Ⓔ	36. Ⓐ Ⓑ Ⓒ Ⓓ Ⓔ	50. Ⓐ Ⓑ Ⓒ Ⓓ Ⓔ
9. Ⓐ Ⓑ Ⓒ Ⓓ Ⓔ	23. Ⓐ Ⓑ Ⓒ Ⓓ Ⓔ	37. Ⓐ Ⓑ Ⓒ Ⓓ Ⓔ	51. Ⓐ Ⓑ Ⓒ Ⓓ Ⓔ
10. Ⓐ Ⓑ Ⓒ Ⓓ Ⓔ	24. Ⓐ Ⓑ Ⓒ Ⓓ Ⓔ	38. Ⓐ Ⓑ Ⓒ Ⓓ Ⓔ	52. Ⓐ Ⓑ Ⓒ Ⓓ Ⓔ
11. Ⓐ Ⓑ Ⓒ Ⓓ Ⓔ	25. Ⓐ Ⓑ Ⓒ Ⓓ Ⓔ	39. Ⓐ Ⓑ Ⓒ Ⓓ Ⓔ	53. Ⓐ Ⓑ Ⓒ Ⓓ Ⓔ
12. Ⓐ Ⓑ Ⓒ Ⓓ Ⓔ	26. Ⓐ Ⓑ Ⓒ Ⓓ Ⓔ	40. Ⓐ Ⓑ Ⓒ Ⓓ Ⓔ	54. Ⓐ Ⓑ Ⓒ Ⓓ Ⓔ
13. Ⓐ Ⓑ Ⓒ Ⓓ Ⓔ	27. Ⓐ Ⓑ Ⓒ Ⓓ Ⓔ	41. Ⓐ Ⓑ Ⓒ Ⓓ Ⓔ	55. Ⓐ Ⓑ Ⓒ Ⓓ Ⓔ
14. Ⓐ Ⓑ Ⓒ Ⓓ Ⓔ	28. Ⓐ Ⓑ Ⓒ Ⓓ Ⓔ	42. Ⓐ Ⓑ Ⓒ Ⓓ Ⓔ	

PART A—CLERICAL ABILITY

Sample Questions

There are four kinds of questions in Part A. Each kind of question has its own set of directions, and each portion of the part is timed separately. The four kinds of questions are:

Sequencing	3 minutes, 20 questions
Comparisons	5 minutes, 30 questions
Spelling	3 minutes, 20 questions
Computations	8 minutes, 15 questions

Directions for sequencing questions: For each question there is a name, number, or code in a box at the left and four other names or codes in alphabetical or numerical order at the right. Find the correct space for the boxed name or number so that it will be in alphabetical and/or numerical order with the others and mark the letter of that space on your answer sheet.

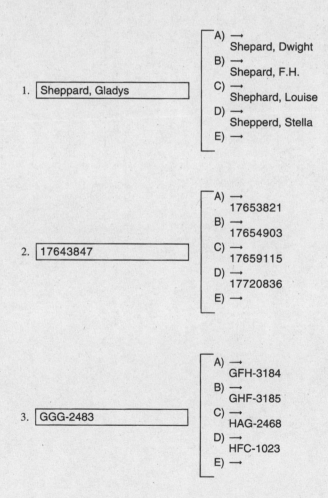

1. Sheppard, Gladys

A) →
   Shepard, Dwight
B) →
   Shepard, F.H.
C) →
   Shephard, Louise
D) →
   Shepperd, Stella
E) →

2. 17643847

A) →
   17653821
B) →
   17654903
C) →
   17659115
D) →
   17720836
E) →

3. GGG-2483

A) →
   GFH-3184
B) →
   GHF-3185
C) →
   HAG-2468
D) →
   HFC-1023
E) →

Directions for comparisons questions: In each line across the page there are three names, addresses, or codes that are very much alike. Compare the three and decide which ones are EXACTLY alike. On your answer sheet, mark:

A if **ALL THREE** names, addresses, or codes are exactly **ALIKE**

B if only the **FIRST** and **SECOND** names, addresses, or codes are exactly **ALIKE**

C if only the **FIRST** and **THIRD** names, addresses, or codes are exactly **ALIKE**

D if only the **SECOND** and **THIRD** names, addresses, or codes are exactly **ALIKE**

E if **ALL THREE** names, addresses, or codes are **DIFFERENT**

4.	H. Merritt Audubon	H. Merriott Audubon	H. Merritt Audubon
5.	2395890	2395890	2395890
6.	3418 W. 42nd St.	3418 W. 42nd Ave.	3148 W. 42nd Ave.

Directions for spelling questions: Find the correct spelling of the word and darken the appropriate space on the answer sheet. If none of the spellings is correct, darken space D.

7. (A) exceed
   (B) excede
   (C) exseed
   (D) none of these
8. (A) maneuver
   (B) manuver
   (C) manuever
   (D) none of these
9. (A) corellation
   (B) corrolation
   (C) corralation
   (D) none of these

Directions for computations questions: *Perform the computation as indicated in the question and find the answer among the list of alternative responses. If the correct answer is not given among the choices, mark E.*

10. $2\sqrt{142}$
   (A) 70
   (B) 72
   (C) 74
   (D) 76
   (E) none of these

11. $\begin{array}{r} 25 \\ -10 \\ \hline \end{array}$
   (A) 5
   (B) 10
   (C) 15
   (D) 20
   (E) none of these

12. $\begin{array}{r} 18 \\ \times\ 6 \\ \hline \end{array}$
   (A) 108
   (B) 116
   (C) 118
   (D) 124
   (E) none of these

Sample Answer Sheet

1 Ⓐ Ⓑ Ⓒ Ⓓ Ⓔ   4 Ⓐ Ⓑ Ⓒ Ⓓ Ⓔ   7 Ⓐ Ⓑ Ⓒ Ⓓ Ⓔ   10 Ⓐ Ⓑ Ⓒ Ⓓ Ⓔ
2 Ⓐ Ⓑ Ⓒ Ⓓ Ⓔ   5 Ⓐ Ⓑ Ⓒ Ⓓ Ⓔ   8 Ⓐ Ⓑ Ⓒ Ⓓ Ⓔ   11 Ⓐ Ⓑ Ⓒ Ⓓ Ⓔ
3 Ⓐ Ⓑ Ⓒ Ⓓ Ⓔ   6 Ⓐ Ⓑ Ⓒ Ⓓ Ⓔ   9 Ⓐ Ⓑ Ⓒ Ⓓ Ⓔ   12 Ⓐ Ⓑ Ⓒ Ⓓ Ⓔ

Correct Answers to Sample Questions

1 Ⓐ Ⓑ Ⓒ ● Ⓔ   4 Ⓐ Ⓑ ● Ⓓ Ⓔ   7 ● Ⓑ Ⓒ Ⓓ Ⓔ   10 Ⓐ Ⓑ Ⓒ Ⓓ ●
2 ● Ⓑ Ⓒ Ⓓ Ⓔ   5 ● Ⓑ Ⓒ Ⓓ Ⓔ   8 ● Ⓑ Ⓒ Ⓓ Ⓔ   11 Ⓐ Ⓑ ● Ⓓ Ⓔ
3 Ⓐ ● Ⓒ Ⓓ Ⓔ   6 Ⓐ Ⓑ Ⓒ Ⓓ ●   9 Ⓐ Ⓑ Ⓒ ● Ⓔ   12 ● Ⓑ Ⓒ Ⓓ Ⓔ

SEQUENCING

Time: 3 Minutes. 20 Questions.

Directions: For each question there is a name, number, or code in a box at the left and four other names, numbers, or codes in alphabetical or numerical order at the right. Find the correct space for the boxed name or number so that it will be in alphabetical and/or numerical order with the others and mark the letter of that space on your answer sheet.

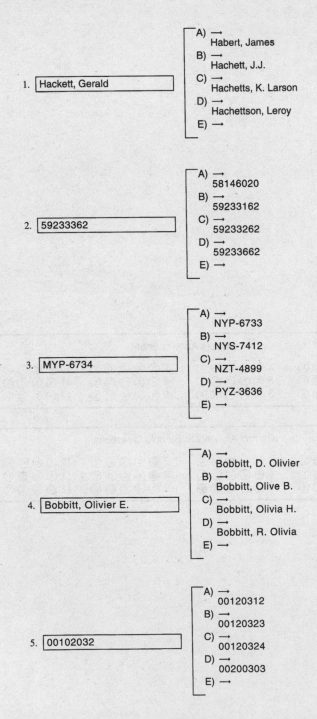

1. | Hackett, Gerald |

A) →
  Habert, James
B) →
  Hachett, J.J.
C) →
  Hachetts, K. Larson
D) →
  Hachettson, Leroy
E) →

2. | 59233362 |

A) →
  58146020
B) →
  59233162
C) →
  59233262
D) →
  59233662
E) →

3. | MYP-6734 |

A) →
  NYP-6733
B) →
  NYS-7412
C) →
  NZT-4899
D) →
  PYZ-3636
E) →

4. | Bobbitt, Olivier E. |

A) →
  Bobbitt, D. Olivier
B) →
  Bobbitt, Olive B.
C) →
  Bobbitt, Olivia H.
D) →
  Bobbitt, R. Olivia
E) →

5. | 00102032 |

A) →
  00120312
B) →
  00120323
C) →
  00120324
D) →
  00200303
E) →

6. | LPD-6100 |

   A) →
      LPD-5865
   B) →
      LPD-6001
   C) →
      LPD-6101
   D) →
      LPD-6106
   E) →

7. | Vanstory, George |

   A) →
      Vanover, Eva
   B) →
      VanSwinderen, Floyd
   C) →
      VanSyckle, Harry
   D) →
      Vanture, Laurence
   E) →

8. | Fitzsimmons, Hugh |

   A) →
      Fitts, Harold
   B) →
      Fitzgerald, June
   C) →
      FitzGibbon, Junius
   D) →
      FitzSimons, Martin
   E) →

9. | 01066010 |

   A) →
      01006040
   B) →
      01006051
   C) →
      01016053
   D) →
      01016060
   E) →

10. | AAZ-2687 |

   A) →
      AAA-2132
   B) →
      AAS-4623
   C) →
      ASA-3216
   D) →
      ASZ-5490
   E) →

11. | Pawlowicz, Ruth M. |

   A) →
      Pawalek, Edward
   B) →
      Pawelek, Flora G.
   C) →
      Pawlowski, Joan M.
   D) →
      Pawtowski, Wanda
   E) →

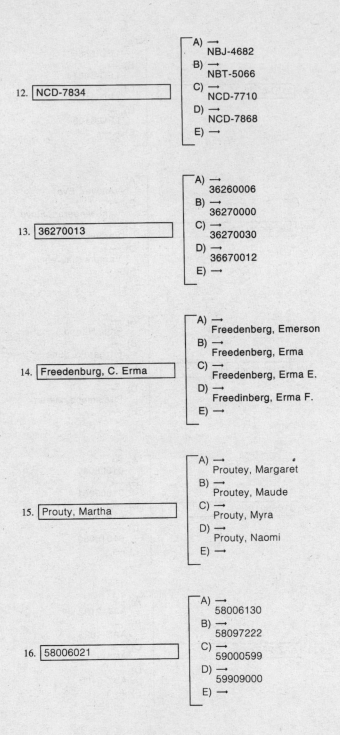

12. NCD-7834

A) → NBJ-4682
B) → NBT-5066
C) → NCD-7710
D) → NCD-7868
E) →

13. 36270013

A) → 36260006
B) → 36270000
C) → 36270030
D) → 36670012
E) →

14. Freedenburg, C. Erma

A) → Freedenberg, Emerson
B) → Freedenberg, Erma
C) → Freedenberg, Erma E.
D) → Freedinberg, Erma F.
E) →

15. Prouty, Martha

A) → Proutey, Margaret
B) → Proutey, Maude
C) → Prouty, Myra
D) → Prouty, Naomi
E) →

16. 58006021

A) → 58006130
B) → 58097222
C) → 59000599
D) → 59909000
E) →

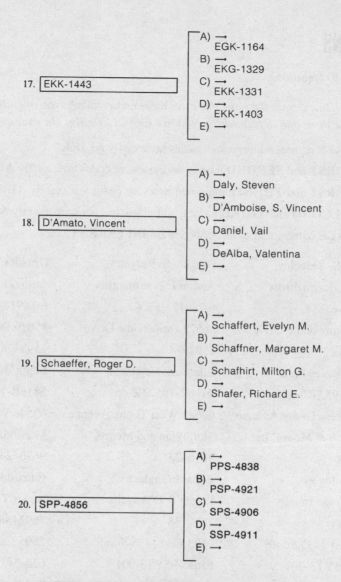

17. EKK-1443

    A) →
       EGK-1164
    B) →
       EKG-1329
    C) →
       EKK-1331
    D) →
       EKK-1403
    E) →

18. D'Amato, Vincent

    A) →
       Daly, Steven
    B) →
       D'Amboise, S. Vincent
    C) →
       Daniel, Vail
    D) →
       DeAlba, Valentina
    E) →

19. Schaeffer, Roger D.

    A) →
       Schaffert, Evelyn M.
    B) →
       Schaffner, Margaret M.
    C) →
       Schafhirt, Milton G.
    D) →
       Shafer, Richard E.
    E) →

20. SPP-4856

    A) →
       PPS-4838
    B) →
       PSP-4921
    C) →
       SPS-4906
    D) →
       SSP-4911
    E) →

END OF SEQUENCING QUESTIONS

COMPARISONS

Time: 5 Minutes. 30 Questions.

Directions: *In each line across the page there are three names, addresses, or codes that are very much alike. Compare the three and decide which ones are EXACTLY alike. On your answer sheet, mark:*

A if **ALL THREE** names, addresses, or codes are exactly **ALIKE**

B if only the **FIRST** and **SECOND** names, addresses, or codes are exactly **ALIKE**

C if only the **FIRST** and **THIRD** names, addresses, or codes are exactly **ALIKE**

D if only the **SECOND** and **THIRD** names, addresses, or codes are exactly **ALIKE**

E if **ALL THREE** names, addresses, or codes are **DIFFERENT**

21.	Drusilla S. Ridgeley	Drusilla S. Ridgeley	Drusilla S. Ridgeley
22.	Andrei I. Toumantzev	Andrei I. Tourmantzev	Andrei I. Toumantzov
23.	6-78912-e3e42	6-78912-3e3e42	6-78912-e3e42
24.	86529 Dunwoodie Drive	86529 Dunwoodie Drive	85629 Dunwoodie Drive
25.	1592514	1592574	1592574
26.	Ella Burk Newham	Ella Burk Newnham	Elena Burk Newnham
27.	5416R-1952TZ-op	5416R-1952TZ-op	5416R-1952TZ-op
28.	60646 West Touhy Avenue	60646 West Touhy Avenue	60646 West Touhey Avenue
29.	Mardikian & Moore, Inc.	Mardikian and Moore, Inc.	Mardikian & Moore, Inc.
30.	9670243	9670423	9670423
31.	Eduardo Ingles	Eduardo Inglese	Eduardo Inglese
32.	Roger T. DeAngelis	Roger T. D'Angelis	Roger T. DeAngeles
33.	7692138	7692138	7692138
34.	2695 East 3435 South	2695 East 3435 South	2695 East 3435 South
35.	63qs5-95YT3-001	63qs5-95YT3-001	63qs5-95YT3-001
36.	2789350	2789350	2798350
37.	Helmut V. Lochner	Helmut V. Lockner	Helmut W. Lochner
38.	2454803	2548403	2454803
39.	Lemberger, WA 28094-9182	Lemberger, VA 28094-9182	Lemberger, VA 28094-9182
40.	4168-GNP-78852	4168-GNP-78852	4168-GNP-78852
41.	Yoshihito Saito	Yoshihito Saito	Yoshihito Saito
42.	5927681	5927861	5927681
43.	O'Reilly Bay, LA 56212	O'Reillys Bay, LA 56212	O'Reilly Bay, LA 56212
44.	Francis Ransdell	Frances Ramsdell	Francis Ramsdell
45.	5634-OotV5a-16867	5634-Ootv5a-16867	5634-Ootv5a-16867
46.	Dolores Mollicone	Dolores Mollicone	Doloras Mollicone
47.	David C. Routzon	David E. Routzon	David C. Routzron

48.	8932 Shimabui Hwy.	8932 Shimabui Hwy.	8932 Shimabui Hwy.
49.	6177396	6177936	6177396
50.	A8987-B73245	A8987-B73245	A8987-B73245

END OF COMPARISONS QUESTIONS

SPELLING

Time: 3 Minutes. 20 Questions.

Directions: Find the correct spelling of the word and darken the appropriate space on your answer sheet. If none of the spellings is correct, darken space D.

51. (A) anticipate
    (B) antisipate
    (C) anticapate
    (D) none of these

52. (A) similiar
    (B) simmilar
    (C) similar
    (D) none of these

53. (A) sufficiantly
    (B) suficeintly
    (C) sufficiently
    (D) none of these

54. (A) intelligence
    (B) inteligence
    (C) intellegence
    (D) none of these

55. (A) referance
    (B) referrence
    (C) referense
    (D) none of these

56. (A) conscious
    (B) consious
    (C) conscius
    (D) none of these

57. (A) paralell
    (B) parellel
    (C) parellell
    (D) none of these

58. (A) abundence
    (B) abundance
    (C) abundants
    (D) none of these

59. (A) corregated
    (B) corrigated
    (C) corrugated
    (D) none of these

60. (A) accumalation
    (B) accumulation
    (C) accumullation
    (D) none of these

61. (A) resonance
    (B) resonence
    (C) resonnance
    (D) none of these

62. (A) benaficial
    (B) benefitial
    (C) beneficial
    (D) none of these

63. (A) spesifically
    (B) specificially
    (C) specifically
    (D) none of these

64. (A) elemanate
    (B) elimenate
    (C) elliminate
    (D) none of these

65. (A) collosal
    (B) colosal
    (C) collossal
    (D) none of these

66. (A) auxillary
    (B) auxilliary
    (C) auxiliary
    (D) none of these

67. (A) inimitable
    (B) inimitible
    (C) inimatable
    (D) none of these

68. (A) disapearance
    (B) dissapearance
    (C) disappearence
    (D) none of these

69. (A) appelate
    (B) appellate
    (C) apellate
    (D) none of these

70. (A) esential
    (B) essential
    (C) essencial
    (D) none of these

END OF SPELLING QUESTIONS

COMPUTATIONS

Time: 8 Minutes. 15 Questions.

Directions: *Perform the computation as indicated in the question and find the answer among the list of alternative responses. If the correct answer is not given among the choices, mark E.*

71. 83
$\underline{-56}$
(A) 23
(B) 29
(C) 33
(D) 37
(E) none of these

72. 15
$\underline{+17}$
(A) 22
(B) 32
(C) 39
(D) 42
(E) none of these

73. 32
$\underline{\times\ 7}$
(A) 224
(B) 234
(C) 324
(D) 334
(E) none of these

74. 39
$\underline{\times\ 2}$
(A) 77
(B) 78
(C) 79
(D) 81
(E) none of these

75. 43
$\underline{-15}$
(A) 23
(B) 32
(C) 33
(D) 35
(E) none of these

76. 50
$\underline{+49}$
(A) 89
(B) 90
(C) 99
(D) 109
(E) none of these

77. $6\sqrt{366}$
(A) 11
(B) 31
(C) 36
(D) 66
(E) none of these

78. 38
$\underline{\times\ 3}$
(A) 111
(B) 113
(C) 115
(D) 117
(E) none of these

79. 19
$\underline{+21}$
(A) 20
(B) 30
(C) 40
(D) 50
(E) none of these

80. 13
$\underline{-\ 6}$
(A) 5
(B) 7
(C) 9
(D) 11
(E) none of these

81. $6\sqrt{180}$
   (A) 29
   (B) 31
   (C) 33
   (D) 39
   (E) none of these

82. $\begin{array}{r} 10 \\ \times\ 1 \\ \hline \end{array}$
   (A) 0
   (B) 1
   (C) 10
   (D) 100
   (E) none of these

83. $7\sqrt{287}$
   (A) 21
   (B) 27
   (C) 31
   (D) 37
   (E) none of these

84. $\begin{array}{r} 12 \\ +11 \\ \hline \end{array}$
   (A) 21
   (B) 22
   (C) 23
   (D) 24
   (E) none of these

85. $\begin{array}{r} 85 \\ -64 \\ \hline \end{array}$
   (A) 19
   (B) 21
   (C) 29
   (D) 31
   (E) none of these

END OF COMPUTATIONS QUESTIONS

END OF PART A

PART B—VERBAL ABILITY

Sample Questions

There are four kinds of questions in Part B. Each kind of question has its own set of directions, but the portions containing the different kinds of questions are not separately timed. There are 55 questions in Part B, and candidates are allowed 50 minutes to complete the entire part. The four kinds of questions are:

Following Written Instructions, 20 questions

Grammar/Punctuation, 20 questions

Vocabulary, 15 questions altogether

Reading Comprehension

Directions for following written instructions: *These questions test your ability to follow instructions. Each question directs you to mark a specific number and letter combination on your answer sheet. The questions require your total concentration because the answers that you are instructed to mark are, for the most part, NOT in numerical sequence (i.e., you would not use Number 1 on your answer sheet to answer Question 1; Number 2 for Question 2; etc.). Instead, you must mark the number and space specifically designated in each test question.*

1. Look at the numbers below. Draw one line under the lowest number. Now, on your answer sheet, find that number and darken letter C for that number.

    4   2   3   6

2. Circle the middle letter in the line below. Now, on your answer sheet, find the number 3 and darken the space for the letter you just circled.

    F   A   D   B   E

3. Subtract 8 from 9 and write your answer on the line below. Now, on your answer sheet, darken space D for the space of the number you wrote.

    _____

The remaining questions are to be answered on the answer sheet in numerical sequence: Question 4 is to be answered in Space 4, Question 5 in Space 5, and so forth.

Directions for Grammar/Punctuation Questions: *Each question consists of a sentence written in four different ways. Choose the sentence that is most appropriate with respect to grammar, usage, and punctuation, so as to be suitable for a business letter or report, and darken its letter on your answer sheet.*

4. (A) Your pen is different from mine.
    (B) Your pen is different to mine.
    (C) Your pen is different than mine.
    (D) Your pen is different with mine.

Directions for Vocabulary Questions: Each question consists of a sentence containing a word in boldface type. Choose the best meaning for the word in boldface type and darken its letter on your answer sheet.

5. A passing grade on the special exam may **exempt** the applicant from the experience requirements for that job. **Exempt** most nearly means
   (A) prohibit
   (B) excuse
   (C) subject
   (D) specify

Directions for Reading Comprehension Questions: Read each paragraph and answer the question that follows it by darkening the letter of the correct answer on your answer sheet.

6. The work goals of an agency can best be reached if the employees understand and agree with these goals. One way to gain such understanding and agreement is for management to encourage and seriously consider suggestions from employees in the setting of agency goals.

   The paragraph best supports the statement that understanding and agreement with agency goals can be gained by
   (A) allowing the employees to set agency goals
   (B) reaching agency goals quickly
   (C) legislative review of agency operations
   (D) employee participation in setting agency goals

Sample Answer Sheet

1. Ⓐ Ⓑ Ⓒ Ⓓ Ⓔ   3. Ⓐ Ⓑ Ⓒ Ⓓ Ⓔ   5. Ⓐ Ⓑ Ⓒ Ⓓ Ⓔ
2. Ⓐ Ⓑ Ⓒ Ⓓ Ⓔ   4. Ⓐ Ⓑ Ⓒ Ⓓ Ⓔ   6. Ⓐ Ⓑ Ⓒ Ⓓ Ⓔ

Correct Answers to Sample Questions

1. Ⓐ Ⓑ Ⓒ ● Ⓔ   3. Ⓐ Ⓑ Ⓒ ● Ⓔ   5. Ⓐ ● Ⓒ Ⓓ Ⓔ
2. Ⓐ Ⓑ ● Ⓓ Ⓔ   4. ● Ⓑ Ⓒ Ⓓ Ⓔ   6. Ⓐ Ⓑ Ⓒ ● Ⓔ

PART B

Time: 50 Minutes. 55 Questions.

Directions: *Questions 1 through 20 test your ability to follow instructions. Each question directs you to mark a specific number and letter combination on your answer sheet. The questions require your total concentration because the answers that you are instructed to mark are, for the most part, NOT in numerical sequence (i.e., you would not use Number 1 on your answer sheet to answer Question 1; Number 2 for Question 2; etc.). Instead, you must mark the number and space specifically designated in each test question.*

1. Look at the letters below. Draw a circle around the letter that comes first in the alphabet. Now, on your answer sheet, find Number 12 and darken the space for the letter you just circled.

    E G D Z B F

2. Draw a line under the odd number below that is more than 5 but less than 10. Find this number on your answer sheet and darken space E.

    8 10 5 6 11 9

3. Divide the number 16 by 4 and write your answer on the line below. Now find this number on your answer sheet and darken space A.

    _____

4. Write the letter C on the line next to the left hand number below. Now, on your answer sheet, darken the space for the number-letter combination you see.

    5_____   19_____   7_____

5. If in any week Wednesday comes before Tuesday, write the number 15 on the line below. If not, write the number 18. Now, on your answer sheet, darken the letter A for the number you just wrote.

    _____

6. Count the number of Bs in the line below and write that number at the end of the line. Now, on your answer sheet, darken the letter D for the number you wrote.

    A D A E B D C A_____

7. Write the letter B on the line with the highest number. Now, on your answer sheet, darken the number-letter combination that appears on that line.

    16_____   9_____   20_____   11_____

8. If the product of 6 × 4 is greater than the product of 8 × 3, write the letter E on the line below. If not, write the letter C. Now, on your answer sheet find number 8 and darken the space for the letter you just wrote.

    _____

9. Write the number 2 in the largest circle below. Now, on your answer sheet, darken the space for the number-letter combination in that circle.

10. Write the letter D on the line next to the number that is the sum of 7 + 4 + 4. Now, on your answer sheet, darken the space for that number-letter combination.

    13_____   14_____   15_____   16_____   17_____

11. If 5 × 5 equals 25 and 5 + 5 equals 10, write the number 17 on the line below. If not, write the number 10. Now, on your answer sheet, darken space E for the number you just wrote.

    _____

12. Circle the second letter below. On the line beside that letter write the number that represents the number of days in a week. Now, on your answer sheet, darken the space for that number-letter combination.

    _____C   _____D   _____B   _____E

13. If a triangle has more angles than a rectangle, write the number 13 in the circle below. If not, write the number 14 in the square. Now, on your answer sheet, darken the space for the number-letter combination in the figure that you just wrote in.

    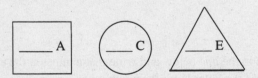

14. Count the number of Bs below and write that number at the end of the line. Subtract 2 from that number. Now, on your answer sheet, darken space E for the number that represents 2 less than the number of Bs in the line.

    B E A D E C C B B B A E B D_____

15. The numbers below represent morning pick-up times from neighborhood letter boxes. Draw a line under the number that represents the latest pick-up time. Now, on your answer sheet, darken space D for the number that is the same as the "minutes" of the time that you underlined.

    9:19   10:16   10:10

16. If a person who is 6 feet tall is taller than a person who is 5 feet tall and if a pillow is softer than a rock, darken space 11A on your answer sheet. If not, darken space 6B.

17. Write the fourth letter of the alphabet on the line next to the third number below. Now, on your answer sheet, darken that number-letter combination.

10_____   19_____   13_____   4_____

18. Write the letter B in the box containing the next to smallest number. On your answer sheet, darken the space for that number-letter combination.

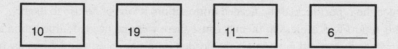

10_____   19_____   11_____   6_____

19. Directly below you will see three boxes and three words. Write the third letter of the first word on the line in the second box. Now, on your answer sheet, darken the space for that number-letter combination.

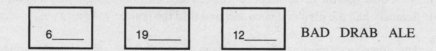

6_____   19_____   12_____   BAD DRAB ALE

20. Count the number of points on the figure below. If there are five or more points, darken the space for 6E on your answer sheet. If there are fewer than five points, darken 6A.

Directions: Each question from 21 through 40 consists of a sentence written in four different ways. Choose the sentence that is most appropriate with respect to grammar, usage, and punctuation, so as to be suitable for a business letter or report and darken its letter on your answer sheet. Answer each question in the answer space with the corresponding number.

21. (A) Double parking is when you park your car alongside one that is already having been parked.
(B) When one double parks, you park your car alongside one that is already parked.
(C) Double parking is parking alongside a car already parked.
(D) To double park is alongside a car already parked.

22. (A) This is entirely among you and he.
(B) This is completely among him and you.
(C) This is between you and him.
(D) This is between he and you.

23. (A) As I said, "neither of them are guilty."
(B) As I said, "neither of them are guilty".
(C) As I said, "neither of them is guilty."
(D) As I said, neither of them is guilty.

24. (A) I think that they will promote whoever has the best record.
    (B) The firm would have liked to have promoted all employees with good records.
    (C) Such of them that have the best records have excellent prospects of promotion.
    (D) I feel sure they will give the promotion to whomever has the best record.

25. (A) The receptionist must answer courteously the questions of all them callers.
    (B) The receptionist must answer courteously the questions what are asked by the callers.
    (C) There would have been no trouble if the receptionist had have always answered courteously.
    (D) The receptionist should answer courteously the questions of all callers.

26. (A) Since the report lacked the needed information, it was of no use to them.
    (B) This report was useless to them because there were no needed information in it.
    (C) Since the report did not contain the needed information, it was not real useful to them.
    (D) Being that the report lacked the needed information, they could not use it.

27. (A) The company had hardly declared the dividend till the notices were prepared for mailing.
    (B) They had no sooner declared the dividend when they sent the notices to the stockholders.
    (C) No sooner had the dividend been declared than the notices were prepared for mailing.
    (D) Scarcely had the dividend been declared than the notices were sent out.

28. (A) The supervisors reprimanded the typists, whom she believed had made careless errors.
    (B) The typists would have corrected the errors had they of known that the supervisor would see the report.
    (C) The errors in the typed reports were so numerous that they could hardly be overlooked.
    (D) Many errors were found in the reports which they typed and could not disregard them.

29. (A) "Are you absolutely certain, she asked, that you are right?"
    (B) "Are you absolutely certain," she asked, "that you are right?"
    (C) "Are you absolutely certain," she asked, "That you are right"?
    (D) "Are you absolutely certain", she asked, "That-you are right?"

30. (A) He goes only to church on Christmas and Easter.
    (B) He only goes to church on Christmas and Easter.
    (C) He goes to only church on Christmas and Easter.
    (D) He goes to church only on Christmas and Easter.

31. (A) Most all these statements have been supported by persons who are reliable and can be depended upon.
    (B) The persons which have guaranteed these statements are reliable.
    (C) Reliable persons guarantee the facts with regards to the truth of these statements.
    (D) These statements can be depended on, for their truth has been guaranteed by reliable persons.

32. (A) The success of the book pleased both the publisher and authors.
    (B) Both the publisher and they was pleased with the success of the book.
    (C) Neither they or their publisher was disappointed with the success of the book.
    (D) Their publisher was as pleased as they with the success of the book.

33. (A) In reviewing the typists' work reports, the job analyst found records of unusual typing speeds.
    (B) It says in the job analyst's report that some employees type with great speed.
    (C) The job analyst found that, in reviewing the typists' work reports, that some unusual typing speeds had been made.
    (D) In the reports of typists' speeds, the job analyst found some records that are kind of unusual.

34. (A) Every carrier should always have something to throw; not something to throw at the dog but something what will divert its attention.
    (B) Every carrier should have something to throw—not something to throw at the dog but something to divert its attention.
    (C) Every carrier should always carry something to throw not something to throw at the dog but something that will divert it's attention.
    (D) Every carrier should always carry something to throw, not something to throw at the dog, but, something that will divert its' attention.

35. (A) Brown's & Company employees have recently received increases in salary.
    (B) Brown & Company recently increased the salaries of all its employees.
    (C) Recently Brown & Company has increased their employees' salaries.
    (D) Brown & Company have recently increased the salaries of all its employees.

36. (A) If properly addressed, the letter will reach my mother and I.
    (B) The letter had been addressed to myself and my mother.
    (C) I believe the letter was addressed to either my mother or I.
    (D) My mother's name, as well as mine, was on the letter.

37. (A) One of us have to make the reply before tomorrow.
    (B) Making the reply before tomorrow will have to be done by one of us.
    (C) One of us has to reply before tomorrow.
    (D) Anyone has to reply before tomorrow.

38. (A) You have got to get rid of some of these people if you expect to have the quality of the work improve.
    (B) The quality of the work would improve if they would leave fewer people do it.
    (C) I believe it would be desirable to have fewer persons doing this work.
    (D) If you had planned on employing fewer people than this to do the work, this situation would not have arose.

39. (A) The paper we use for this purpose must be light, glossy, and stand hard usage as well.
    (B) Only a light and a glossy, but durable, paper must be used for this purpose.
    (C) For this purpose, we want a paper that is light, glossy, but that will stand hard wear.
    (D) For this purpose, paper that is light, glossy, and durable is essential.

40. (A) This letter, together with the reports, are to be sent to the postmaster.
    (B) The reports, together with this letter, is to be sent to the postmaster.
    (C) The reports and this letter is to be sent to the postmaster.
    (D) This letter, together with the reports, is to be sent to the postmaster.

Directions: Each question from 41 through 48 consists of a sentence containing a word in boldface type. Choose the best meaning for the word in boldface type and darken its letter on your answer sheet. Answer each question in the answer space with the corresponding number.

41. Please consult your office **manual** to learn the proper operation of our copying machine. **Manual** means most nearly
(A) labor
(B) handbook
(C) typewriter
(D) handle

42. There is a specified punishment for each **infraction** of the rules. **Infraction** means most nearly
(A) violation
(B) use
(C) interpretation
(D) part

43. The order was **rescinded** within the week. **Rescinded** means most nearly
(A) revised
(B) canceled
(C) misinterpreted
(D) confirmed

44. If you have a question, please raise your hand to **summon** the test proctor. **Summon** means most nearly
(A) ticket
(B) fine
(C) give
(D) call

45. We dared not prosecute the terrorist for fear of **reprisal. Reprisal** means most nearly
(A) retaliation
(B) advantage
(C) warning
(D) denial

46. The increased use of dictation machines has severely **reduced** the need for office stenographers. **Reduced** means most nearly
(A) enlarged
(B) cut out
(C) lessened
(D) expanded

47. Frequent use of marijuana may **impair** your judgment. **Impair** means most nearly
(A) weaken
(B) conceal
(C) improve
(D) expose

48. It is altogether **fitting** that the parent discipline the child. **Fitting** means most nearly
  (A) illegal
  (B) bad practice
  (C) appropriate
  (D) required

Directions: For questions 49 through 55, read each paragraph and answer the question that follows it by darkening the letter of the correct answer on your answer sheet. Answer each question in the answer space with the corresponding number.

49. A survey to determine the subjects that have helped students most in their jobs shows that typewriting leads all other subjects in the business group. It also leads among the subjects college students consider most valuable and would take again if they were to return to high school.

The paragraph best supports the statement that
  (A) the ability to type is an asset in business and in school
  (B) students who return to night school take typing
  (C) students with a knowledge of typing do superior work in college
  (D) success in business is assured those who can type

50. Telegrams should be clear, concise, and brief. Omit all unnecessary words. The parts of speech most often used in telegrams are nouns, verbs, adjectives, and adverbs. If possible, do pronouns, prepositions, articles, and copulative verbs. Use simple sentences, rather than complex and compound.

The paragraph best supports the statement that in writing telegrams one should always use
  (A) common and simple words
  (B) only nouns, verbs, adjectives, and adverbs
  (C) incomplete sentences
  (D) only words essential to the meaning

51. Since the government can spend only what it obtains from the people, and this amount is ultimately limited by their capacity and willingness to pay taxes, it is very important that people be given full information about the work of the government.

The paragraph best supports the statement that
  (A) governmental employees should be trained not only in their own work, but also in how to perform the duties of other employees in their agency
  (B) taxation by the government rests upon the consent of the people
  (C) the release of full information on the work of the government will increase the efficiency of governmental operations
  (D) the work of the government, in recent years, has been restricted because of reduced tax collections.

52. Both the high school and the college should take the responsibility for preparing the student to get a job. Since the ability to write a good application letter is one of the first steps toward this goal, every teacher should be willing to do what he can to help the student learn to write such letters.

    The paragraph best supports the statement that
    (A) inability to write a good letter often reduces one's job prospects
    (B) the major responsibility of the school is to obtain jobs for its students
    (C) success is largely a matter of the kind of work the student applies for first
    (D) every teacher should teach a course in the writing of application letters

53. Direct lighting is the least satisfactory lighting arrangement. The desk or ceiling light with a reflector that diffuses all the rays downward is sure to cause a glarc on the working surface.

    The paragraph best supports the statement that direct lighting is least satisfactory as a method of lighting chiefly because
    (A) the light is diffused causing eye strain
    (B) the shade on the individual desk lamp is not constructed along scientific lines
    (C) the working surface is usually obscured by the glare
    (D) direct lighting is injurious to the eyes

54. "White collar" is a term used to describe one of the largest groups of workers in American industry and trade. It distinguishes those who work with the pencil and the mind from those who depend on their hands and the machine. It suggests occupations in which physical exertion and handling of materials are not primary features of the job.

    The paragraph best supports the statement that "white collar" workers are
    (A) not so strong physically as those who work with their hands
    (B) those who supervise workers handling materials
    (C) all whose work is entirely indoors
    (D) not likely to use machines as much as are other groups of workers

55. In large organizations some standardized, simple, inexpensive method of giving employees information about company policies and rules, as well as specific instructions regarding their duties, is practically essential. This is the purpose of all office manuals of whatever type.

    The paragraph best supports the statement that office manuals
    (A) are all about the same
    (B) should be simple enough for the average employee to understand
    (C) are necessary to large organizations
    (D) act as constant reminders to the employee of his duties

END OF PART B

PART C—STENOGRAPHY

Sample Dictation

Have someone dictate the sample passage below to you. It should take 3 minutes. Take notes on your own paper.

Directions to person dictating: This practice dictation should be dictated at the rate of 80 words a minute. Do not dictate the punctuation except for periods, but dictate with the expression the punctuation indicates. Use a watch with a second hand to enable you to read the exercises at the proper speed.

Exactly on a minute start dictating.	Finish reading each two lines at the number of seconds indicated below.
I realize that this practice dictation is not a part of the examination	10
proper and is not to be scored. (Period) The work of preventing and correcting	20
physical defects in children is becoming more effective as a result of change	30
in the attitude of many parents. (Period) In order to bring about this change,	40
parents have been invited to visit the schools when their children are being examined	50
and to discuss the treatment necessary for the correction of defects. (Period)	1 min.
There is a distinct value in having a parent see that his or her child is not the	10
only one who needs attention. (Period) Otherwise a few parents might feel that they	20
were being criticized by having the defects of their children singled out for medical	30
treatment. (Period) The special classes that have been set up have shown the value of	40
the scientific knowledge that has been applied in the treatment of children. (Period)	50
In these classes the children have been taught to exercise by a trained teacher	2 min.
under medical supervision. (Period) The hours of the school day have been divided	10
between school work and physical activity that helps not only to correct their defects	20
but also to improve their general physical condition. (Period) This method of treatment	30

has been found to be very effective except
for those who have severe medical   40

defects. (Period) Most parents now see how
desirable it is to have these classes   50

that have been set up in the regular school
system to meet special needs. (Period)   3 min.

After dictating the practice, pause for 15 seconds to permit the competitor to complete notetaking. Then continue in accordance with the directions. After the sample dictation transcript has been completed, dictate the test on page 167.

Sample Dictation Transcript Sheet

The transcript below is part of the material that was dictated to you for practice, except that many of the words have been left out. From your notes, you are to tell what the missing words are. Proceed as follows:

Compare your notes with the transcript and, when you come to a blank in the transcript, decide what word (or words) belongs there. For example, you will find that the word "practice" belongs in blank number 1. Look at the word list to see whether you can find the same word there. Notice what letter (A, B, C, or D) is printed beside it, and write that letter in the blank. For example, the word "practice" is listed, followed by the letter B. We have already written B in blank number 1 to show you how you are to record your choice. Now decide what belongs in each of the other blanks. (You may also write the word or words, or the shorthand for them, if you wish.) The same word may belong in more than one blank. If the exact answer is not listed, write E in the blank.

ALPHABETIC WORD LIST
Write E if the answer is **not** listed.

about—B	paper—B
against—C	parents—B
attitude—A	part—C
being—D	physical—D
childhood—B	portion—D
children—A	practical—A
correcting—C	practice—B
doctors—B	preliminary—D
effective—D	preventing—B
efficient—A	procedure—A
examination—A	proper—C
examining—C	reason for—A
for—B	result—B
health—B	result of—C
mothers—C	schools—C
never—C	to be—C
not—D	to prevent—A

TRANSCRIPT

I realize that this _B_ dictation is__
              1   2

a __ of the __ __ and is __ __
 3   4 5   6 7

scored

    The work __ and __ __ defects
            8   9 10

in ___ is becoming more ___ as a ___
 11   12   13

a change in the ___ of many ___.
            14   15

ALPHABETIC WORD LIST

Write E if the answer is **not** listed.

all—A	reducing—A
at—C	satisfied—D
bring—A	say—C
collection—B	see—B
correction—C	soon—C
discuss—C	their—D
during—D	to discover—A
friend—A	to discuss—D
indicated—C	to endorse—C
insisted—D	to visit—B
is—B	treatments—A
is not—A	understand—D
know—A	undertake—B
knows—D	virtue—D
needed—B	visit—A
promote—B	volume—B
recognizing—D	young—C

TRANSCRIPT (continued)

In order to ___ ___ this change,
      16 17

parents have been invited ___ the
                18

schools when ___ children are being
         19

examined and ___ the ___ necessary for
         20   21

the ___ of defects. There is a distinct
    22

___ in having a parent ___ that his or her
  23   24

child ___ the only one who needs
      25

attention…. (The rest of the sample
dictation is not transcribed here.)

Answer Sheet for Sample Dictation

1. Ⓐ Ⓑ Ⓒ Ⓓ Ⓔ   8. Ⓐ Ⓑ Ⓒ Ⓓ Ⓔ   14. Ⓐ Ⓑ Ⓒ Ⓓ Ⓔ   20. Ⓐ Ⓑ Ⓒ Ⓓ Ⓔ
2. Ⓐ Ⓑ Ⓒ Ⓓ Ⓔ   9. Ⓐ Ⓑ Ⓒ Ⓓ Ⓔ   15. Ⓐ Ⓑ Ⓒ Ⓓ Ⓔ   21. Ⓐ Ⓑ Ⓒ Ⓓ Ⓔ
3. Ⓐ Ⓑ Ⓒ Ⓓ Ⓔ   10. Ⓐ Ⓑ Ⓒ Ⓓ Ⓔ   16. Ⓐ Ⓑ Ⓒ Ⓓ Ⓔ   22. Ⓐ Ⓑ Ⓒ Ⓓ Ⓔ
4. Ⓐ Ⓑ Ⓒ Ⓓ Ⓔ   11. Ⓐ Ⓑ Ⓒ Ⓓ Ⓔ   17. Ⓐ Ⓑ Ⓒ Ⓓ Ⓔ   23. Ⓐ Ⓑ Ⓒ Ⓓ Ⓔ
5. Ⓐ Ⓑ Ⓒ Ⓓ Ⓔ   12. Ⓐ Ⓑ Ⓒ Ⓓ Ⓔ   18. Ⓐ Ⓑ Ⓒ Ⓓ Ⓔ   24. Ⓐ Ⓑ Ⓒ Ⓓ Ⓔ
6. Ⓐ Ⓑ Ⓒ Ⓓ Ⓔ   13. Ⓐ Ⓑ Ⓒ Ⓓ Ⓔ   19. Ⓐ Ⓑ Ⓒ Ⓓ Ⓔ   25. Ⓐ Ⓑ Ⓒ Ⓓ Ⓔ
7. Ⓐ Ⓑ Ⓒ Ⓓ Ⓔ

The correct answers for the sample dictation are:

1.	B	8.	B	14.	A	20.	D
2.	D	9.	C	15.	B	21.	E
3.	C	10.	D	16.	A	22.	C
4.	A	11.	A	17.	E	23.	E
5.	C	12.	D	18.	B	24.	B
6.	D	13.	C	19.	D	25.	A
7.	C						

Compare your answers with the correct ones. If one of your answers does not agree with the correct answer, again compare your notes with the samples and make certain you understand the instructions.

Your notes should show that the word "bring" goes in blank 16, and "about" in blank 17. But "about" is *not in the list;* so E should be your answer for question 17.

The two words, "to visit—B," are needed for 18, and the one word "visit—A," would be an incorrect answer.

For the actual test you will use a separate answer sheet. As scoring will be done by an electronic machine, it is important that you follow directions carefully. Use the special pencil if one is furnished by the examiner. If no pencil is furnished, use only a number 2 pencil, as directed. Make a heavy mark for each answer. If you have to change your mark for any question, be sure to erase the first mark completely (do not merely cross it out) before making another.

Correctly Filled Transcripts for Sample Dictation

Check your notes against the dictation; check your notes against the alphabetic list of words and the transcript sheet; check the transcript against your answer grid. Identify your errors.

I realize that this <u>B</u> dictation is <u>D</u>
             1   2

a <u>C</u> of the <u>A</u> <u>C</u> and is <u>D</u> <u>C</u>
3   4 5   6 7

scored

      The work <u>B</u> and <u>C</u> <u>D</u> defects
             8   9 10

in <u>A</u> is becoming more <u>D</u> as a <u>C</u>
  11   12   13

a change in the <u>A</u> of many <u>B</u>.
             14   15

In order to <u>A</u> <u>E</u> this change,
          16 17

parents have been invited <u>B</u> the
                    18

schools when <u>D</u> children are being
          19

examined and <u>D</u> the <u>E</u> necessary for
          20   21

the <u>C</u> of defects. There is a distinct
    22

<u>E</u> in having a parent <u>B</u> that his or her
23   24

child <u>A</u> the only one who needs
     25

attention…. (The rest of the sample

dictation is not transcribed here.)

PART C

Dictation Time: 3 Minutes.

Exactly on a minute start dictating.

Finish reading each two lines at the number of seconds indicated below.

In recent years there has been a great increase in the need for capable stenographers,	10
not only in business offices but also in public service agencies, both	20
governmental and private. (Period) The high schools and business schools in many parts of	30
the country have tried to meet this need by offering complete commercial courses. (Period)	40
The increase in the number of persons who are enrolled in these courses shows that	50
students have become aware of the great demand for stenographers. (Period) A person	1 min.
who wishes to secure employment in this field must be able to take dictation	10
and to transcribe the notes with both speed and accuracy. (Period) The rate of	20
speed at which dictation is given in most offices is somewhat less than that of	30
ordinary speech. (Period) Thus, one who has had a thorough training in shorthand	40
should have little trouble in taking complete notes. (Period) Skill in taking dictation	50
at a rapid rate is of slight value if the stenographer cannot also type the notes	2 min.
in proper form. (Period) A manager sometimes dictates a rough draft of the ideas	10
he/she wishes to have included in a letter, and leaves to the stenographer the task	20
of putting them in good form. (Period) For this reason, knowledge of the essentials	30
of grammar and of composition is as important as the ability to take	40
dictation. (Period) In addition, a stenographer should be familiar with the sources of	50
general information that are most likely to be used in office work. (Period)	3 min.

Dictation Transcript

Time: 30 Minutes. 125 Questions.

ALPHABETIC WORD LIST
Write E if the answer is **not** listed.

also—A	offering—C
also in—C	officials—D
business—C	one—C
busy—D	only—B
capable—A	parts—A
commerce—C	private—C
commercial—D	public—D
county—B	recent—B
culpable—D	recurrent—A
decrease—A	school—C
governing—D	schools—B
governmental—C	servant—D
had been—B	stenographers—D
has been—D	stenos—A
many—A	their—D
most—D	there—B
need—C	tied—A
needy—D	to beat—C
offending—A	tried—B

TRANSCRIPT

In ___ years ___ ___ a great ___ in the
   1   2 3   4

___ for ___ ___, not ___ in ___ ___
 5   6   7   8   9 10

but ___ in ___ ___ agencies, both ___
     11   12 13   14

and ___. The high ___ and ___ schools
    15   16   17

in ___ ___ of the ___ have ___ ___
  18 19   20   21 22

this ___ by ___ complete ___ courses.
    23   24   25

Continue on the next page without waiting for a signal.

ALPHABETIC WORD LIST
Write E if the answer is **not** listed.

awake—C	in a—B
aware—B	in the—A
be able—A	increase—C
be able to—C	increment—A
became—B	notations—B
better—A	notes—C
both—D	number—C
courses—D	numbers—D
curses—C	people—A
demand—C	person—C
demean—A	seclude—C
dictation—B	secure—B
dictation notes—C	speech—C
employing—A	speed—B
employment—D	students—C
enrolled—B	studies—D
enroute—D	the—C
feel—A	this—A
felt—D	transcribe—C
grate—D	transcript—D
great—A	who desires—C

TRANSCRIPT (continued)

The ___ ___ ___ of ___ who are ___ in
   26 27 28   29   30

these ___ shows ___ ___ have ___ ___
     31   32 33   34 35

of the ___ ___ for stenographers. A ___
     36 37   38

___ to ___ ___ in ___ ___ must ___
 39   40 41   42 43   44

to take ___ and to ___ the ___ with ___
        45   46   47   48

___ and ___.
 49   50

Continue on the next page without waiting for a signal.

ALPHABETIC WORD LIST
Write E if the answer is **not** listed.

also—D	rampant—B
also can—B	rate—C
at a—A	ratio—D
at the—C	should—D
compete—B	should not—A
complete—D	sight—C
dictates—B	slight—B
dictation—D	somehow—D
firm—C	speech—A
form—D	speed—A
gained—A	stenographer—C
give—D	taking—C
has—C	that—D
have—B	thorough—C
less—B	through—B
less than—A	treble—D
many—A	trial—A
most—D	typed—D
note—C	typewriter—A
notes—B	valuate—A
offices—C	value—C
orderly—C	what—C
ordinary—D	which—B
proffer—C	who gets—A
proper—A	who had—C

TRANSCRIPT (continued)

The ___ of ___ at ___ dictation is ___
    51   52   53   54

in ___ ___ is ___ ___ than ___ of ___
   55 56   57 58   59   60

___. Thus, one ___ had a ___ ___ in
 61   62   63 64

shorthand ___ ___ little ___ in ___ ___
          65 66   67   68 69

___. Skill in ___ ___ ___ ___ ___ is
 70   71 72 73 74 75

of ___ ___ if the ___ cannot ___ ___
   76 77   78   79 80

the ___ in ___ ___.
   81   82 83

Continue on the next page without waiting for a signal.

ALPHABETIC WORD LIST

Write E if the answer is **not** listed.

ability—B	letter—D
adding—C	like—A
addition—A	likely—C
are—D	manager—A
as—A	management—B
composing—A	of the —D
composition—C	of these—A
dictates—B	office—A
essence—B	official—B
essentials—C	put in—D
form—A	putting—C
familial—C	reasoning—B
familiar—A	rough—A
general—C	roughly—D
generous—A	sauces—A
good—C	shall—D
grammatical—D	should—B
great—A	some times—A
had—A	somethings—D
have—B	source—D
ideals—C	stenographic—A
ideas—A	take—D
included—C	task—D
inclusive—A	this—A
information—D	to—A
important—B	to be—B
impotent—A	used—C
knowledge—B	useful—A
knowledgeable—C	wished—D
leaves—B	wishes—A
lets—C	with the—D

TRANSCRIPT (continued)

A ___ ___ ___ a ___ ___ ___ ___
  84 85 86   87 88 89 90

s/he ___ to ___ ___ in a ___, and ___
   91   92 93   94   95

to the ___ the ___ of ___ them in ____
    96   97   98   99

____. For ____ ____ ____ ____ ____ of ____
 100   101 102 103 104 105   106

and of ____ is ____ ____ ____ ____ to ____
     107   108 109 110 111   112

dictation. In ____ ____ stenographer ____
            113 114   115

be ____ ____ ____ of____ ____ that ____
   116 117 118   119 120   121

most ____ ____ ____ in ____ work.
    122 123 124   125

You will now have ten minutes to transfer your answers to the Part C answer sheet.

END OF EXAM

CORRECT ANSWERS FOR MODEL EXAMINATION 2

PART A—CLERICAL ABILITY

1.	E	12.	D	23.	C	34.	A	45.	D	56.	A	67.	A	78.	E
2.	D	13.	C	24.	B	35.	A	46.	B	57.	D	68.	D	79.	C
3.	A	14.	D	25.	D	36.	B	47.	E	58.	B	69.	B	80.	B
4.	D	15.	C	26.	E	37.	E	48.	A	59.	C	70.	B	81.	E
5.	A	16.	A	27.	A	38.	C	49.	C	60.	B	71.	E	82.	C
6.	C	17.	E	28.	B	39.	D	50.	A	61.	A	72.	B	83.	E
7.	B	18.	B	29.	C	40.	A	51.	A	62.	C	73.	A	84.	C
8.	D	19.	A	30.	D	41.	A	52.	C	63.	C	74.	B	85.	B
9.	E	20.	C	31.	D	42.	C	53.	C	64.	D	75.	E		
10.	C	21.	A	32.	E	43.	C	54.	A	65.	D	76.	C		
11.	C	22.	E	33.	A	44.	E	55.	D	66.	C	77.	E		

Explanations

1. **(E)** Ha<u>ch</u>ettson; Ha<u>ck</u>ett

2. **(D)** 59233<u>2</u>62; 59233<u>3</u>362

3. **(A)** <u>M</u>YP; <u>N</u>YP

4. **(D)** Olivi<u>a</u> H.; Olivi<u>er</u> E.; <u>R</u>. Olivia

5. **(A)** 00<u>10</u>; 00<u>12</u>

6. **(C)** 6<u>001</u>; 6<u>100</u>; 6<u>101</u>

7. **(B)** Va<u>n</u>over; Va<u>n</u>story; Van<u>S</u>winderen

8. **(D)** Fit<u>z</u>Gibbon; Fit<u>z</u>simmons; Fit<u>zS</u>imons

9. **(E)** 01<u>0</u>16060; 01<u>066</u>010

10. **(C)** A<u>AS</u>; A<u>AZ</u>; A<u>SA</u>

11. **(C)** Pa<u>we</u>lek; Pa<u>wlo</u>wicz; Pa<u>wlo</u>wski

12. **(D)** 7<u>710</u>; 7<u>834</u>; 7<u>868</u>

13. **(C)** 36270<u>000</u>; 36270<u>013</u>; 36270<u>030</u>

14. **(D)** Freed<u>en</u>berg; Freed<u>en</u>burg; Freed<u>in</u>berg

15. **(C)** Prout<u>ey</u>; Prouty, <u>Ma</u>rtha; Prouty, <u>My</u>ra

16. **(A)** 58006021; 58006130

17. **(E)** EKK-1403; EKK-1443

18. **(B)** Daly; D'Amato; D'Amboise

19. **(A)** Schaeffer; Schaffert

20. **(C)** PSP; SPP; SPS

21. **(A)** Drusilla S. Ridgeley   Drusilla S. Ridgeley   Drusilla S. Ridgeley

22. **(E)** Andrei I. Toumantzev   Andrei I. Tourmantzev   Andrei I. Toumantzov

23. **(C)** 6-78912-e3e42   6-78912-3e3e42   6-78912-e3e42

24. **(B)** 86529 Dunwoodie Drive   86529 Dunwoodie Drive   85629 Dunwoodie Drive

25. **(D)** 1592514   1592574   1592574

26. **(E)** Ella Burk Newham   Ella Burk Newnham   Elena Burk Newnham

27. **(A)** 5416R-1952TZ-op   5416R-1952TZ-op   5416R-1952TZ-op

28. **(B)** 60646 West Touhy Avenue   60646 West Touhy Avenue   60646 West Touhey Avenue

29. **(C)** Mardikian & Moore, Inc.   Mardikian and Moore, Inc.   Mardikian & Moore, Inc.

30. **(D)** 9670243   9670423   9670423

31. **(D)** Eduardo Ingles_   Eduardo Inglese   Eduardo Inglese

32. **(E)** Roger T. DeAngelis   Roger T. D'Angelis   Roger T. DeAngeles

33. **(A)** 7692138   7692138   7692138

34. **(A)** 2695 East 3435 South   2695 East 3435 South   2695 East 3435 South

35. **(A)** 63qs5-95YT3-001   63qs5-95YT3-001   63qs5-95YT3-001

36. **(B)** 2789350   2789350   2798350

37. **(E)** Helmut V. Lochner   Helmut V. Lockner   Helmut W. Lochner

38. **(C)** 2454803   2548403   2454803

39. **(D)** Lemberger, WA 28094-9182   Lemberger, VA 28094-9182   Lemberger, VA 28094-9182

40. **(A)** 4168-GNP-78852   4168-GNP-78852   4168-GNP-78852

41. **(A)** Yoshihito Saito   Yoshihito Saito   Yoshihito Saito

42. **(C)** 5927681   5927861   5927681

43. **(C)** O'Reilly Bay, LA 56212   O'Reillys Bay, LA 56212   O'Reilly Bay, LA 56212

44. **(E)** Francis Ransdell   Frances Ramsdell   Francis Ramsdell

45. **(D)** 5634-OotV5a-16867   5634-Ootv5a-16867   5634-Ootv5a-16867

46. **(B)** Dolores Mollicone   Dolores Mollicone   Doloras Mollicone

47. **(E)** David C. Routzon   David E. Routzon   David C. Routzron

48. **(A)** 8932 Shimabui Hwy.   8932 Shimabui Hwy.   8932 Shimabui Hwy.

49. **(C)** 6177396   6177936   6177396

50. **(A)** A8987-B73245   A8987-B73245   A8987-B73245

51. **(A)** anticipate

52. **(C)** similar

53. **(C)** sufficiently

54. **(A)** intelligence

55. **(D)** reference

56. **(A)** conscious

57. **(D)** parallel

58. **(B)** abundance

59. **(C)** corrugated

60. **(B)** accumulation

61. **(A)** resonance

62. **(C)** beneficial

63. **(C)** specifically

64. **(D)** eliminate

65. **(D)** colossal

66. **(C)** auxiliary

67. **(A)** inimitable

68. **(D)** disappearance

69. **(B)** appellate

70. **(B)** essential

71. **(E)**
$$\begin{array}{r} 83 \\ -56 \\ \hline 27 \end{array}$$

72. **(B)**
$$\begin{array}{r} 15 \\ +17 \\ \hline 32 \end{array}$$

73. **(A)**
$$\begin{array}{r} 32 \\ \times\ 7 \\ \hline 224 \end{array}$$

74. **(B)**
$$\begin{array}{r} 39 \\ \times\ 2 \\ \hline 78 \end{array}$$

75. **(E)**
$$\begin{array}{r} 43 \\ -15 \\ \hline 28 \end{array}$$

76. **(C)**
$$\begin{array}{r} 50 \\ +49 \\ \hline 99 \end{array}$$

77. **(E)**
$$6\sqrt{366} \overset{61}{} $$

78. **(E)**
$$\begin{array}{r} 38 \\ \times\ 3 \\ \hline 114 \end{array}$$

79. **(C)**
$$\begin{array}{r} 19 \\ +21 \\ \hline 40 \end{array}$$

80. **(B)** $\begin{array}{r} 13 \\ -6 \\ \hline 7 \end{array}$

81. **(E)** $6\sqrt{180}$ $= 30$

82. **(C)** $\begin{array}{r} 10 \\ \times\ 1 \\ \hline 10 \end{array}$

83. **(E)** $7\sqrt{287}$ $= 41$

84. **(C)** $\begin{array}{r} 12 \\ +11 \\ \hline 23 \end{array}$

85. **(B)** $\begin{array}{r} 85 \\ -64 \\ \hline 21 \end{array}$

PART B—VERBAL ABILITY

1.	D	12.	B	23.	D	34.	B	45.	A
2.	C	13.	D	24.	A	35.	B	46.	C
3.	E	14.	A	25.	D	36.	D	47.	A
4.	A	15.	D	26.	A	37.	C	48.	C
5.	C	16.	D	27.	C	38.	C	49.	A
6.	E	17.	E	28.	C	39.	D	50.	D
7.	D	18.	A	29.	B	40.	D	51.	B
8.	C	19.	D	30.	D	41.	B	52.	A
9.	E	20.	B	31.	D	42.	A	53.	C
10.	B	21.	C	32.	D	43.	B	54.	D
11.	A	22.	C	33.	A	44.	D	55.	C

Explanations

Questions 1–20. If you made any errors in the Following Written Instructions portion, go back and reread those questions more carefully.

21. **(C)** Sentence (C) is the best expression of the idea. Sentence (A) has two grammatical errors: the use of *when* to introduce a definition and the unacceptable verb form *is already having been parked.* Sentence (B) incorrectly shifts subjects from *one* to *you.* Sentence (D) does not make sense.

22. **(C)** Choice (B) is incorrect because only two persons are involved in this statement. *Between* is used when there are only two, *among* is reserved for three or more. (A) makes a similar error. In addition, both (A) and (D) use the pronoun *he.* The object of a preposition, in this case *between,* must be in the objective case, hence *him.*

23. **(D)** Punctuation aside, both (A) and (B) incorrectly place the verb in the plural, *are. Neither* is a singular indefinite pronoun. It means *not one and not the other* and requires a singular verb. The choice between (C) and (D) is more difficult, but basically this is a simple statement and not a direct quote.

24. **(A)** *Whoever* is the subject of the phrase *whoever has the best record.* Hence (A) is the correct answer and (D) is wrong. Both (B) and (C) are wordy and awkward.

25. **(D)** All the other choices contain obvious errors.

26. **(A)** Choice (B) uses the plural verb *were* with the singular subject *report.* (C) and (D) are colloquial and incorrect even for informal speech. They have no place in business writing.

27. **(C)** Choices (A) and (B) use adverbs incorrectly; choice (D) is awkward and unidiomatic.

28. **(C)** Choices (B) and (D) are obviously incorrect. In (A), the pronoun *who* should be the subject of the phrase, *who had made careless errors.*

29. **(B)** Only the quoted material should appear enclosed by quotation marks, so (A) is incorrect. Only the first word of a sentence should begin with a capital letter, so both (C) and (D) are wrong.

    In addition, only the quoted material itself is a question; the entire sentence is a statement. Therefore, the question mark must be placed inside the quotes.

30. **(D)** Choices (A) and (B) imply that he stays in church all day on Christmas and Easter and goes nowhere else. Choice (C) makes the same implication and in addition splits the infinitive awkwardly. In (D) the modifier *only* is correctly placed to tell us that the only times he goes to church are on Christmas and Easter.

31. **(D)** Choice (A) might state either *most* or *all* but not both; choice (B) should read *persons who;* choice (C) should read *with regard to*….

32. **(D)** Choice (A) is incorrect because *both* can refer to only two, but the publisher and authors implies at least three; choice (B) requires the plural verb *were*; choice (C) requires the correlative construction *neither…nor*.

33. **(A)** Choices (C) and (D) are glaringly poor. Choice (B) is not incorrect, but choice (A) is far better.

34. **(B)** Choice (A) incorrectly uses a semicolon to separate a complete clause from a sentence fragment. Additionally, (A) incorrectly uses *what* in place of *that*. Choice (C) is a run-on sentence that also misuses an apostrophe: *It's* is the contraction for *it is*, not the possessive of *it*. Choice (D) uses commas indiscriminately; it also misuses the apostrophe.

35. **(B)** In choice (A) the placement of the apostrophe is inappropriate; choices (C) and (D) use the plural, but there is only one company.

36. **(D)** Choices (A) and (C) are incorrect in use of the subject form *I* instead of the object of the preposition *me*. Choice (B) incorrectly uses the reflexive *myself*. Only I can address a letter to myself.

37. **(C)** Choice (A) incorrectly uses the plural verb form *have* with the singular subject *one*. (B) is awkward and wordy. (D) incorrectly changes the subject from *one of us* to *anyone*.

38. **(C)** (A) is wordy. In (B), the correct verb should be *have* in place of *leave*. In (D), the word *arose* should be *arisen*.

39. **(D)** The first three sentences lack parallel construction. All the words that modify *paper* must appear in the same form.

40. **(D)** The phrase, *together with*…, is extra information and not a part of the subject; therefore, both (A) and (B) represent similar errors of agreement. Choice (C) also presents disagreement in number between subject and verb, but in this case the compound subject, indicated by the use of the conjunction, *and,* requires a plural verb.

41. **(B)** Even if you do not recognize the root *manu* meaning *hand* and relating directly to *handbook,* you should have no trouble getting this question right. If you substitute each of the choices in the sentence, you will readily see that only one makes sense.

42. **(A)** Within the context of the sentence, the thought of a specified punishment for use, interpretation, or an edition of the rules does not make too much sense. *Fraction* gives a hint of *part,* but you must also contend with the negative prefix *in*. Since it is reasonable to expect punishment for negative behavior with relation to the rules, *violation,* which is the meaning of INFRACTION, is the proper answer.

43. **(B)** The prefix should help you narrow your choices. The prefix *re* meaning *back* or *again* narrows the choices to (A) or (B). To RESCIND is to *take back* or to *cancel.*

44. **(D)** First eliminate (C) since it does not make sense in the sentence. Your experience with the word *summons* may be with relation to *tickets* and *fines,* but tickets and fines have nothing to do with asking questions while taking a test. Even if you are unfamiliar with the word SUMMON, you should be able to choose *call* as the best synonym in this context.

45. **(A)** REPRISAL means injury done for injury received or *retaliation.*

46. **(C)** To REDUCE is to *make smaller* or to *lessen.*

47. **(A)** To IMPAIR is to *make worse,* to *injure,* or to *weaken.*

48. **(C)** FITTING in this context means *suitable* or *appropriate.*

49. **(A)** The survey showed that of all subjects typing has helped most in business. It was also considered valuable by college students in their schoolwork.

50. **(D)** See the second sentence.

51. **(B)** According to the paragraph, the government can spend only what it obtains from the people. The government obtains money from the people by taxation. If the people are unwilling to pay taxes, the government has no source of funds.

52. **(A)** Step one in the job application process is often the application letter. If the letter is not effective, the applicant will not move on to the next step and job prospects will be greatly lessened.

53. **(C)** The second sentence states that direct lighting causes glare on the working surface.

54. **(D)** While all the answer choices are likely to be true, the answer suggested by the paragraph is that "white collar" workers work with their pencils and their minds rather than with their hands and machines.

55. **(C)** All the paragraph says is that office manuals are a necessity in large organizations.

PART C—STENOGRAPHY

1.	B	26.	C	51.	C	76.	B	101.	A
2.	B	27.	A	52.	A	77.	C	102.	E
3.	D	28.	C	53.	B	78.	C	103.	B
4.	E	29.	E	54.	E	79.	D	104.	D
5.	C	30.	B	55.	D	80.	E	105.	C
6.	A	31.	D	56.	C	81.	B	106.	E
7.	D	32.	E	57.	E	82.	A	107.	C
8.	B	33.	C	58.	B	83.	D	108.	A
9.	C	34.	E	59.	D	84.	A	109.	B
10.	E	35.	B	60.	D	85.	E	110.	E
11.	A	36.	A	61.	A	86.	B	111.	B
12.	D	37.	C	62.	E	87.	A	112.	D
13.	E	38.	C	63.	C	88.	E	113.	A
14.	C	39.	E	64.	E	89.	D	114.	E
15.	C	40.	B	65.	D	90.	A	115.	B
16.	B	41.	D	66.	B	91.	A	116.	A
17.	C	42.	A	67.	E	92.	B	117.	D
18.	A	43.	E	68.	C	93.	C	118.	E
19.	A	44.	A	69.	D	94.	D	119.	C
20.	E	45.	B	70.	B	95.	B	120.	D
21.	E	46.	C	71.	C	96.	E	121.	D
22.	E	47.	C	72.	D	97.	D	122.	C
23.	C	48.	D	73.	A	98.	C	123.	B
24.	C	49.	B	74.	E	99.	C	124.	C
25.	D	50.	E	75.	C	100.	A	125.	A

Correctly Filled Transcript

In <u>B</u> years <u>B</u> <u>D</u> a great <u>E</u> in the
    1   2   3   4

<u>C</u> for <u>A</u> <u>D</u>, not <u>B</u> in <u>C</u> <u>E</u>
 5   6   7   8   9   10

but <u>A</u> in <u>D</u> <u>E</u> agencies, both <u>C</u>
    11   12 13   14

and <u>C</u>. The high <u>B</u> and <u>C</u> schools
   15   16   17

in <u>A</u> <u>A</u> of the <u>E</u> have <u>E</u> <u>E</u>
  18 19   20   21 22

this <u>C</u> by <u>C</u> complete <u>D</u> courses.
    23   24   25

The <u>C</u> <u>A</u> <u>C</u> of <u>E</u> who are <u>B</u> in
    26 27 28   29   30

these <u>D</u> shows <u>E</u> <u>C</u> have <u>E</u> <u>B</u>
    31   32 33   34 35

of the <u>A</u> <u>C</u> for stenographers. A <u>C</u>
      36 37   38

<u>E</u> to <u>B</u> <u>D</u> in <u>A</u> <u>E</u> must <u>A</u>
39   40 41   42 43   44

to take <u>B</u> and to <u>C</u> the <u>C</u> with <u>D</u>
     45   46   47   48

<u>B</u> and <u>E</u>.
49   50

The <u>C</u> of <u>A</u> at <u>B</u> dictation is <u>E</u>
    51   52   53   54

in <u>D</u> <u>C</u> is <u>E</u> <u>B</u> than <u>D</u> of <u>D</u>
  55 56   57 58   59   60

<u>A</u>. Thus, one <u>E</u> had a <u>C</u> <u>E</u> in
61   62   63 64

shorthand <u>D</u> <u>B</u> little <u>E</u> in <u>C</u> <u>D</u>
        65 66   67   68 69

<u>B</u>. Skill in <u>C</u> <u>D</u> <u>A</u> <u>E</u> <u>C</u> is
70   71 72 73 74 75

of <u>B</u> <u>C</u> if the <u>C</u> cannot <u>D</u> <u>E</u>
 76 77   78   79 80

the <u>B</u> in <u>A</u> <u>D</u>.
   81   82 83

A <u>A</u> E <u>B</u> a <u>A</u> E <u>D</u> <u>A</u>
84 85 86   87 88 89 90

s/he <u>A</u> to <u>B</u> <u>C</u> in a <u>D</u>, and <u>B</u>
  91   92 93   94   95

to the <u>E</u> the <u>D</u> of <u>C</u> them in <u>C</u>
   96   97   98   99

<u>A</u> . For <u>A</u> <u>E</u> <u>B</u> <u>D</u> <u>C</u> of <u>E</u>
100   101 102 103 104 105   106

and of <u>C</u> is <u>A</u> <u>B</u> <u>E</u> <u>B</u> to <u>D</u>
    107   108 109 110 111   112

dictation. In <u>A</u> <u>E</u> stenographer <u>B</u>
     113 114   115

be <u>A</u> <u>D</u> <u>E</u> of <u>C</u> <u>D</u> that <u>D</u>
116 117 118   119 120   121

most <u>C</u> <u>B</u> <u>C</u> in <u>A</u> work.
   122 123 124   125

Arco's *Practice for Clerical, Typing, and Stenographic Tests* offers techniques, strategies, and tips for taking dictation and answering stenography questions, along with lots of practice.

SCORE SHEET

Your score on Part A and Part B of the examination for Clerk-Typist, Clerk-Stenographer, and Data Conversion Operator is based only on the number of correct answers. Wrong answers have no effect on the score. Part A and Part B are timed and administered as two separate units, but they are not scored separately. There is no Clerical Ability score and no Verbal Ability score; there is only a single Exam 710 score.

To determine your raw score on this exam, count up all of your correct answers on the full exam.

Number Right equals Raw Score

_____ = _____

Since there is only a single Exam 710 score, your performance on any single question type does not matter. In order to earn a high score, however, you must do well on all parts of the exam. Enter your scores below to chart your performance on each question type. Then concentrate your efforts toward improvement in the areas with which you had the most difficulty.

Part A

Sequencing, Questions 1–20.   Number right _____ out of 20.

Comparisons, Questions 21–50.   Number right _____ out of 30.

Spelling, Questions 51–70.   Number right _____ out of 20.

Computations, Questions 71–85.   Number right _____ out of 15.

Part B

Following Written Instructions, Questions 1–20.   Number right _____ out of 20.

Grammar/Punctuation, Questions 21–40.   Number right _____ out of 20.

Vocabulary/Reading Comprehension, Questions 41–55.   Number right _____ out of 15.

Now use the self evaluation chart below to see where your total score falls on a scale from Poor to Excellent.

Self Evaluation Chart

	Excellent	Good	Average	Fair	Poor
Exam 710	125–140	109–124	91–108	61–90	0–60

Part C

Your score on Part C, the stenography test, is based on your number of correct answers minus one fourth of your wrong answers. To determine your score, divide the number of answers you got wrong by 4 and subtract that number from the number of answers you got right.

Number Right		minus	Number Wrong (÷4)		equals	Raw Score
_____	−		_____	=		_____

Evaluate your performance on the stenography test by darkening the space in which your raw score falls in the chart below.

Self Evaluation Chart

Part C	**Excellent**	**Good**	**Average**	**Fair**	**Poor**
Stenography	111–125	96–110	81–95	51–80	0–50

Answer Sheet

Exam 911

Cleaner
Custodian
Custodial Laborer

1 Ⓐ Ⓑ Ⓒ Ⓓ Ⓔ	23 Ⓐ Ⓑ Ⓒ Ⓓ Ⓔ	45 Ⓐ Ⓑ Ⓒ Ⓓ Ⓔ	67 Ⓐ Ⓑ Ⓒ Ⓓ Ⓔ
2 Ⓐ Ⓑ Ⓒ Ⓓ Ⓔ	24 Ⓐ Ⓑ Ⓒ Ⓓ Ⓔ	46 Ⓐ Ⓑ Ⓒ Ⓓ Ⓔ	68 Ⓐ Ⓑ Ⓒ Ⓓ Ⓔ
3 Ⓐ Ⓑ Ⓒ Ⓓ Ⓔ	25 Ⓐ Ⓑ Ⓒ Ⓓ Ⓔ	47 Ⓐ Ⓑ Ⓒ Ⓓ Ⓔ	69 Ⓐ Ⓑ Ⓒ Ⓓ Ⓔ
4 Ⓐ Ⓑ Ⓒ Ⓓ Ⓔ	26 Ⓐ Ⓑ Ⓒ Ⓓ Ⓔ	48 Ⓐ Ⓑ Ⓒ Ⓓ Ⓔ	70 Ⓐ Ⓑ Ⓒ Ⓓ Ⓔ
5 Ⓐ Ⓑ Ⓒ Ⓓ Ⓔ	27 Ⓐ Ⓑ Ⓒ Ⓓ Ⓔ	49 Ⓐ Ⓑ Ⓒ Ⓓ Ⓔ	71 Ⓐ Ⓑ Ⓒ Ⓓ Ⓔ
6 Ⓐ Ⓑ Ⓒ Ⓓ Ⓔ	28 Ⓐ Ⓑ Ⓒ Ⓓ Ⓔ	50 Ⓐ Ⓑ Ⓒ Ⓓ Ⓔ	72 Ⓐ Ⓑ Ⓒ Ⓓ Ⓔ
7 Ⓐ Ⓑ Ⓒ Ⓓ Ⓔ	29 Ⓐ Ⓑ Ⓒ Ⓓ Ⓔ	51 Ⓐ Ⓑ Ⓒ Ⓓ Ⓔ	73 Ⓐ Ⓑ Ⓒ Ⓓ Ⓔ
8 Ⓐ Ⓑ Ⓒ Ⓓ Ⓔ	30 Ⓐ Ⓑ Ⓒ Ⓓ Ⓔ	52 Ⓐ Ⓑ Ⓒ Ⓓ Ⓔ	74 Ⓐ Ⓑ Ⓒ Ⓓ Ⓔ
9 Ⓐ Ⓑ Ⓒ Ⓓ Ⓔ	31 Ⓐ Ⓑ Ⓒ Ⓓ Ⓔ	53 Ⓐ Ⓑ Ⓒ Ⓓ Ⓔ	75 Ⓐ Ⓑ Ⓒ Ⓓ Ⓔ
10 Ⓐ Ⓑ Ⓒ Ⓓ Ⓔ	32 Ⓐ Ⓑ Ⓒ Ⓓ Ⓔ	54 Ⓐ Ⓑ Ⓒ Ⓓ Ⓔ	76 Ⓐ Ⓑ Ⓒ Ⓓ Ⓔ
11 Ⓐ Ⓑ Ⓒ Ⓓ Ⓔ	33 Ⓐ Ⓑ Ⓒ Ⓓ Ⓔ	55 Ⓐ Ⓑ Ⓒ Ⓓ Ⓔ	77 Ⓐ Ⓑ Ⓒ Ⓓ Ⓔ
12 Ⓐ Ⓑ Ⓒ Ⓓ Ⓔ	34 Ⓐ Ⓑ Ⓒ Ⓓ Ⓔ	56 Ⓐ Ⓑ Ⓒ Ⓓ Ⓔ	78 Ⓐ Ⓑ Ⓒ Ⓓ Ⓔ
13 Ⓐ Ⓑ Ⓒ Ⓓ Ⓔ	35 Ⓐ Ⓑ Ⓒ Ⓓ Ⓔ	57 Ⓐ Ⓑ Ⓒ Ⓓ Ⓔ	79 Ⓐ Ⓑ Ⓒ Ⓓ Ⓔ
14 Ⓐ Ⓑ Ⓒ Ⓓ Ⓔ	36 Ⓐ Ⓑ Ⓒ Ⓓ Ⓔ	58 Ⓐ Ⓑ Ⓒ Ⓓ Ⓔ	80 Ⓐ Ⓑ Ⓒ Ⓓ Ⓔ
15 Ⓐ Ⓑ Ⓒ Ⓓ Ⓔ	37 Ⓐ Ⓑ Ⓒ Ⓓ Ⓔ	59 Ⓐ Ⓑ Ⓒ Ⓓ Ⓔ	81 Ⓐ Ⓑ Ⓒ Ⓓ Ⓔ
16 Ⓐ Ⓑ Ⓒ Ⓓ Ⓔ	38 Ⓐ Ⓑ Ⓒ Ⓓ Ⓔ	60 Ⓐ Ⓑ Ⓒ Ⓓ Ⓔ	82 Ⓐ Ⓑ Ⓒ Ⓓ Ⓔ
17 Ⓐ Ⓑ Ⓒ Ⓓ Ⓔ	39 Ⓐ Ⓑ Ⓒ Ⓓ Ⓔ	61 Ⓐ Ⓑ Ⓒ Ⓓ Ⓔ	83 Ⓐ Ⓑ Ⓒ Ⓓ Ⓔ
18 Ⓐ Ⓑ Ⓒ Ⓓ Ⓔ	40 Ⓐ Ⓑ Ⓒ Ⓓ Ⓔ	62 Ⓐ Ⓑ Ⓒ Ⓓ Ⓔ	84 Ⓐ Ⓑ Ⓒ Ⓓ Ⓔ
19 Ⓐ Ⓑ Ⓒ Ⓓ Ⓔ	41 Ⓐ Ⓑ Ⓒ Ⓓ Ⓔ	63 Ⓐ Ⓑ Ⓒ Ⓓ Ⓔ	85 Ⓐ Ⓑ Ⓒ Ⓓ Ⓔ
20 Ⓐ Ⓑ Ⓒ Ⓓ Ⓔ	42 Ⓐ Ⓑ Ⓒ Ⓓ Ⓔ	64 Ⓐ Ⓑ Ⓒ Ⓓ Ⓔ	86 Ⓐ Ⓑ Ⓒ Ⓓ Ⓔ
21 Ⓐ Ⓑ Ⓒ Ⓓ Ⓔ	43 Ⓐ Ⓑ Ⓒ Ⓓ Ⓔ	65 Ⓐ Ⓑ Ⓒ Ⓓ Ⓔ	87 Ⓐ Ⓑ Ⓒ Ⓓ Ⓔ
22 Ⓐ Ⓑ Ⓒ Ⓓ Ⓔ	44 Ⓐ Ⓑ Ⓒ Ⓓ Ⓔ	66 Ⓐ Ⓑ Ⓒ Ⓓ Ⓔ	88 Ⓐ Ⓑ Ⓒ Ⓓ Ⓔ

TEAR HERE

SCORE SHEET

The worksheet is *not* scored. Raw score is based only upon the number of answers correctly gridded.

Number correctly gridded = Raw Score

_____ = _____

The best possible score on this test is 28. If your score is lower than 24, you might find it helpful to purchase Arco's *Postal Clerk and Carrier*. There you will find useful instructions and lots of practice in answering Following Oral Instructions Questions.

FOLLOWING ORAL INSTRUCTIONS

Directions and Sample Instructions

Listening to Instructions: When you are ready to try these sample questions, give the following instructions to a friend and have the friend read them aloud to you at the rate of 80 words per minute. Do not read them to yourself. Your friend will need a watch with a second hand. Listen carefully and do exactly what your friend tells you to do with the worksheet and answer sheet. Your friend will tell you some things to do with each item on the worksheet. After each set of instructions, your friend will give you time to mark your answer by darkening a circle on the sample answer sheet. Since B and D sound very much alike, your friend will say "B as in baker" when he or she means B and "D as in dog" when he or she means D.

Before proceeding further, tear out the worksheet on page 189. Then hand this book to your friend.

To the Person Who Is to Read the Instructions: The instructions are to be read at the rate of 80 words per minute. Do not read aloud the material that is in parentheses. Do not repeat any directions.

Read Aloud to the Candidate

Look at line 1 on the worksheet. (Pause slightly.)Write a D as in dog beside the middle number on line 1. (Pause 2 seconds.) Now, on your answer sheet, find the number beside which you just wrote the letter D and darken the space for that number-letter combination. (Pause 5 seconds.)

Look at line 2 on your worksheet. (Pause slightly.) Draw a circle around the largest number on the line. (Pause 2 seconds.) Now, on your answer sheet, find the number that you just circled and darken space A for that number. (Pause 5 seconds.)

Look at line 3 on your worksheet. (Pause slightly.) Draw two lines under the first letter in the word on line 3. (Pause 2 seconds.) Now, on your answer sheet, find the number 11 and darken the space for the letter under which you just drew two lines. (Pause 5 seconds.)

Look at line 4 on your worksheet. (Pause slightly.) Write the number 7 in the largest circle in line 4. (Pause 2 seconds.) Now, on your answer sheet, darken the space for the number-letter combination in the circle in which you just wrote. (Pause 5 seconds.)

Sample Worksheet

Directions: Listening carefully to each set of instructions, mark each item on this worksheet as directed. Then complete each question by marking the sample answer sheet below as directed. For each answer you will darken the answer for a number-letter combination. Should you fall behind and miss an instruction, don't become excited. Let that one go and listen for the next one. If, when you start to darken a space for a number, you find that you have already darkened another space for that number, either erase the first mark and darken the space for the new combination or let the first mark stay and do not darken a space for the new combination. Write with a pencil that has a clean eraser. When you finish, you should have no more than one space darkened for each number.

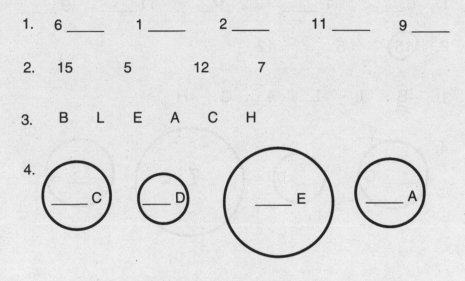

1. 6 _____   1 _____   2 _____   11 _____   9 _____

2. 15   5   12   7

3. B L E A C H

4. _____ C   _____ D   _____ E   _____ A

SAMPLE ANSWER SHEET

TEAR HERE

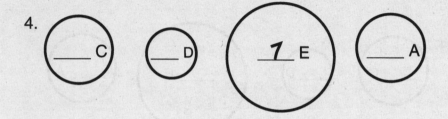

CORRECT ANSWERS TO SAMPLE QUESTIONS

Correctly Filled Worksheet

1. 6 ____   1 ____   2 _D_   11 ____   9 ____

2. (15)   5   12   7

3. B̲   L   E   A   C   H

4. ____ C   ____ D   _1_ E   ____ A

FOLLOWING ORAL INSTRUCTIONS

Time: 25 Minutes.

Listening to Instructions

Directions: When you are ready to try this test, give the following instructions to a friend and have the friend read them aloud to you at the rate of 80 words per minute. Do NOT read them to yourself. Your friend will need a watch with a second hand. Listen carefully and do exactly what your friend tells you to do with the worksheet and with the answer sheet. Your friend will tell you some things to do with each item on the worksheet. After each set of instructions, your friend will give you time to mark your answer by darkening a circle on the answer sheet. Since B and D sound very much alike, your friend will say "B as in baker" when he or she means B and "D as in dog" when he or she means D.

Before proceeding further, tear out the worksheet on page 195. Then hand this book to your friend.

To the Person Who Is to Read the Instructions: The instructions are to be read at the rate of 80 words per minute. Do not read aloud the material that is in parentheses. Once you have begun the test itself, do not repeat any instructions. The next three paragraphs consist of approximately 120 words. Read these three paragraphs aloud to the candidate in about one and one-half minutes. You may reread these three paragraphs as often as necessary to establish an 80-words-per-minute reading speed.

Read Aloud to the Candidate

On the job you will have to listen to directions and then do what you have been told to do. In this test, I will read instructions to you. Try to understand them as I read them; I cannot repeat them. Once we begin, you may not ask any questions until the end of the test.

On the job you won't have to deal with pictures, numbers, and letters like those in the test, but you will have to listen to instructions and follow them. We are using this test to see how well you can follow instructions.

You are to mark your test booklet according to the instructions that I'll read to you. After each set of instructions, I'll give you time to record your answers on the separate answer sheet.

The actual test begins now.

Look at line 1 on your worksheet. Each number represents a length of rope. (Pause slightly.) Draw two lines under the number that represents the longest length of rope. (Pause 2 seconds.) Now, on your answer sheet, find the number under which you just drew two lines and darken B as in baker for that number. (Pause 5 seconds.)

Look at line 1 again. (Pause slightly.) Find the number that represents the shortest length of rope and draw one wavy line above that number. (Pause 2 seconds.) Now, on your answer sheet, darken space A for the number over which you just drew the wavy line. (Pause 5 seconds.)

Look at line 2 on your worksheet. The number in each carton represents the number of boxes of soap powder in the carton. (Pause slightly.) Write the letter D as in dog in the carton that is closest to empty. (Pause 2 seconds.) Now, on your answer sheet, darken the space for the number-letter combination in the carton you just wrote in. (Pause 5 seconds.)

Look at line 3 on your worksheet. (Pause slightly.) If Christmas is always on a Thursday, write the letter C next to the first number on line 3; if not, write the letter E next to the second number. (Pause 5 seconds.) Now, on your answer sheet, darken the space for the number next to which you just wrote a letter. (Pause 5 seconds.)

Look at line 3 again. (Pause slightly.) Write the second letter of the alphabet next to the lowest number on line 3. (Pause 2 seconds.) Now, on your answer sheet, darken the space for the number-letter combination you just wrote. (Pause 5 seconds.)

Look at line 4 on your worksheet. (Pause slightly.) Count the number of letters in the word and write the number of letters at the end of line 4. (Pause 2 seconds.) Now, on your answer sheet, darken letter C for the number you just wrote. (Pause 5 seconds.)

Look at line 4 again. (Pause slightly.) Draw a circle around the fifth letter in the word. (Pause 2 seconds.) Now, on your answer sheet, find number 64 and darken the space for the letter you just circled. (Pause 5 seconds.)

Look at line 5 on your worksheet. The numbers represent days of the month. Floors are to be washed on odd-numbered days. (Pause slightly.) Draw one line under the number of each day on which floors should be washed. (Pause 5 seconds.) Now, on your answer sheet, darken letter D as in dog for each number under which you drew a line. (Pause 10 seconds.)

Look at line 6 on your worksheet. (Pause slightly.) Write the letter C on the line in the bucket with the highest number. (Pause 2 seconds.) Now, on your answer sheet, darken the space for the number-letter combination in that bucket. (Pause 5 seconds.)

Look at line 6 again. (Pause slightly.) Write the letter B as in baker on the line in the middle bucket. (Pause 2 seconds.) Now, on your answer sheet, darken the space for the number-letter combination in that bucket. (Pause 5 seconds.)

Look at line 7 on your worksheet. (Pause slightly.) Count the number of times the letter A appears on line 7 and write that number at the end of the line. (Pause 2 seconds.) Add 10 to the number you just wrote. Now, on your answer sheet, find the number that represents the sum of the number you wrote plus 10 and darken space E for that number. (Pause 10 seconds.)

Look at line 8 on your worksheet. Each item on line 8 represents a key code. Only keys with odd-numbered codes open the restroom doors in the post office. (Pause slightly.) Draw two lines under the code for each key that will open a restroom door. (Pause 5 seconds.) Now, on your answer sheet, darken each space that represents a key that will open a restroom. (Pause 15 seconds.)

Look at line 9 on your worksheet. Each box contains a different kind of screw. (Pause slightly.) The box with the higher number holds wood screws, and the box with the lower number holds sheet-metal screws. (Pause 2 seconds.) Write the letter A in the box that holds sheet-metal screws. (Pause 2 seconds.) Write the letter E in the box that holds wood screws. (Pause 2 seconds.) Now, on your answer sheet, darken the spaces for the number-letter combinations in the boxes. (Pause 10 seconds.)

Look at line 10 on your worksheet. (Pause slightly.) If brooms are used for sweeping floors, write B as in baker in the triangle. If not, write D as in dog in the square. (Pause 2 seconds.) Now, on your answer sheet, darken the space for the number-letter combination in the figure you just wrote in. (Pause 5 seconds.)

Look at line 10 again. (Pause slightly.) Write the letter C in every figure that has no angles. (Pause 5 seconds.) Now, on your answer sheet, darken the number-letter combination in each figure that you just wrote in. (Pause 10 seconds.)

Look at line 11 on your worksheet. (Pause slightly.) The third mailbox on line 11 has a broken lock and must be reported for repair. Write the letter D as in dog on the line in the broken mailbox. (Pause 2 seconds.) Now, on your answer sheet, darken the space for the number-letter combination in the mailbox with the broken lock. (Pause 5 seconds.)

Look at line 11 again. (Pause slightly.) The first mailbox belongs to Mr. and Mrs. Dana. Write the second letter of the Danas's name in their mailbox. (Pause 2 seconds.) Now, on your answer sheet, darken the space for the number-letter combination in the Danas's mailbox. (Pause 5 seconds.)

Look at line 12 on your worksheet. (Pause slightly.) Write the number of minutes in an hour next to the fourth letter of the alphabet. (Pause 2 seconds.) Now, on your answer sheet, darken the space for the number-letter combination you just wrote. (Pause 5 seconds.)

Look at the brooms on line 13 on your worksheet. (Pause slightly.) Write the first letter of the word "broom" on the line under the first broom. (Pause 2 seconds.) Now, on your answer sheet, darken the space for the number-letter combination under the broom. (Pause 5 seconds.)

Look at the brooms on line 13 again. (Pause slightly.) Write the letter E on the line under the broom that is different from the other brooms. (Pause 2 seconds.) Now, on your answer sheet, darken the space for the number-letter combination under the broom. (Pause 5 seconds.)

FOLLOWING ORAL INSTRUCTIONS

Worksheet

Directions: *Listening carefully to each set of instructions, mark each item on this worksheet as directed. Then complete each question by marking the answer sheet as directed. For each answer you will darken the space for a number-letter combination. Should you fall behind and miss an instruction, don't get excited. Let that one go and listen for the next one. If, when you start to darken a space for a number, you find that you have already darkened another space for that number, either erase the first mark and darken the space for the new combination or let the first mark stay and do not darken a space for the new combination. Write with a pencil that has a clean eraser. When you finish, you should have no more than one space darkened for each number. Correct answers are on pages 197–199.*

1.   3ft.   5yds.   10 in.   7 yds.

2.   ☐ 6__   ☐ 2__   ☐ 12__   ☐ 3__

3.   51___   77___   46___

4.   I N F L A M M A B L E __

5.   19   24   25   26   27   30

6.   55__   87__   42__   18__   63__

7.   G A D A G G A A D ___

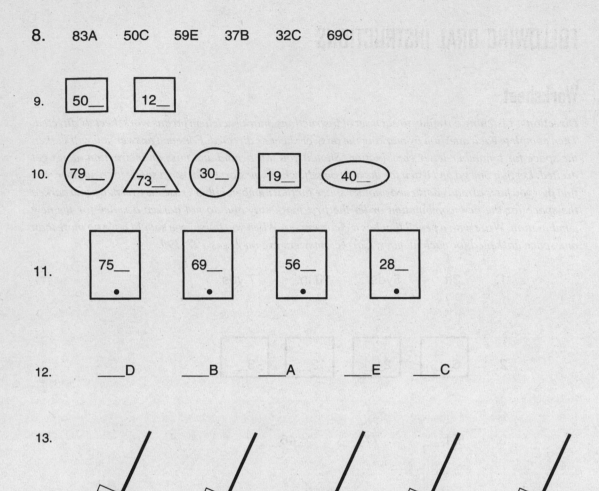

8.   83A   50C   59E   37B   32C   69C

9.   [50__]   [12__]

10.   (79__)   (73__)   (30__)   [19__]   (40__)

11.   [75__ •]   [69__ •]   [56__ •]   [28__ •]

12.   ___D   ___B   ___A   ___E   ___C

13.   53__   21__   33__   85__   46__

END OF EXAM

Correctly Filled Worksheet

1.   3ft.   5yds.   10 in.   <u>7 yds.</u>

2.   6__   2 _D_   12__   3__

3.   51___   77 _E_   46 _B_

4.   I N F L (A) M M A B L E   II

5.   <u>19</u>   24   <u>25</u>   26   <u>27</u>   30

6.   55__   87 _C_   42 _B_   18__   63__

7.   G A D A G G A A D   <u>4</u>

8. <u>83A</u>   50C   <u>59E</u>   <u>37B</u>   32C   <u>69C</u>

9. 50 *E*   22 *A*

10. 79 *C*   73 *B*   30 *C*   19 ___   40 *C*

11. 75 *A*   69 ___   56 *D*   28 ___

12. *60* D   ___ B   ___ A   ___ E   ___ C

13.
53 *B*   21 ___   33 *E*   85 ___   46 ___

Correctly Filled Answer Grid

#		#		#		#	
1	Ⓐ Ⓑ Ⓒ Ⓓ Ⓔ	23	Ⓐ Ⓑ Ⓒ Ⓓ Ⓔ	45	Ⓐ Ⓑ Ⓒ Ⓓ Ⓔ	67	Ⓐ Ⓑ Ⓒ Ⓓ Ⓔ
2	Ⓐ Ⓑ Ⓒ ● Ⓔ	24	Ⓐ Ⓑ Ⓒ Ⓓ Ⓔ	46	Ⓐ ● Ⓒ Ⓓ Ⓔ	68	Ⓐ Ⓑ Ⓒ Ⓓ Ⓔ
3	Ⓐ Ⓑ Ⓒ Ⓓ Ⓔ	25	Ⓐ Ⓑ Ⓒ ● Ⓔ	47	Ⓐ Ⓑ Ⓒ Ⓓ Ⓔ	69	Ⓐ Ⓑ ● Ⓓ Ⓔ
4	Ⓐ Ⓑ Ⓒ Ⓓ Ⓔ	26	Ⓐ Ⓑ Ⓒ Ⓓ Ⓔ	48	Ⓐ Ⓑ Ⓒ Ⓓ Ⓔ	70	Ⓐ Ⓑ Ⓒ Ⓓ Ⓔ
5	Ⓐ Ⓑ Ⓒ Ⓓ Ⓔ	27	Ⓐ Ⓑ Ⓒ ● Ⓔ	49	Ⓐ Ⓑ Ⓒ Ⓓ Ⓔ	71	Ⓐ Ⓑ Ⓒ Ⓓ Ⓔ
6	Ⓐ Ⓑ Ⓒ Ⓓ Ⓔ	28	Ⓐ Ⓑ Ⓒ Ⓓ Ⓔ	50	Ⓐ Ⓑ Ⓒ Ⓓ ●	72	Ⓐ Ⓑ Ⓒ Ⓓ Ⓔ
7	Ⓐ ● Ⓒ Ⓓ Ⓔ	29	Ⓐ Ⓑ Ⓒ Ⓓ Ⓔ	51	Ⓐ Ⓑ Ⓒ Ⓓ Ⓔ	73	Ⓐ ● Ⓒ Ⓓ Ⓔ
8	Ⓐ Ⓑ Ⓒ Ⓓ Ⓔ	30	Ⓐ Ⓑ ● Ⓓ Ⓔ	52	Ⓐ Ⓑ Ⓒ Ⓓ Ⓔ	74	Ⓐ Ⓑ Ⓒ Ⓓ Ⓔ
9	Ⓐ Ⓑ Ⓒ Ⓓ Ⓔ	31	Ⓐ Ⓑ Ⓒ Ⓓ Ⓔ	53	Ⓐ ● Ⓒ Ⓓ Ⓔ	75	● Ⓑ Ⓒ Ⓓ Ⓔ
10	● Ⓑ Ⓒ Ⓓ Ⓔ	32	Ⓐ Ⓑ Ⓒ Ⓓ Ⓔ	54	Ⓐ Ⓑ Ⓒ Ⓓ Ⓔ	76	Ⓐ Ⓑ Ⓒ Ⓓ Ⓔ
11	Ⓐ Ⓑ ● Ⓓ Ⓔ	33	Ⓐ Ⓑ Ⓒ Ⓓ ●	55	Ⓐ Ⓑ Ⓒ Ⓓ Ⓔ	77	Ⓐ Ⓑ Ⓒ Ⓓ ●
12	Ⓐ Ⓑ Ⓒ Ⓓ Ⓔ	34	Ⓐ Ⓑ Ⓒ Ⓓ Ⓔ	56	Ⓐ Ⓑ Ⓒ ● Ⓔ	78	Ⓐ Ⓑ Ⓒ Ⓓ Ⓔ
13	Ⓐ Ⓑ Ⓒ Ⓓ Ⓔ	35	Ⓐ Ⓑ Ⓒ Ⓓ Ⓔ	57	Ⓐ Ⓑ Ⓒ Ⓓ Ⓔ	79	Ⓐ Ⓑ ● Ⓓ Ⓔ
14	Ⓐ Ⓑ Ⓒ Ⓓ ●	36	Ⓐ Ⓑ Ⓒ Ⓓ Ⓔ	58	Ⓐ Ⓑ Ⓒ Ⓓ Ⓔ	80	Ⓐ Ⓑ Ⓒ Ⓓ Ⓔ
15	Ⓐ Ⓑ Ⓒ Ⓓ Ⓔ	37	Ⓐ ● Ⓒ Ⓓ Ⓔ	59	Ⓐ Ⓑ Ⓒ Ⓓ ●	81	Ⓐ Ⓑ Ⓒ Ⓓ Ⓔ
16	Ⓐ Ⓑ Ⓒ Ⓓ Ⓔ	38	Ⓐ Ⓑ Ⓒ ● Ⓔ	60	Ⓐ Ⓑ Ⓒ ● Ⓔ	82	Ⓐ Ⓑ Ⓒ Ⓓ Ⓔ
17	Ⓐ Ⓑ Ⓒ Ⓓ Ⓔ	39	Ⓐ Ⓑ Ⓒ Ⓓ Ⓔ	61	Ⓐ Ⓑ Ⓒ Ⓓ Ⓔ	83	● Ⓑ Ⓒ Ⓓ Ⓔ
18	Ⓐ Ⓑ Ⓒ Ⓓ Ⓔ	40	Ⓐ Ⓑ ● Ⓓ Ⓔ	62	Ⓐ Ⓑ Ⓒ Ⓓ Ⓔ	84	Ⓐ Ⓑ Ⓒ Ⓓ Ⓔ
19	Ⓐ Ⓑ Ⓒ Ⓓ Ⓔ	41	Ⓐ Ⓑ Ⓒ Ⓓ Ⓔ	63	Ⓐ Ⓑ Ⓒ Ⓓ Ⓔ	85	Ⓐ Ⓑ Ⓒ Ⓓ Ⓔ
20	Ⓐ Ⓑ Ⓒ Ⓓ Ⓔ	42	Ⓐ ● Ⓒ Ⓓ Ⓔ	64	● Ⓑ Ⓒ Ⓓ Ⓔ	86	Ⓐ Ⓑ Ⓒ Ⓓ Ⓔ
21	Ⓐ Ⓑ Ⓒ Ⓓ Ⓔ	43	Ⓐ Ⓑ Ⓒ Ⓓ Ⓔ	65	Ⓐ Ⓑ Ⓒ Ⓓ Ⓔ	87	Ⓐ Ⓑ ● Ⓓ Ⓔ
22	● Ⓑ Ⓒ Ⓓ Ⓔ	44	Ⓐ Ⓑ Ⓒ Ⓓ Ⓔ	66	Ⓐ Ⓑ Ⓒ Ⓓ Ⓔ	88	Ⓐ Ⓑ Ⓒ Ⓓ Ⓔ

Answer Sheet

Exam 91

Garageman-Driver

Tractor-Trailer Operator

Motor Vehicle Operator

The exam that follows is very much like the actual examination. Tear out the answer sheets and use them to record your answers to the examination questions. There are two parts to this exam. Each part has its own directions and time limits. Correct answers for all questions are on pages 225–228.

PART ONE

1. _____
2. _____
   _____
3. _____
   _____
4. _____
   _____
5. _____
   _____
6. _____
   _____
7. _____
   _____
8. _____
   _____
9. _____
10.

11. _____

12. _____

13. _____

14. _____
15. _____

16. _____

17. _____
18. _____
19. _____
20. _____
21. _____
22. _____

Chart A

	Truck License Number	Kind of Service	Odometer Reading When Serviced
	835 XYZ	tune up	22,305
23.			
24.			

Chart B

	Driver ID Number	Truck License Number	Odometer Reading
	8723	997 IUP	88,141
25.			
26.			

Chart C

	Driver ID Number	Odometer Reading When Taken Out	Odometer Reading When Returned
	3406	12,562	12,591
27.			
28.			

Chart D

	Vehicle License Number	Kind of Service	Serviceperson ID Number
	592 TJD	grease job	8452
29.			
30.			

TEAR HERE

Chart E

	Truck License Number	Driver ID Number	Serviceperson ID Number
	042 RVB	5842	4307
31.			
32.			

33. _____

34. _____

35. _____

36. _____

37. _____

38. _____

39. _____

40. _____

PART TWO

41. Ⓐ Ⓑ Ⓒ Ⓓ Ⓔ   49. Ⓐ Ⓑ Ⓒ Ⓓ Ⓔ   57. Ⓐ Ⓑ Ⓒ Ⓓ Ⓔ   65. Ⓐ Ⓑ Ⓒ Ⓓ Ⓔ   73. Ⓐ Ⓑ Ⓒ Ⓓ Ⓔ
42. Ⓐ Ⓑ Ⓒ Ⓓ Ⓔ   50. Ⓐ Ⓑ Ⓒ Ⓓ Ⓔ   58. Ⓐ Ⓑ Ⓒ Ⓓ Ⓔ   66. Ⓐ Ⓑ Ⓒ Ⓓ Ⓔ   74. Ⓐ Ⓑ Ⓒ Ⓓ Ⓔ
43. Ⓐ Ⓑ Ⓒ Ⓓ Ⓔ   51. Ⓐ Ⓑ Ⓒ Ⓓ Ⓔ   59. Ⓐ Ⓑ Ⓒ Ⓓ Ⓔ   67. Ⓐ Ⓑ Ⓒ Ⓓ Ⓔ   75. Ⓐ Ⓑ Ⓒ Ⓓ Ⓔ
44. Ⓐ Ⓑ Ⓒ Ⓓ Ⓔ   52. Ⓐ Ⓑ Ⓒ Ⓓ Ⓔ   60. Ⓐ Ⓑ Ⓒ Ⓓ Ⓔ   68. Ⓐ Ⓑ Ⓒ Ⓓ Ⓔ   76. Ⓐ Ⓑ Ⓒ Ⓓ Ⓔ
45. Ⓐ Ⓑ Ⓒ Ⓓ Ⓔ   53. Ⓐ Ⓑ Ⓒ Ⓓ Ⓔ   61. Ⓐ Ⓑ Ⓒ Ⓓ Ⓔ   69. Ⓐ Ⓑ Ⓒ Ⓓ Ⓔ   77. Ⓐ Ⓑ Ⓒ Ⓓ Ⓔ
46. Ⓐ Ⓑ Ⓒ Ⓓ Ⓔ   54. Ⓐ Ⓑ Ⓒ Ⓓ Ⓔ   62. Ⓐ Ⓑ Ⓒ Ⓓ Ⓔ   70. Ⓐ Ⓑ Ⓒ Ⓓ Ⓔ   78. Ⓐ Ⓑ Ⓒ Ⓓ Ⓔ
47. Ⓐ Ⓑ Ⓒ Ⓓ Ⓔ   55. Ⓐ Ⓑ Ⓒ Ⓓ Ⓔ   63. Ⓐ Ⓑ Ⓒ Ⓓ Ⓔ   71. Ⓐ Ⓑ Ⓒ Ⓓ Ⓔ   79. Ⓐ Ⓑ Ⓒ Ⓓ Ⓔ
48. Ⓐ Ⓑ Ⓒ Ⓓ Ⓔ   56. Ⓐ Ⓑ Ⓒ Ⓓ Ⓔ   64. Ⓐ Ⓑ Ⓒ Ⓓ Ⓔ   72. Ⓐ Ⓑ Ⓒ Ⓓ Ⓔ   80. Ⓐ Ⓑ Ⓒ Ⓓ Ⓔ

Score Yourself

How did you do? This exam is machine scored. Your official score will therefore be based on the number of questions you answered correctly in *Part Two only*. Because answering Part One questions correctly is so important to getting the correct answers in Part Two, however, it will be helpful to you to find your raw score for each section so you can identify and correct your problems.

Part One   40 Questions   Number Right _____
Part Two   40 Questions   Number Right _____

On a scale of Poor to Excellent, where does your score fall?

Self Evaluation Chart

	Excellent	Good	Average	Fair	Poor
Part One	36–40	32–35	28–31	24–27	0–23
Part Two	36–40	32–35	28–31	24–27	0–23

PART ONE

Time: 60 Minutes. 40 Questions.

Directions: *Read the questions carefully. Be sure you know what the questions are about and then answer each question in the way you are told. Write or diagram your answers on the separate answer sheet for Part One. Correct answers are on pages 225–227.*

Questions 1 and 2 are about Picture 1 below. Look at the picture.

Picture 1

1. How many vehicles are shown in the picture?
2. What is happening in this picture?

Question 3 is about Picture 2 below. Look at the picture.

Picture 2

3. What does the driver see in his rearview mirror? Be as complete as possible in your description. When you answer the questions in Part Two, you may not look back at the pictures.

Questions 4 and 5 are about Picture 3 below. Look at the picture.

Picture 3

4. Describe the man on the left. Take special note of his seat belt.
5. Describe the man on the right.

Question 6 is about Picture 4 below. Look at the picture.

Picture 4

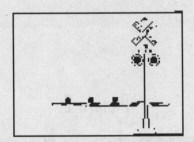

6. If you come upon the scene shown in Picture 4 as you are driving along the road, what must you do?

Question 7 is about Picture 5 below. Look at the picture.

Picture 5

7. What are the vehicles in the picture doing?

Question 8 is about Picture 6 below. Look at the picture.

Picture 6

8. How is the sign on the left related to the vehicle on the right? What does it mean?

Questions 9 and 10 are about Picture 7 below. Look at the picture.

Picture 7

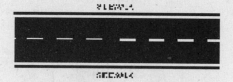

9. The roadway in Picture 7 is
    (A) a four-lane superhighway
    (B) a no-passing zone
    (C) a two-way street
    (D) a single-lane street
    (Write the letter of your answer on the answer sheet.)

10. On your answer sheet, draw arrows in the roadway indicating the direction of traffic flow.

Question 11 is about Picture 8 below. Look at the picture.

Picture 8

11. Write as complete a description as you can of the objects and activities in Picture 8.

Question 12 is about Picture 9 below. Look at the picture.

Picture 9

12. Describe the pattern of wear on this tire.

Question 13 is about Picture 10 below. Look at the picture.

Picture 10

13. The meaning of this sign is
   (A)   no parking
   (B)   no truck parking
   (C)   no trucks
   (D)   trucks only
   (Write the letter of your answer on the answer sheet.)

Question 14 is about Picture 11 below. Look at the picture.

Picture 11

14. What should you look for when you see this sign?

Questions 15 and 16 are about Picture 12 below. Look at the picture.

Picture 12

15. What is the boy doing?
16. What else is happening in this picture?

Question 17 is about Picture 13 below. Look at the picture.

Picture 13

17. The purpose of this sign is to caution you against
    (A) a winding road
    (B) drunk drivers
    (C) a road that may be slippery when wet
    (D) a steep hill
(Write the letter of your answer on the answer sheet.)

Question 18 is about the words on Picture 14 below. Look at the picture.

Picture 14

18. The words on this sign mean the same as
   (A)   Dead End, No Exit
   (B)   One Way Traffic
   (C)   No U Turn, Keep Out
   (D)   Special Parking Rules Today, Do Not Park Here
   (Write the letter of your answer on the answer sheet.)

Questions 19 and 20 are about Picture 15 below. Look at the picture.

Picture 15

19.   What is the vehicle in the picture?
20.   Who are the passengers?

Question 21 is about words that might appear on a traffic sign. Decide which line—A, B, C, or D—means most nearly the same as the first line, and write the letter of that line on the answer sheet.

21.   Bridge Freezes Before Roadway
   (A)   Bridge May Be Icy
   (B)   Detour—Bridge Under Repair
   (C)   Yield to Road Maintenance Crews
   (D)   Cold Weather Forecast for Tonight

Question 22 is about Picture 16 below. Look at the picture.

Picture 16

22. The words on this sign mean that
    (A) 500 people are working in the road
    (B) for the next 1000 feet, people will be working in the road
    (C) in 1000 feet, expect to find people working in the road
    (D) please help the people working in the road for the next 1000 feet
    (Write the letter of your answer on the answer sheet.)

Questions 23 and 24 have to do with filling in a chart. You are given the following information to put in Chart A.

Truck, license number 835 XZY, had a tune up at odometer reading 22,305.

Truck, license number 673 PUR, received a new fuel pump at odometer reading 67,422.

Truck, license number 441 RTG, had an oil change at odometer reading 46,098.

The information for the first truck has already been filled in. For question 23, write the information for the second truck in the proper columns in Chart A on the answer sheet. For question 24, write the information for the third truck in the proper columns in Chart A on the answer sheet.

Questions 25 and 26 have to do with filling in another chart. You are given the following information to put in Chart B.

Driver, ID number 8723, took truck license number 997 IUP at odometer reading 88,141.

Driver, ID number 6309, took truck license number 534 TRE at odometer reading 35,790.

Driver, ID number 7342, took truck license number 256 TAE at odometer reading 56,798.

The information for the first driver has already been filled in. For question 25, write the information for the second driver in the proper columns in Chart B on the answer sheet. For question 26, write the information for the third driver in the proper columns in Chart B on the answer sheet.

Questions 27 and 28 have to do with filling in another chart. You are given the following information to put in Chart C.

Driver, ID number 3406, took his jeep at odometer reading 12,562 and returned it at odometer reading 12,591.

Driver, ID number 9845, took his jeep at odometer reading 54,970 and returned it at odometer reading 54,997.

Driver, ID number 4785, took her jeep at odometer reading 43,054 and returned it at odometer reading 43,086.

The information for the first driver has already been filled in. For question 27, write the information for the second driver in the proper columns in Chart C on the answer sheet. For question 28, write the information for the third driver in the proper columns in Chart C on the answer sheet.

Questions 29 and 30 have to do with filling in another chart. You are given the following information to put in Chart D.

Vehicle license number 592 TJD had a grease job by mechanic ID number 8452.

Vehicle license number 447 IKT had its carburetor adjusted by serviceperson ID number 7092.

Vehicle license number 837 PRE had a tire changed by serviceperson ID number 6052.

The information for the first vehicle has already been filled in. For question 29, write the information for the second vehicle in the proper columns in Chart D on the answer sheet. For question 30, write the information for the third vehicle in the proper columns in Chart D on the answer sheet.

Questions 31 and 32 have to do with filling in one more chart. You are given the following information to put in Chart E.

Truck license number 042 RVB is to be driven into the yard by driver ID number 5842 and turned over to serviceperson ID number 4307 for service.

Truck license number 759 YUX is to be driven into the yard by driver ID number 8372 and turned over to serviceperson ID number 3987 for service.

Truck license number 943 WCG is to be driven into the yard by driver ID number 6241 and turned over to serviceperson ID number 4273 for service.

The information for the first truck has already been filled in. For question 31, write the information for the second truck in the proper columns in Chart E on the answer sheet. For question 32, write the information for the third truck in the proper columns in Chart E on the answer sheet.

Questions 33 and 34 are about pictures of lane-control lights. Each picture has a letter. You are to tell what each picture shows by writing a short description of the picture on the answer sheet.

X

Y

33. What does Picture X show?
34. What does Picture Y show?

Question 35 is about Picture 17 below. Look at the picture.

Picture 17

35. Describe this picture in the space on the answer sheet.

Question 36 is about the word on Picture 18 below. Look at the picture.

Picture 18

36. The word on this sign means that the driver should
   (A) stop
   (B) turn around
   (C) let merging traffic enter the roadway
   (D) look carefully before proceeding
   (Write the letter of your answer on the answer sheet.)

Question 37 is about Picture 19 below. Look at the picture.

Picture 19

37. The meaning of this sign is
 (A) Right Turn Only
 (B) No Right Turn
 (C) No Left Turn
 (D) Left Turn Only
 (Write the letter of your answer on the answer sheet.)

Question 38 is about Picture 20 below. Look at the picture.

Picture 20

38. Describe what is happening in this picture.

Question 39 is about Picture 21 below. Look at the picture.

Picture 21

39. What is happening in this picture? Write your description in the space on the answer sheet.

Question 40 is about the sign in Picture 22 below. Look at the picture.

Picture 22

40. The driver who approaches this sign must
(A) stop
(B) slow down and look both ways
(C) turn around
(D) back up
(Write the letter of your answer on the answer sheet.)

PART TWO

Time: 60 Minutes. 40 Questions.

Directions: To answer the questions in Part Two, you must use the information that you wrote in answer to the questions in Part One. Refer to your answer sheet for Part One to answer these questions. Mark the answers to questions 41 to 80 on the Part Two answer sheet by blackening the letter of your answer. You may not look back at the pictures while answering the questions in Part Two. The correct answers are on page 228.

Question 41 below is about question 1, and question 42 below is about question 2.

41. For number 41 on the answer sheet, mark space
    (A) if there are no vehicles in the picture
    (B) if there is one vehicle in the picture
    (C) if there are two vehicles in the picture
    (D) if there are three vehicles in the picture
    (E) if there are four vehicles in the picture

42. For number 42 on the answer sheet, mark space
    (A) if there is about to be a crash
    (B) if a vehicle just went through a stop sign
    (C) if a car is driving on the wrong side of the street
    (D) if there are no vehicles in the intersection
    (E) if one car has stopped at a stop sign

Question 43 is about question 3.

43. For number 43 on the answer sheet, mark space
    (A) if a motorcycle is passing a car
    (B) if a motorcycle is directly behind a car
    (C) if a truck is behind a car
    (D) if two motorcycles are in the left lane
    (E) if there is nothing in the rearview mirror

Question 44 below is about question 4, and question 45 below is about question 5.

44. For number 44 on the answer sheet, mark space
    (A) if the man is likely to suffer internal injuries in case of a crash
    (B) if the man is wearing his seat belt properly
    (C) if the man is well protected in case of auto crash
    (D) if the man is wearing his seat belt across his right shoulder
    (E) if the man is likely to be thrown from the car in an accident

45. For number 45 on the answer sheet, mark space
    (A) if the man's shoulder strap goes under his tie
    (B) if the man's lap strap is unfastened
    (C) if the man is likely to be thrown through the windshield in a crash
    (D) if the man is wearing his seat belt and shoulder harness properly
    (E) if the man is wearing a jacket

Question 46 below is about question 6.

46. For number 46 on the answer sheet, mark space
    (A) if you should blow your horn
    (B) if you should get out of your car and move the barrier
    (C) if you should come to a full stop and wait
    (D) if you should accelerate and continue
    (E) if you should stop, look, and proceed

Question 47 below is about question 7.

47. For number 47 on the answer sheet, mark space
    (A) if a car is about to hit a pedestrian
    (B) if a person is jaywalking
    (C) if a police officer is directing traffic
    (D) if a cyclist is going the wrong way on a one-way street
    (E) if a woman and child are crossing in the crosswalk

Question 48 below is about question 8.

48. For number 48 on the answer sheet, mark space
    (A) if the sign should be blue and orange
    (B) if the sign signifies that this is a slow-moving vehicle
    (C) if the sign means "pass when safe"
    (D) if the sign should be worn on the driver's back
    (E) if the sign means that you should yield the right of way to the vehicle to which it is attached

For number 49 on the answer sheet, mark the space that has the same letter as the letter you wrote on the answer line for question 9.

Question 50 below is about question 10.

50. For number 50 on the answer sheet, mark space
    (A) if the arrow in one lane points in one direction and the arrow in the other lane points in the opposite direction
    (B) if the arrows in both lanes point to the right
    (C) if the arrows in both lanes point to the left
    (D) if there are arrows pointing in both directions in both lanes
    (E) if there is an arrow in only one lane

Question 51 below is about question 11.

51. For number 51 on the answer sheet, mark space
  (A) if it is raining
  (B) if there is one balloon on the ground
  (C) if there are four balloons
  (D) if there is heavy road traffic
  (E) if it would be wise for the motorist to pull over to the side of the road to watch the show

Question 52 below is about question 12.

52. For number 52 on the answer sheet, mark space
  (A) if the wear on the tire indicates the effect of overinflation
  (B) if the wear on the tire indicates the effect of excessive caster
  (C) if the wear on the tire indicates the effect of improper balance
  (D) if the wear on the tire indicates the effect of underinflation
  (E) if the wear on the tire indicates the effect of toe-out

For number 53 on the answer sheet, mark the space that has the same letter as the letter you wrote on the answer line for question 13.

Question 54 below is about question 14.

54. For number 54 on the answer sheet, mark space
  (A) if you should look for hitchhikers
  (B) if you should look for schoolchildren
  (C) if you should look for a garage sale
  (D) if you should watch out for a flagman
  (E) if you should watch for deaf pedestrians

Question 55 below is about question 15, and question 56 below is about question 16.

55. For number 55 on the answer sheet, mark space
  (A) if a little boy is running across the street
  (B) if a little boy is sleeping
  (C) if a little boy is helping an old lady cross the street
  (D) if a little boy is lying in the street
  (E) if a little boy is getting out of the car

56. For number 56 on the answer sheet, mark space
  (A) if an ambulance has just pulled up
  (B) if a man is getting out of the car
  (C) if there has been a hit-and-run accident
  (D) if a crowd is gathering around the little boy
  (E) if a woman is crying

For number 57 on the answer sheet, mark the space that has the same letter as the letter you wrote on the answer line for question 17.

For Number 58 on the answer sheet, mark the space that has the same letter as the letter you wrote on the answer line for question 18.

Question 59 below is about question 19, and question 60 below is about question 20.

59. For number 59 on the answer sheet, mark space
    (A) if the vehicle is a taxicab
    (B) if the vehicle is a bus
    (C) if the vehicle is a tractor-trailer
    (D) if the vehicle is a farm tractor
    (E) if the vehicle is a jeep

60. For number 60 on the answer sheet, mark space
    (A) if the passengers are schoolchildren
    (B) if the passengers are campers
    (C) if the passengers are farmers
    (D) if the passengers are military personnel
    (E) if the passengers are senior citizens

For number 61 on the answer sheet, mark the space that has the same letter as the letter you wrote on the answer line for question 21.

For number 62 on the answer sheet, mark the space that has the same letter as the letter you wrote on the answer line for question 22.

Questions 63 and 64 below are about Chart A, which you filled in. Mark on the answer sheet the letter of the answer.

63. What is the license number of the truck that received a new fuel pump? Look at what you wrote on the chart. Do not try to answer from memory.
    (A) 673 PUR
    (B) 835 XZY
    (C) 441 RTG
    (D) 637 RUP

64. At what odometer reading did truck 441 RTG have its oil changed?
    (A) 46,908
    (B) 64,809
    (C) 46,098
    (D) 46,089

Questions 65 and 66 below are about Chart B, which you filled in. Look at what you wrote on the chart and mark the answer sheet with the letter of the correct answer.

65. What was the ID number of the driver who took truck license number 534 TRE?
    (A) 6390
    (B) 6309
    (C) 7342
    (D) 7243

66. At what odometer reading did driver number 7342 take out his truck?
    (A) 56,798
    (B) 88,141
    (C) 35,790
    (D) 65,798

Questions 67 and 68 below are about Chart C, which you filled in. Look at what you wrote on the chart and mark the answer sheet with the letter of the correct answer.

67. What was the odometer reading when driver number 9845 returned her jeep?
    (A) 54,997
    (B) 54,970
    (C) 15,591
    (D) 43,086

68. What was the odometer reading when driver number 4785 took out his jeep?
    (A) 12,562
    (B) 43,086
    (C) 54,970
    (D) 43,054

Questions 69 and 70 below are about Chart D, which you filled in. Look at what you wrote on the chart and mark the answer sheet with the letter of the correct answer.

69. What service was performed on vehicle license number 447 IKT?
    (A) lubrication
    (B) replacement of air hose
    (C) carburetor adjustment
    (D) tire change

70. What was the ID number of the serviceperson who changed a tire?
    (A) 837 PRE
    (B) 6052
    (C) 6025
    (D) 7092

Questions 71 and 72 below are about Chart E, which you filled in. Look at what you wrote on the chart and mark the answer sheet with the letter of the correct answer.

71. What was the ID number of the serviceperson to whom driver ID number 8372 turned over her truck?
  (A) 3978
  (B) 3987
  (C) 3897
  (D) 3879

72. What was the ID number of the driver who turned over her truck to serviceperson ID 4273?
  (A) 943 WCG
  (B) 5842
  (C) 959 YUX
  (D) 6241

Question 73 below is about question 33 under Picture X, and question 74 below is about question 34 under Picture Y.

73. For number 73 on the answer sheet, mark space
  (A) if there are no lanes open in Picture X
  (B) if there is only one lane open in Picture X
  (C) if there are only two lanes open in Picture X
  (D) if there are only three lanes open in Picture X
  (E) if there is only one lane closed in Picture X

74. For number 74 on the answer sheet, mark space
  (A) if there is only one lane closed in Picture Y
  (B) if there are only two lanes closed in Picture Y
  (C) if there are only three lanes closed in Picture Y
  (D) if there are only four lanes closed in Picture Y
  (E) if there are only five lanes closed in Picture Y

Question 75 below is about question 35.

75. For number 75 on the answer sheet, mark space
  (A) if drivers approaching from the right cannot see any traffic signals
  (B) if drivers approaching this light straight ahead have a green arrow pointing to the right
  (C) if drivers approaching from the left are guided by five different traffic signals
  (D) if drivers approaching this light straight ahead have a red arrow pointing to the left
  (E) if drivers approaching this light straight ahead have a green arrow pointing to the left

For number 76 on the answer sheet, mark the space that has the same letter as the letter you wrote on the answer line for question 36.

For number 77 on the answer sheet, mark the space that has the same letter as the letter you wrote on the answer line for question 37.

Question 78 below is about question 38.

78. For number 78 on the answer sheet, mark space
    (A) if a person is being pushed in a wheelchair
    (B) if there has been a traffic accident
    (C) if two men are putting a person into an ambulance
    (D) if a police officer is directing traffic
    (E) if a woman is wringing her hands in despair

Question 79 below is about question 39.

79. For number 79 on the answer sheet, mark space
    (A) if there is a mail truck in the picture
    (B) if a car is about to enter an intersection
    (C) if three people are walking abreast
    (D) if children are playing in the street
    (E) if a young man is walking with an elderly woman

For number 80 on the answer sheet, mark the space that has the same letter as the letter you wrote on the answer line for question 40.

END OF EXAM

CORRECT ANSWERS FOR MODEL EXAMINATION IV

PART ONE

1. Two

2. The car on the left has stopped at the stop sign; the car on the right is passing through the intersection.

3. In the rearview mirror, the driver sees that there is a motorcycle directly behind the car.

4. The man on the left is wearing his seat belt incorrectly. The shoulder strap is under his arm instead of across his shoulder.

5. The man on the right is wearing his seat belt correctly.

6. Stop and wait for the train to pass and the barrier to be lifted.

7. The vehicles have stopped for pedestrians in the crosswalk.

8. The sign on the left should be mounted on the tractor. The sign is a warning to other vehicles on the road that the vehicle upon which it is mounted is a slow-moving vehicle.

9. **(C)**

10.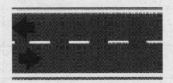

11. There is one car on the road. There are three hot air balloons in the sky. The sun is peeking from behind some clouds.

12. The tire is worn right down the middle.

13. **(C)**

14. Look for a flagman.

15. The young boy is lying in the roadway.

16. A man is getting out of a car.

17. **(C)**

18. **(B)**

19. The vehicle is a bus.

20. The passengers are a group of well-dressed elderly men and women, some with suitcases.

21. **(A)**

22. **(C)**

Chart A

	Truck License Number	Kind of Service	Odometer Reading When Serviced
	835 XYZ	tune up	22,305
23.	673 PUR	new fuel pump	67,422
24.	441 RTG	oil change	46,098

Chart B

	Driver ID Number	Truck License Number	Odometer Reading
	8723	997 IUP	88,141
25.	6309	534 TRE	35,790
26.	7342	256 TAE	56,798

Chart C

	Driver ID Number	Odometer Reading When Taken Out	Odometer Reading When Returned
	3406	12,562	12,591
27.	9845	54,970	54,997
28.	4785	43,054	43,086

Chart D

Vehicle License Number	Kind of Service	Serviceperson ID Number
592 TJD	grease job	8452
447 IKT	carburetor adjustment	7092
837 PRE	tire change	6052

(29. is to the left of the 447 IKT row; 30. is to the left of the 837 PRE row.)

Chart E

Truck License Number	Driver ID Number	Serviceperson ID Number
042 RVB	5842	4307
759 YUX	8372	3987
943 WCG	6241	4273

(31. is to the left of the 759 YUX row; 32. is to the left of the 943 WCG row.)

33. Picture X shows the left lane is open to traffic (shown by arrow) and the two lanes to the right are closed to traffic (shown by Xs).

34. Picture Y shows six traffic lanes. Starting from the left, lanes 1 and 2 are open to traffic, lanes 3 and 4 are closed to traffic, lane 5 is open, and lane 6 is closed.

35. There is a signal light at a three- or four-way intersection. Cars coming straight at the signal light can have a red, yellow, or green light, or a green arrow pointing left. Cars coming from left and right probably have only a red, yellow, or green light.

36. **(C)**

37. **(B)**

38. Two men are putting a person on a stretcher into an ambulance.

39. A young man and an older woman are walking together.

40. **(A)**

PART TWO

41.	C	55.	D	69.	C
42.	E	56.	B	70.	B
43.	B	57.	C	71.	B
44.	A	58.	B	72.	D
45.	D	59.	B	73.	B
46.	C	60.	E	74.	C
47.	E	61.	A	75.	E
48.	B	62.	C	76.	C
49.	C	63.	A	77.	B
50.	A	64.	C	78.	C
51.	E	65.	B	79.	E
52.	A	66.	A	80.	A
53.	C	67.	A		
54.	D	68.	D		

Answer Sheet

Exam 630

Postal Police Officer

The exam that follows is very much like the actual postal police officer examination. Tear out the answer sheet and use it to record your answers to the examination questions. Listen carefully and follow the additional instructions as given by the examiner. Correct answers for Book A questions are on pages 251–264.

BOOK A

Part A—Name and Number Comparisons

1. Ⓐ Ⓑ Ⓒ Ⓓ Ⓔ 11. Ⓐ Ⓑ Ⓒ Ⓓ Ⓔ 21. Ⓐ Ⓑ Ⓒ Ⓓ Ⓔ 31. Ⓐ Ⓑ Ⓒ Ⓓ Ⓔ 41. Ⓐ Ⓑ Ⓒ Ⓓ Ⓔ
2. Ⓐ Ⓑ Ⓒ Ⓓ Ⓔ 12. Ⓐ Ⓑ Ⓒ Ⓓ Ⓔ 22. Ⓐ Ⓑ Ⓒ Ⓓ Ⓔ 32. Ⓐ Ⓑ Ⓒ Ⓓ Ⓔ 42. Ⓐ Ⓑ Ⓒ Ⓓ Ⓔ
3. Ⓐ Ⓑ Ⓒ Ⓓ Ⓔ 13. Ⓐ Ⓑ Ⓒ Ⓓ Ⓔ 23. Ⓐ Ⓑ Ⓒ Ⓓ Ⓔ 33. Ⓐ Ⓑ Ⓒ Ⓓ Ⓔ 43. Ⓐ Ⓑ Ⓒ Ⓓ Ⓔ
4. Ⓐ Ⓑ Ⓒ Ⓓ Ⓔ 14. Ⓐ Ⓑ Ⓒ Ⓓ Ⓔ 24. Ⓐ Ⓑ Ⓒ Ⓓ Ⓔ 34. Ⓐ Ⓑ Ⓒ Ⓓ Ⓔ 44. Ⓐ Ⓑ Ⓒ Ⓓ Ⓔ
5. Ⓐ Ⓑ Ⓒ Ⓓ Ⓔ 15. Ⓐ Ⓑ Ⓒ Ⓓ Ⓔ 25. Ⓐ Ⓑ Ⓒ Ⓓ Ⓔ 35. Ⓐ Ⓑ Ⓒ Ⓓ Ⓔ 45. Ⓐ Ⓑ Ⓒ Ⓓ Ⓔ
6. Ⓐ Ⓑ Ⓒ Ⓓ Ⓔ 16. Ⓐ Ⓑ Ⓒ Ⓓ Ⓔ 26. Ⓐ Ⓑ Ⓒ Ⓓ Ⓔ 36. Ⓐ Ⓑ Ⓒ Ⓓ Ⓔ 46. Ⓐ Ⓑ Ⓒ Ⓓ Ⓔ
7. Ⓐ Ⓑ Ⓒ Ⓓ Ⓔ 17. Ⓐ Ⓑ Ⓒ Ⓓ Ⓔ 27. Ⓐ Ⓑ Ⓒ Ⓓ Ⓔ 37. Ⓐ Ⓑ Ⓒ Ⓓ Ⓔ 47. Ⓐ Ⓑ Ⓒ Ⓓ Ⓔ
8. Ⓐ Ⓑ Ⓒ Ⓓ Ⓔ 18. Ⓐ Ⓑ Ⓒ Ⓓ Ⓔ 28. Ⓐ Ⓑ Ⓒ Ⓓ Ⓔ 38. Ⓐ Ⓑ Ⓒ Ⓓ Ⓔ 48. Ⓐ Ⓑ Ⓒ Ⓓ Ⓔ
9. Ⓐ Ⓑ Ⓒ Ⓓ Ⓔ 19. Ⓐ Ⓑ Ⓒ Ⓓ Ⓔ 29. Ⓐ Ⓑ Ⓒ Ⓓ Ⓔ 39. Ⓐ Ⓑ Ⓒ Ⓓ Ⓔ 49. Ⓐ Ⓑ Ⓒ Ⓓ Ⓔ
10. Ⓐ Ⓑ Ⓒ Ⓓ Ⓔ 20. Ⓐ Ⓑ Ⓒ Ⓓ Ⓔ 30. Ⓐ Ⓑ Ⓒ Ⓓ Ⓔ 40. Ⓐ Ⓑ Ⓒ Ⓓ Ⓔ 50. Ⓐ Ⓑ Ⓒ Ⓓ Ⓔ

Part B—Reading Comprehension

1. Ⓐ Ⓑ Ⓒ Ⓓ Ⓔ 7. Ⓐ Ⓑ Ⓒ Ⓓ Ⓔ 13. Ⓐ Ⓑ Ⓒ Ⓓ Ⓔ 19. Ⓐ Ⓑ Ⓒ Ⓓ Ⓔ 25. Ⓐ Ⓑ Ⓒ Ⓓ Ⓔ
2. Ⓐ Ⓑ Ⓒ Ⓓ Ⓔ 8. Ⓐ Ⓑ Ⓒ Ⓓ Ⓔ 14. Ⓐ Ⓑ Ⓒ Ⓓ Ⓔ 20. Ⓐ Ⓑ Ⓒ Ⓓ Ⓔ 26. Ⓐ Ⓑ Ⓒ Ⓓ Ⓔ
3. Ⓐ Ⓑ Ⓒ Ⓓ Ⓔ 9. Ⓐ Ⓑ Ⓒ Ⓓ Ⓔ 15. Ⓐ Ⓑ Ⓒ Ⓓ Ⓔ 21. Ⓐ Ⓑ Ⓒ Ⓓ Ⓔ 27. Ⓐ Ⓑ Ⓒ Ⓓ Ⓔ
4. Ⓐ Ⓑ Ⓒ Ⓓ Ⓔ 10. Ⓐ Ⓑ Ⓒ Ⓓ Ⓔ 16. Ⓐ Ⓑ Ⓒ Ⓓ Ⓔ 22. Ⓐ Ⓑ Ⓒ Ⓓ Ⓔ 28. Ⓐ Ⓑ Ⓒ Ⓓ Ⓔ
5. Ⓐ Ⓑ Ⓒ Ⓓ Ⓔ 11. Ⓐ Ⓑ Ⓒ Ⓓ Ⓔ 17. Ⓐ Ⓑ Ⓒ Ⓓ Ⓔ 23. Ⓐ Ⓑ Ⓒ Ⓓ Ⓔ 29. Ⓐ Ⓑ Ⓒ Ⓓ Ⓔ
6. Ⓐ Ⓑ Ⓒ Ⓓ Ⓔ 12. Ⓐ Ⓑ Ⓒ Ⓓ Ⓔ 18. Ⓐ Ⓑ Ⓒ Ⓓ Ⓔ 24. Ⓐ Ⓑ Ⓒ Ⓓ Ⓔ 30. Ⓐ Ⓑ Ⓒ Ⓓ Ⓔ

TEAR HERE

Part C—Arithmetic Reasoning

1. Ⓐ Ⓑ Ⓒ Ⓓ Ⓔ   5. Ⓐ Ⓑ Ⓒ Ⓓ Ⓔ   9. Ⓐ Ⓑ Ⓒ Ⓓ Ⓔ   13. Ⓐ Ⓑ Ⓒ Ⓓ Ⓔ   17. Ⓐ Ⓑ Ⓒ Ⓓ Ⓔ
2. Ⓐ Ⓑ Ⓒ Ⓓ Ⓔ   6. Ⓐ Ⓑ Ⓒ Ⓓ Ⓔ   10. Ⓐ Ⓑ Ⓒ Ⓓ Ⓔ   14. Ⓐ Ⓑ Ⓒ Ⓓ Ⓔ   18. Ⓐ Ⓑ Ⓒ Ⓓ Ⓔ
3. Ⓐ Ⓑ Ⓒ Ⓓ Ⓔ   7. Ⓐ Ⓑ Ⓒ Ⓓ Ⓔ   11. Ⓐ Ⓑ Ⓒ Ⓓ Ⓔ   15. Ⓐ Ⓑ Ⓒ Ⓓ Ⓔ   19. Ⓐ Ⓑ Ⓒ Ⓓ Ⓔ
4. Ⓐ Ⓑ Ⓒ Ⓓ Ⓔ   8. Ⓐ Ⓑ Ⓒ Ⓓ Ⓔ   12. Ⓐ Ⓑ Ⓒ Ⓓ Ⓔ   16. Ⓐ Ⓑ Ⓒ Ⓓ Ⓔ   20. Ⓐ Ⓑ Ⓒ Ⓓ Ⓔ

BOOK B

There are 122 questions in Book B of the Postal Police Officer Exam. The questions in Book B are questions about you—about your school and work records, about your likes and dislikes, and about your personality. There arc no right and wrong answers to these Book B questions, so there is no answer key and no scoring method. In this model exam we include forty questions that are typical of the questions you'll be asked. You may want to look at old report cards or yearbooks so that you are prepared to answer these questions.

1. Ⓐ Ⓑ Ⓒ Ⓓ Ⓔ   26. Ⓐ Ⓑ Ⓒ Ⓓ Ⓔ   51. Ⓐ Ⓑ Ⓒ Ⓓ Ⓔ   76. Ⓐ Ⓑ Ⓒ Ⓓ Ⓔ   101. Ⓐ Ⓑ Ⓒ Ⓓ Ⓔ
2. Ⓐ Ⓑ Ⓒ Ⓓ Ⓔ   27. Ⓐ Ⓑ Ⓒ Ⓓ Ⓔ   52. Ⓐ Ⓑ Ⓒ Ⓓ Ⓔ   77. Ⓐ Ⓑ Ⓒ Ⓓ Ⓔ   102. Ⓐ Ⓑ Ⓒ Ⓓ Ⓔ
3. Ⓐ Ⓑ Ⓒ Ⓓ Ⓔ   28. Ⓐ Ⓑ Ⓒ Ⓓ Ⓔ   53. Ⓐ Ⓑ Ⓒ Ⓓ Ⓔ   78. Ⓐ Ⓑ Ⓒ Ⓓ Ⓔ   103. Ⓐ Ⓑ Ⓒ Ⓓ Ⓔ
4. Ⓐ Ⓑ Ⓒ Ⓓ Ⓔ   29. Ⓐ Ⓑ Ⓒ Ⓓ Ⓔ   54. Ⓐ Ⓑ Ⓒ Ⓓ Ⓔ   79. Ⓐ Ⓑ Ⓒ Ⓓ Ⓔ   104. Ⓐ Ⓑ Ⓒ Ⓓ Ⓔ
5. Ⓐ Ⓑ Ⓒ Ⓓ Ⓔ   30. Ⓐ Ⓑ Ⓒ Ⓓ Ⓔ   55. Ⓐ Ⓑ Ⓒ Ⓓ Ⓔ   80. Ⓐ Ⓑ Ⓒ Ⓓ Ⓔ   105. Ⓐ Ⓑ Ⓒ Ⓓ Ⓔ
6. Ⓐ Ⓑ Ⓒ Ⓓ Ⓔ   31. Ⓐ Ⓑ Ⓒ Ⓓ Ⓔ   56. Ⓐ Ⓑ Ⓒ Ⓓ Ⓔ   81. Ⓐ Ⓑ Ⓒ Ⓓ Ⓔ   106. Ⓐ Ⓑ Ⓒ Ⓓ Ⓔ
7. Ⓐ Ⓑ Ⓒ Ⓓ Ⓔ   32. Ⓐ Ⓑ Ⓒ Ⓓ Ⓔ   57. Ⓐ Ⓑ Ⓒ Ⓓ Ⓔ   82. Ⓐ Ⓑ Ⓒ Ⓓ Ⓔ   107. Ⓐ Ⓑ Ⓒ Ⓓ Ⓔ
8. Ⓐ Ⓑ Ⓒ Ⓓ Ⓔ   33. Ⓐ Ⓑ Ⓒ Ⓓ Ⓔ   58. Ⓐ Ⓑ Ⓒ Ⓓ Ⓔ   83. Ⓐ Ⓑ Ⓒ Ⓓ Ⓔ   108. Ⓐ Ⓑ Ⓒ Ⓓ Ⓔ
9. Ⓐ Ⓑ Ⓒ Ⓓ Ⓔ   34. Ⓐ Ⓑ Ⓒ Ⓓ Ⓔ   59. Ⓐ Ⓑ Ⓒ Ⓓ Ⓔ   84. Ⓐ Ⓑ Ⓒ Ⓓ Ⓔ   109. Ⓐ Ⓑ Ⓒ Ⓓ Ⓔ
10. Ⓐ Ⓑ Ⓒ Ⓓ Ⓔ   35. Ⓐ Ⓑ Ⓒ Ⓓ Ⓔ   60. Ⓐ Ⓑ Ⓒ Ⓓ Ⓔ   85. Ⓐ Ⓑ Ⓒ Ⓓ Ⓔ   110. Ⓐ Ⓑ Ⓒ Ⓓ Ⓔ
11. Ⓐ Ⓑ Ⓒ Ⓓ Ⓔ   36. Ⓐ Ⓑ Ⓒ Ⓓ Ⓔ   61. Ⓐ Ⓑ Ⓒ Ⓓ Ⓔ   86. Ⓐ Ⓑ Ⓒ Ⓓ Ⓔ   111. Ⓐ Ⓑ Ⓒ Ⓓ Ⓔ
12. Ⓐ Ⓑ Ⓒ Ⓓ Ⓔ   37. Ⓐ Ⓑ Ⓒ Ⓓ Ⓔ   62. Ⓐ Ⓑ Ⓒ Ⓓ Ⓔ   87. Ⓐ Ⓑ Ⓒ Ⓓ Ⓔ   112. Ⓐ Ⓑ Ⓒ Ⓓ Ⓔ
13. Ⓐ Ⓑ Ⓒ Ⓓ Ⓔ   38. Ⓐ Ⓑ Ⓒ Ⓓ Ⓔ   63. Ⓐ Ⓑ Ⓒ Ⓓ Ⓔ   88. Ⓐ Ⓑ Ⓒ Ⓓ Ⓔ   113. Ⓐ Ⓑ Ⓒ Ⓓ Ⓔ
14. Ⓐ Ⓑ Ⓒ Ⓓ Ⓔ   39. Ⓐ Ⓑ Ⓒ Ⓓ Ⓔ   64. Ⓐ Ⓑ Ⓒ Ⓓ Ⓔ   89. Ⓐ Ⓑ Ⓒ Ⓓ Ⓔ   114. Ⓐ Ⓑ Ⓒ Ⓓ Ⓔ
15. Ⓐ Ⓑ Ⓒ Ⓓ Ⓔ   40. Ⓐ Ⓑ Ⓒ Ⓓ Ⓔ   65. Ⓐ Ⓑ Ⓒ Ⓓ Ⓔ   90. Ⓐ Ⓑ Ⓒ Ⓓ Ⓔ   115. Ⓐ Ⓑ Ⓒ Ⓓ Ⓔ
16. Ⓐ Ⓑ Ⓒ Ⓓ Ⓔ   41. Ⓐ Ⓑ Ⓒ Ⓓ Ⓔ   66. Ⓐ Ⓑ Ⓒ Ⓓ Ⓔ   91. Ⓐ Ⓑ Ⓒ Ⓓ Ⓔ   116. Ⓐ Ⓑ Ⓒ Ⓓ Ⓔ
17. Ⓐ Ⓑ Ⓒ Ⓓ Ⓔ   42. Ⓐ Ⓑ Ⓒ Ⓓ Ⓔ   67. Ⓐ Ⓑ Ⓒ Ⓓ Ⓔ   92. Ⓐ Ⓑ Ⓒ Ⓓ Ⓔ   117. Ⓐ Ⓑ Ⓒ Ⓓ Ⓔ
18. Ⓐ Ⓑ Ⓒ Ⓓ Ⓔ   43. Ⓐ Ⓑ Ⓒ Ⓓ Ⓔ   68. Ⓐ Ⓑ Ⓒ Ⓓ Ⓔ   93. Ⓐ Ⓑ Ⓒ Ⓓ Ⓔ   118. Ⓐ Ⓑ Ⓒ Ⓓ Ⓔ
19. Ⓐ Ⓑ Ⓒ Ⓓ Ⓔ   44. Ⓐ Ⓑ Ⓒ Ⓓ Ⓔ   69. Ⓐ Ⓑ Ⓒ Ⓓ Ⓔ   94. Ⓐ Ⓑ Ⓒ Ⓓ Ⓔ   119. Ⓐ Ⓑ Ⓒ Ⓓ Ⓔ
20. Ⓐ Ⓑ Ⓒ Ⓓ Ⓔ   45. Ⓐ Ⓑ Ⓒ Ⓓ Ⓔ   70. Ⓐ Ⓑ Ⓒ Ⓓ Ⓔ   95. Ⓐ Ⓑ Ⓒ Ⓓ Ⓔ   120. Ⓐ Ⓑ Ⓒ Ⓓ Ⓔ
21. Ⓐ Ⓑ Ⓒ Ⓓ Ⓔ   46. Ⓐ Ⓑ Ⓒ Ⓓ Ⓔ   71. Ⓐ Ⓑ Ⓒ Ⓓ Ⓔ   96. Ⓐ Ⓑ Ⓒ Ⓓ Ⓔ   121. Ⓐ Ⓑ Ⓒ Ⓓ Ⓔ
22. Ⓐ Ⓑ Ⓒ Ⓓ Ⓔ   47. Ⓐ Ⓑ Ⓒ Ⓓ Ⓔ   72. Ⓐ Ⓑ Ⓒ Ⓓ Ⓔ   97. Ⓐ Ⓑ Ⓒ Ⓓ Ⓔ   122. Ⓐ Ⓑ Ⓒ Ⓓ Ⓔ
23. Ⓐ Ⓑ Ⓒ Ⓓ Ⓔ   48. Ⓐ Ⓑ Ⓒ Ⓓ Ⓔ   73. Ⓐ Ⓑ Ⓒ Ⓓ Ⓔ   98. Ⓐ Ⓑ Ⓒ Ⓓ Ⓔ
24. Ⓐ Ⓑ Ⓒ Ⓓ Ⓔ   49. Ⓐ Ⓑ Ⓒ Ⓓ Ⓔ   74. Ⓐ Ⓑ Ⓒ Ⓓ Ⓔ   99. Ⓐ Ⓑ Ⓒ Ⓓ Ⓔ
25. Ⓐ Ⓑ Ⓒ Ⓓ Ⓔ   50. Ⓐ Ⓑ Ⓒ Ⓓ Ⓔ   75. Ⓐ Ⓑ Ⓒ Ⓓ Ⓔ   100. Ⓐ Ⓑ Ⓒ Ⓓ Ⓔ

BOOK A

PART A—NAME AND NUMBER COMPARISONS

Time: 8 Minutes. 50 Questions.

Directions: For each question, compare the three names or numbers and mark your answer:

A if **ALL THREE** names or numbers are exactly **ALIKE**

B if only the **FIRST** and **SECOND** names or numbers are exactly **ALIKE**

C if only the **FIRST** and **THIRD** names or numbers are exactly **ALIKE**

D if only the **SECOND** and **THIRD** names or numbers are exactly **ALIKE**

E if **ALL THREE** names or numbers are **DIFFERENT**

1.	Thomas L. Kershaw	Thomas L. Kershaw	Thomas J. Kershaw
2.	Takahide E. Moro	Takahide E. Moru	Takahide E. Moru
3.	Carlota Cosentino	Carlotta Cosentino	Carlotta Constentino
4.	Albertina Andriuolo	Albertina Andriuolo	Albertina Andriuolo
5.	Francis J. Czukor	Francis Z. Czukor	Frances J. Czukor
6.	7692138	7692138	7692138
7.	2633342	2633342	2633342
8.	2454803	2548403	2454803
9.	9670243	9670423	9670423
10.	2789350	2789350	2798350
11.	Darlene P. Tenenbaum	Darlene P. Tenenbaum	Darlene P. Tanenbaum
12.	Maxwell Macmillan	Maxwell MacMillan	Maxwell Macmillian
13.	Frank D. Stanick	Frank D. Satanic	Frank D. Satanich
14.	J. Robert Schunk	J. Robert Schunh Robert	J. Schunk
15.	Fernando Silva, Jr.	Fernando Silva, Jr.	Fernand Silva, Jr.
16.	2797630	2797360	2797360
17.	6312192	6312192	6312192
18.	7412032	7412032	7412032
19.	2789327	2879327	2789327
20.	5927681	5927861	5927681
21.	Wendy A. Courtney	Wendy A. Courtney	Wendy A. Courtnay
22.	Lambert Forman, MD	Lambert Forman, MD	Lambert Forman, MD
23.	Joseph A. Gurreri	Joseph A. Gurreri	Joseph A. Gurreri
24.	Sylnette Lynch	Sylnette Lynch	Sylnette Lynch
25.	Zion McKenzie, Jr.	Zion McKenzie, Sr.	Zion MacKenzie, Jr.
26.	6932976	6939276	6932796

27.	9631695	9636195	9631695
28.	7370527	7375027	7370537
29.	2799379	2739779	2799379
30.	5261383	5261383	5261338
31.	J. Randolph Rea	J. Randolph Rea	J. Randolphe Rea
32.	W.E. Johnston	W.E. Johnson	W.E. Johnson
33.	Vergil L. Muller	Vergil L. Muller	Vergil L. Muller
34.	Atherton R. Warde	Asheton R. Warde	Atherton P. Warde
35.	E. Owens McVey	E. Owen McVey	E. Owen McVay
36.	8125690	8126690	8125609
37.	2395890	2395890	2395890
38.	1926341	1926347	1926314
39.	6219354	6219354	6219354
40.	2312793	2312793	2312793
41.	Alexander Majthenyi	Alexander Majthenyi	Alexander Majthenyi
42.	James T. Harbison	James T. Harbinson	James T. Harbison
43.	Margareta Goldenkoff	Margaretta Goldenkoff	Margaretha Goldenkoff
44.	Cornelius Detwiler	Cornelius Detwiler	Cornelius Detwiler
45.	Benjamin A. D'Ortona	Benjamin A. D'Ortoni	Benjamin D'Ortonia
46.	1065407	1065407	1065047
47.	6452054	6452654	6452054
48.	8501268	8501268	8501286
49.	3457988	3457986	3457986
50.	4695682	4695862	4695682

END OF PART A

PART B—READING COMPREHENSION

Time: 60 Minutes. 30 Questions.

Directions: *For each reading question you will be given a paragraph that contains all the information necessary to infer the correct answer. Use only the information provided in the paragraph. Do not speculate or make assumptions that go beyond this information. Also, assume that all information given in the paragraph is true, even if it conflicts with some fact known to you. Only one correct answer can be validly inferred from the information contained in the paragraph. Mark its letter on your answer sheet.*

1. A member of the department shall not indulge in liquor while in uniform. A member of the department not required to wear a uniform and a uniformed member while out of uniform shall not indulge in intoxicants to an extent unfitting the member for duty.

    The paragraph best supports the statement that
    (A) an off-duty member, not in uniform, may drink liquor to the extent that it does not unfit the member for duty
    (B) a member not on duty, but in uniform and not unfit for duty, may drink liquor
    (C) an on-duty member, unfit for duty in uniform, may drink intoxicants
    (D) a uniformed member in civilian clothes may not drink intoxicants unless unfit for duty
    (E) a civilian member of the department, in uniform, may drink liquor if fit for duty

2. Tax law specialists may authorize their assistants to sign their names to reports, letters, and papers that are not specially required to be signed personally by the tax law specialist. The signature should be: "Jane Doe, tax law specialist, by Richard Roe, tax technician." The name of the tax law specialist may be written or stamped, but the signature of the tax technician shall be in ink.

    The paragraph best supports the statement that
    (A) if a tax law specialist's assistant signs official papers both by rubber stamp and in ink, the assistant has authority to sign
    (B) if a tax technician does not neglect to include his or her title in ink along with his or her signature following the word "by," the technician may sign papers that are not specially required to be signed personally by the tax law specialist
    (C) no signatory authority delegated to the tax technician by the tax law specialist may be redelegated by the tax technician to an assistant unless so authorized in ink by the tax law specialist
    (D) if a tax law specialist personally signs written requisitions in ink, the technician is not required to identify the source of the order with a rubber stamp
    (E) when a tax technician signs authorized papers for a tax law specialist, the tax technician must write out the tax law specialist's signature in full with pen and ink

3. Upon retirement from service, a member shall receive a retirement allowance consisting of an annuity that shall be the actuarial equivalent of his accumulated deductions at the time of retirement; a pension in addition to his annuity that shall be one service-fraction of his final compensation multiplied by the number of years of government service since he last became a member; and a pension that is the actuarial equivalent of the reserve-for-increased-take-home-pay to which he may then be entitled, if any.

    The paragraph best supports the statement that
    (A) a retirement allowance shall consist of an annuity plus a pension plus an actuarial equivalent of a service-fraction
    (B) upon retirement from service, a member shall receive an annuity plus a pension plus an actuarial equivalent of reserve-for-increased-take-home-pay if he is entitled
    (C) a retiring member shall receive an annuity plus reserve-for-increased-take-home-pay, if any, plus final compensation
    (D) a retirement allowance shall consist of a pension plus reserve-for-increased-take-home-pay, if any, plus accumulated deductions
    (E) a retirement allowance shall consist of an annuity that is equal to one service-fraction of final compensation, a pension multiplied by the number of years of government service, and the actuarial equivalent of accumulated deductions from increased take-home-pay

4. If you are in doubt as to whether any matter is legally mailable, you should ask the postmaster. Even though the Postal Service has not expressly declared any matter to be nonmailable, the sender of such matter may be held fully liable for violation of law if he or she does actually send nonmailable matter through the mail.

    The paragraph best supports the statement that
    (A) if the postmaster is in doubt as to whether any matter is legally mailable, the postmaster may be held liable for any sender's sending nonmailable matter through the mail
    (B) if the sender is ignorant of what it is that constitutes nonmailable matter, the sender is relieved of all responsibility for mailing nonmailable matter
    (C) if a sender sends nonmailable matter, the sender is fully liable for law violation even though doubt may have existed about the mailability of the matter
    (D) if the Postal Service has not expressly declared material mailable, it is nonmailable
    (E) if the Postal Service has not expressly declared material nonmailable, it is mailable

5. In evaluating education for a particular position, education in and of itself is of no value except to the degree in which it contributes to knowledges, skills and abilities needed in the particular job. On its face, such a statement would seem to contend that general educational development need not be considered in evaluating education and training. Much to the contrary, such a proposition favors the consideration of any and all training, but only as it pertains to the position for which the applicant applies.

    The paragraph best supports the statement that
    (A) if general education is supplemented by specialized education, it is of no value
    (B) if a high school education is desirable in any occupation, special training need not be evaluated
    (C) in evaluating education, a contradiction arises in assigning equal weight to general and specialized education
    (D) unless it is supplemented by general education, specialized education is of no value
    (E) education is of value to the degree to which it is needed in the particular position

6. Statistics tell us that heart disease kills more people than any other illness, and the death rate continues to rise. People over 30 have a fifty-fifty chance of escaping, for heart disease is chiefly an illness of people in late middle age and advanced years. Because there are more people in this age group living today than there were some years ago, heart disease is able to find more victims.

    The paragraph best supports the statement that
    (A) if a person has heart disease, there is a 50 percent chance that he or she is over 30 years of age
    (B) according to statistics, more middle-aged and elderly people die of heart disease than of all other causes
    (C) because heart disease is chiefly an illness of people in late middle age, young people are less likely to be the victims of heart disease
    (D) the rising birth rate has increased the possibility that the average person will die of heart disease
    (E) if the stress of modern living were not increasing, there would be a slower increase in the risk of heart disease.

7. Racketeers are primarily concerned with business affairs, legitimate or otherwise, and prefer those that are close to the margin of legitimacy. They get their best opportunities from business organizations that meet the need of large sections of the public for goods or services that are defined as illegitimate by the same public, such as prostitution, gambling, illicit drugs or liquor. In contrast to the thief, the racketeer and the establishments he or she controls deliver goods and services for money received.

The paragraph best supports the statement that
(A) since racketeers deliver goods and services for money received, their business affairs are not illegitimate
(B) since racketeering involves objects of value, it is unlike theft
(C) victims of racketeers are not guilty of violating the law, therefore racketeering is a victimless crime
(D) since many people want services which are not obtainable through legitimate sources, they contribute to the difficulty of suppressing racketeers
(E) if large sections of the public are engaged in legitimate business with racketeers, the businesses are not illegitimate

8. The housing authority not only faces every problem of the private developer, it must also assume responsibilities of which private building is free. The authority must account to the community; it must conform to federal regulations; it must provide durable buildings of good standard at low cost; and it must overcome the prejudices of contractors, bankers and prospective tenants against public operations. These authorities are being watched by antihousing enthusiasts for the first error of judgment or the first evidence of high costs that can be torn to bits before a Congressional committee.

The paragraph best supports the statement that
(A) since private developers are not accountable to the community, they do not have the opposition of contractors, bankers, and prospective tenants
(B) if Congressional committees are watched by antihousing enthusiasts, they may discover errors of judgment and high costs on the part of a housing authority
(C) while a housing authority must deal with all the difficulties encountered by a private builder, it must also deal with antihousing enthusiasts
(D) if housing authorities are not immune to errors in judgment, they must provide durable buildings of good standard and low cost just like private developers
(E) if a housing authority is to conform to federal regulations, it must overcome the prejudices of contractors, builders and prospective tenants

9.   Security of tenure in the public service must be viewed in the context of the universal quest for security. If we narrow our application of the term to employment, the problem of security in the public service is seen to differ from that in private industry only in the need to meet the peculiar threats to security in governmental organizations—principally the danger of making employment contingent upon factors other than the performance of the workers.

The paragraph best supports the statement that
(A) if workers seek security, they should enter public service
(B) if employment is contingent upon factors other than work performance, workers will feel more secure
(C) if employees believe that their security is threatened, they are employed in private industry
(D) the term of employment in public service differs from that in private industry
(E) the employment status of the public servant with respect to security of tenure differs from that of the private employee by encompassing factors beyond those affecting the private employee

10. The wide use of antibiotics has presented a number of problems. Some patients become allergic to the drugs, so that they cannot be used when they are needed. In other cases, after prolonged treatment with antibiotics, certain organisms no longer respond to them. This is one of the reasons for the constant search for more potent drugs.

The paragraph best supports the statement that
(A) since a number of problems have been presented by long term treatment with antibiotics, antibiotics should never be used on a long term basis
(B) because some people have developed an allergy to specific drugs, potent antibiotics cannot always be used
(C) since antibiotics have been used successfully for certain allergies, there must be a constant search for more potent drugs
(D) if antibiotics are used for a prolonged period of time, certain organisms become allergic to them
(E) since so many diseases have been successfully treated with antibiotics, there must be a constant search for new drugs

11. The noncompetitive class consists of positions for which there are minimum qualifications but for which no reliable exam has been developed. In the noncompetitive class, every applicant must meet minimum qualifications in terms of education, experience, and medical or physical qualifications. There may even be an examination on a pass/fail basis.

The paragraph best supports the statement that
(A) if an exam is unreliable, the position is in the noncompetitive class
(B) if an applicant has met minimum qualifications in terms of education, experience, medical, or physical requirements, the applicant must pass a test
(C) if an applicant has met minimum qualifications in terms of education, experience, medical, or physical requirements, the applicant may fail a test
(D) if an applicant passes an exam for a noncompetitive position, the applicant must also meet minimum qualifications
(E) if there are minimum qualifications for a position, the position is in the non-competitive class

12. Two independent clauses cannot share one sentence without some form of connective. If they do, they form a run-on sentence. Two principal clauses may be joined by a coordinating conjunction, by a comma followed by a coordinating conjunction, or by a semicolon. They may also form two distinct sentences. Two main clauses may never be joined by a comma without a coordinating conjunction. This error is called a comma splice.

The paragraph best supports the statement that
(A) if the violation is called a comma splice, two main clauses are joined by a comma without a coordinating conjunction
(B) if two distinct sentences share one sentence and are joined by a coordinating conjunction, the result is a run-on sentence
(C) when a coordinating conjunction is not followed by a semicolon, the writer has committed an error of punctuation
(D) while a comma and a semicolon may not be used in the same principal clause, they may be used in the same sentence
(E) a bad remedy for a run-on sentence is not a comma splice

13. The pay in some job titles is hourly; in others it is annual. Official work weeks vary from 35 hours to $37^1/_2$ hours to 40 hours. In some positions, overtime is earned for all time worked beyond the set number of hours, and differentials are paid for night, weekend, and holiday work. Other positions offer compensatory time off for overtime or for work during unpopular times. Still other positions require the jobholder to devote as must extra time as needed to do the work without any extra compensation. And in some positions, employees who work overtime are given a meal allowance.

The paragraph best supports the statement that
(A) if a meal allowance is given, there is compensation for overtime
(B) if the work week is 35 hours long, the job is unpopular
(C) if overtime is earned, pay in the job title is hourly
(D) if a jobholder has earned a weekend differential, the employee has worked beyond the set number of hours
(E) if compensatory time is offered, it is offered as a substitute for overtime pay

14. All applicants must be of satisfactory character and reputation and must meet all requirements set forth in the Notice of Examination for the position for which they are applying. Applicants may be summoned for the written test prior to investigation of their qualifications and background. Admission to the test does not mean that the applicant has met the qualifications for the position.

The paragraph best supports the statement that
(A) if an applicant has been admitted to the test, the applicant has not met requirements for the position
(B) if an applicant has not been investigated, the applicant will not be admitted to the written test
(C) if an applicant has met all requirements for the position, the applicant will be admitted to the test
(D) if an applicant has satisfactory character and reputation, the applicant will not have his or her background investigated
(E) if an applicant has met all the requirements set forth in the Notice of Examination, the applicant will pass the test

15. Although it has in the past been illegal for undocumented aliens to work in the United States, it has not, until now, been unlawful for employers to hire these aliens. With the passage of the new immigration law, employers will now be subject to civil penalties and ultimately imprisonment if they "knowingly" hire, recruit, or refer for a fee any unauthorized alien. Similarly, it is also unlawful for employers to continue to employ an undocumented alien who was hired after November 6, 1986, knowing that he or she was or is unauthorized to work.

The paragraph best supports the statement that
- (A) under the new immigration law, it is no longer illegal for undocumented aliens to be denied employment in the United States
- (B) if an undocumented alien is not remaining on the job illegally, the worker was not hired after November 6, 1986
- (C) if a person wishes to avoid the penalties of the new immigration law, the person must not knowingly employ aliens
- (D) if an employer inadvertently hires undocumented aliens, the employer may be subject to fine or imprisonment but not both
- (E) if an unauthorized alien is able to find an employer who will hire him or her after November 6, 1986, the alien is welcome to go to work

16. The law requires that the government offer employees, retirees, and their families the opportunity to continue group health and/or welfare fund coverage at 102 percent of the group rate in certain instances where the coverage would otherwise terminate. All group benefits, including optional benefits riders, are available. Welfare fund benefits that can be continued under COBRA are dental, vision, prescription drugs, and other related medical benefits. The period of coverage varies from 18 to 36 months, depending on the reason for continuation.

The paragraph best supports the statement that
- (A) the period of coverage continuation varies depending on the reason for termination
- (B) upon retirement, welfare fund benefits continue at a 102 percent rate
- (C) the law requires employees, retirees, and their families to continue health coverage
- (D) COBRA is a program for acquiring welfare fund benefits
- (E) if retirees or their families do not desire to terminate them, they can continue group benefits at 102 percent of the group rate

17. Historical records as such rarely constitute an adequate or, more importantly, a reliable basis for estimating earthquake potential. In most regions of the world, recorded history is short relative to the time between the largest earthquakes. Thus, the fact that there have been no historic earthquakes larger than a given size does not make us confident that they will also be absent in the future. It may, alternatively, be due to the short length of available historical records relative to the long repeat time for large earthquakes.

The paragraph best supports the statement that
(A) if historic earthquakes are no larger than a given size, they are unlikely to recur
(B) potential earthquakes do not inspire confidence in historical records as predictors of time between earthquakes
(C) if the time span between major earthquakes were not longer than the length of available records, history would have greater predictive value
(D) since there have been no historic earthquakes larger than a given size, we are confident that there will be a long time span between major earthquakes
(E) in those regions of the world where recorded history is long, the time between the largest earthquakes is short

18. A language can be thought of as a number of strings or sequences of symbols. The definition of a language defines which strings belong to the language, but since most languages of interest consist of an infinite number of strings, this definition is impossible to accomplish by listing the strings (or sentences). While the number of *sentences* in a language can be infinite, the rules by which they are constructed are not. This may explain why we are able to speak sentences in a language that we have never spoken before, and to understand sentences that we have never heard before.

The paragraph best supports the statement that
(A) if there is an infinite number of sequences of symbols in a language, there is an infinite number of rules for their construction
(B) if we have never spoken a language, we can understand its sentences provided that we know the rules by which they were constructed
(C) a language is defined by its strings
(D) if the number of sentences in an unnatural language were not infinite, we would be able to define it
(E) if sequences of symbols are governed by rules of construction, then the number of sentences can be determined

19. An assumption commonly made in regard to the reliability of testimony is that when a number of persons report the same matter, those details upon which there is an agreement may generally be considered substantiated. Experiments have shown, however, that there is a tendency for the same errors to appear in the testimony of different individuals, and that, apart from any collusion, agreement of testimony is no proof of dependability.

The paragraph best supports the statement that
(A) if details of the testimony are true, all witnesses will agree to it
(B) unless there is collusion, it is impossible for a number of persons to give the same report
(C) if most witnesses do not independently attest to the same facts, the facts cannot be true
(D) if the testimony of a group of people is in substantial agreement, it cannot be ruled out that those witnesses have not all made the same mistake
(E) under experimental conditions, witnesses tend to give reliable testimony

20. In some instances, changes are made in a contract after it has been signed and accepted by both parties. This is done either by inserting a new clause in a contract or by annexing a *rider* to the contract. If a contract is changed by a rider, both parties must sign the rider in order for it to be legal. The basic contract should also note that a rider is attached by inserting new words to the contract, and both parties should also initial and date the new insertion. The same requirement applies if they later change any wording in the contract. What two people agree to do, they can mutually agree not to do—as long as they both agree.

The paragraph best supports the statement that
(A) if two people mutually agree not to do something, they must sign a rider
(B) if both parties to a contract do not agree to attach a rider, they must initial the contract to render it legal
(C) if a rider to a contract is to be legal, that rider must be agreed to and signed by both parties, who must not neglect to initial and date that portion of the contract to which the rider refers
(D) if a party to a contract does not agree to a change, that party should initial the change and annex a rider detailing the disagreement
(E) if the wording of a contract is not to be changed, both parties must initial and date a rider

21. Personnel administration begins with the process of defining the quantities of people needed to do the job. Thereafter, people must be recruited, selected, trained, directed, rewarded, transferred, promoted, and perhaps released or retired. However, it is not true that all organizations are structured so that workers can be dealt with as individuals. In some organizations, employees are represented by unions, and managers bargain directly only with these associations.

The paragraph best supports the statement that
(A) no organizations are structured so that workers cannot be dealt with as individuals
(B) some working environments other than organizations are structured so that workers can be dealt with as individuals
(C) all organizations are structured so that employees are represented by unions
(D) no organizations are structured so that managers bargain with unions
(E) some organizations are not structured so that workers can be dealt with as individuals

22. Explosives are substances or devices capable of producing a volume of rapidly expanding gases that exert a sudden pressure on their surroundings. Chemical explosives are the most commonly used, although there are mechanical and nuclear explosives. All mechanical explosives are devices in which a physical reaction is produced, such as that caused by overloading a container with compressed air. While nuclear explosives are by far the most powerful, all nuclear explosives have been restricted to military weapons.

The paragraph best supports the statement that
(A) all explosives that have been restricted to military weapons are nuclear explosives
(B) no mechanical explosives are devices in which a physical reaction is produced, such as that caused by overloading a container with compressed air
(C) some nuclear explosives have not been restricted to military weapons
(D) all mechanical explosives have been restricted to military weapons
(E) some devices in which a physical reaction is produced, such as that caused by overloading a container with compressed air, are mechanical explosives

23. The modern conception of the economic role of the public sector (government), as distinct from the private sector, is that every level of government is a link in the economic process. Government's contribution to political and economic welfare must, however, be evaluated not merely in terms of its technical efficiency, but also in the light of its acceptability to a particular society at a particular state of political and economic development. Even in a dictatorship, this principle is formally observed, although the authorities usually destroy the substance by presuming to interpret to the public its collective desires.

The paragraph best supports the statement that
(A) it is not true that some levels of government are not links in the economic process
(B) all dictatorships observe the same economic principles as other governments
(C) all links in the economic process are levels of government
(D) the contributions of some levels of government do not need to be evaluated for technical efficiency and acceptability to society
(E) no links in the economic process are institutions other than levels of government

24. All property is classified as either personal property or real property, but not both. In general, if something is classified as personal property, it is transient and transportable in nature, while real property is not. Things such as leaseholds, animals, money, and intangible and other moveable goods are examples of personal property. Permanent buildings and land, on the other hand, are fixed in nature and are not transportable.

The paragraph best supports the statement that
(A) if something is classified as personal property, it is not transient and transportable in nature
(B) some forms of property are considered to be both personal property and real property
(C) permanent buildings and land are real property
(D) permanent buildings and land are personal property
(E) tangible goods are considered to be real property

25. The Supreme Court's power to invalidate legislation that violates the Constitution is a strong restriction on the powers of Congress. If an Act of Congress is deemed unconstitutional by the Supreme Court, then the Act is voided. Unlike a presidential veto, which can be overridden by a two-thirds vote of the House and the Senate, a constitutional ruling by the Supreme Court must be accepted by the Congress.

The paragraph best supports the statement that
(A) if an Act of Congress is voided, then it has been deemed unconstitutional by the Supreme Court
(B) if an Act of Congress has not been voided, then it has not been deemed unconstitutional by the Supreme Court
(C) if an Act of Congress has not been deemed unconstitutional by the Supreme Court, then it is voided
(D) if an Act of Congress is deemed unconstitutional by the Supreme Court, then it is not voided
(E) if an Act of Congress has not been voided, then it has been deemed unconstitutional by the Supreme Court

26. All child-welfare agencies are organizations that seek to promote the healthy growth and development of children. Supplying or supplementing family income so that parents can maintain a home for their children is usually the first such service to be provided. In addition to programs of general family relief, some special programs for broken families are offered when parental care is temporarily or permanently unavailable.

The paragraph best supports the statement that
(A) it is not true that some organizations that seek to promote the healthy growth and development of children are child-welfare agencies
(B) some programs offered when parental care is temporarily or permanently unavailable are not special programs for broken families
(C) it is not true that no special programs for broken families are offered when temporary or permanent parental care is unavailable
(D) all programs offered when parental care is temporarily or permanently unavailable are special programs for broken families
(E) some organizations that seek to promote the healthy growth and development of children are not child-welfare agencies

27. Information centers can be categorized according to the primary activity or service they provide. For example, some information centers are document depots. These depots, generally government-sponsored, serve as archives for the acquisition, storage, retrieval, and dissemination of a variety of documents. All document depots have the capacity to provide a great range of user services, which may include preparing specialized bibliographies, publishing announcements, indexes, and abstracts, as well as providing copies.

The paragraph best supports the statement that
(A) some information centers are categorized by features other than the primary activity or service they provide
(B) some document depots lack the capacity to provide a great range of user services
(C) no document depot lacks the capacity to provide a great range of user services
(D) all information centers are document depots
(E) some places that provide a great range of user services are not document depots

28. Authorities generally agree that the use of hyphens tends to defy most rules. The best advice that can be given is to consult the dictionary to determine whether a given prefix is joined solidly to a root word or is hyphenated. One reliable rule, however, is that if an expression is a familiar one, such as overtime and hatchback, then it is a nonhyphenated compound.

The paragraph best supports the statement that
(A) if an expression is a familiar one, then it is a hyphenated compound
(B) if an expression is a nonhyphenated compound, then it is a familiar expression
(C) if an expression is not a familiar one, then it is a hyphenated compound
(D) if an expression is a hyphenated compound, containing a suffix rather than a prefix, then it is not a familiar one
(E) if an expression is a hyphenated compound, then it is not a familiar one

29. One use for wild land is the protection of certain species of wild animals or plants in wildlife refuges or in botanical reservations. Some general types of land use are activities that conflict with this stated purpose. All activities that exhibit such conflict are, of course, excluded from refuges and reservations.

The paragraph best supports the statement that
(A) all activities that conflict with the purpose of wildlife refuges or botanical reservations are general types of land use
(B) all activities excluded from wildlife refuges and botanical reservations are those that conflict with the purpose of the refuge or reservation
(C) some activities excluded from wildlife refuges and botanical reservations are general types of land use
(D) no activities that conflict with the purpose of wildlife refuges and botanical reservations are general types of land use
(E) some general types of land use are not excluded from wildlife refuges and botanical reservations

30. Many kinds of computer programming languages have been developed over the years. Initially, programmers had to write instructions in machine language. If a computer programming language is a machine language, then it is a code that can be read directly by a computer. Most high-level computer programming languages, such as Fortran and Cobol, use strings of common English phrases that communicate with the computer only after being converted or translated into a machine code.

The paragraph best supports the statement that
(A) all high-level computer programming languages use strings of common English phrases that are converted to a machine code
(B) if a computer programming language is a machine language, then it is not a code that can be read directly by a computer
(C) if a computer programming language is a code that can be read directly by a computer, then it is not a machine language
(D) if a computer programming language is not a code that can be read directly by a computer, then it is not a machine language
(E) if a computer programming language is not a machine language, then it is a code that can be read directly by a computer

END OF PART B

PART C—ARITHMETIC REASONING

Time: 50 Minutes. 20 Questions.

Directions: Analyze each paragraph to set up each problem; then solve it. Mark your answer sheet with the letter of the correct answer. If the correct answer is not given as one of the response choices, you should select response E, "none of these."

1. Twelve clerks are assigned to enter certain data on index cards. This number of clerks could perform the task in 18 days. After these clerks have worked on this assignment for 6 days, 4 more clerks are added to the staff to do this work. Assuming that all the clerks work at the same rate of speed, the entire task, instead of taking 18 days, will be performed in
   (A) 9 days
   (B) 12 days
   (C) 15 days
   (D) 16 days
   (E) none of these

2. In a low-cost public-health dental clinic, an adult cleaning costs twice as much as the same treatment for a child. If a family of three children and two adults can visit the clinic for cleanings for a cost of $49, what is the cost for each adult?
   (A) $7
   (B) $10
   (C) $12
   (D) $14
   (E) none of these

3. A government employee is relocated to a new region of the country and purchases a new home. The purchase price of the house is $87,250. Taxes to be paid on this house include: county tax of $424 per year; town tax of $783 per year; and school tax of $466 every six months. The aggregate tax rate is $.132 per $1000 of assessed value. The assessed value of this house is what percent of the purchase price?
   (A) 14.52%
   (B) 18.57%
   (C) 22.81%
   (D) 29.05%
   (E) none of these

4. The Social Security Administration has ordered an intensive check of 756 SSI payment recipients who are suspected of having above-standard incomes. Four clerical assistants have been assigned to this task. At the end of six days at 7 hours each, they have checked on 336 recipients. In order to speed up the investigation, two more assistants are assigned at this point. If they work at the same rate, the number of additional 7-hour days it will take to complete the job is, most nearly
   (A) 1
   (B) 2
   (C) 3
   (D) 4
   (E) none of these

5. A family spends 30 percent of its take-home income for food, 8 percent for clothing, 25 percent for shelter, 4 percent for recreation, 13 percent for education, and 5 percent for miscellaneous items. The remainder goes into the family savings account. If the weekly net earnings of this household are $500, how many weeks will it take this family to accumulate $15,000 in savings, before interest?
    (A) 200
    (B) 175
    (C) 150
    (D) 100
    (E) none of these

6. An Internal Revenue Service (IRS) officer is making spot-checks of income reported on income tax returns. A cab driver being audited works on a commission basis, receiving $42\frac{1}{2}$ percent of fares collected. The IRS allocates that earnings from tips should be valued at 29 percent of commissions. If the cab driver's weekly fare collections average $520, then the IRS projects his reportable monthly earnings to be
    (A) between $900 and $1000
    (B) between $1000 and $1100
    (C) between $1100 and $1200
    (D) between $1200 and $1250
    (E) none of these

7. A department head hired a total of 60 temporary employees to handle a seasonal increase in the department's workload. The following lists the number of temporary employees hired, their rates of pay, and the duration of their employment:

    One-third of the total were hired as clerks, each at the rate of $12,700 a year, for two months

    30 percent of the total were hired as office machine operators, each at the rate of $13,150 a year, for four months

    22 stenographers were hired, each at the rate of $13,000 a year, for three months. The total amount paid to these temporary employees to the nearest dollar was

    (A) $194,499
    (B) $192,900
    (C) $130,000
    (D) $127,500
    (E) none of these

8. A government worker whose personal car gets 24 miles to the gallon was required to use this car for government business. He filled the tank before he began, requiring 18 gallons, for which he paid $1.349 per gallon. He drove 336 miles, then filled the tank again at a cost of $1.419 per gallon. The government reimburses him at the rate of $.20 per mile. What was the actual cost of gasoline for this trip?
    (A) $19.87
    (B) $23.05
    (C) $24.28
    (D) $44.15
    (E) none of these

9. The visitors' section of a courtroom seats 105 people. The court is in session 6 hours a day. On one particular day, 486 people visited the court and were given seats. What is the average length of time spent by each visitor in the court? Assume that as soon as a person leaves a seat it is immediately filled and that at no time during the day is one of the 105 seats vacant. Express your answer in hours and minutes.
   - (A) 1 hour 18 minutes
   - (B) 1 hour 20 minutes
   - (C) 1 hour 30 minutes
   - (D) 2 hours
   - (E) none of these

10. A worker is paid at the rate of $8.60 per hour for the first 40 hours worked in a week and time-and-a-half for overtime. The FICA (social security) deduction is 7.13 percent; federal tax withholding is 15 percent; state tax withholding, 5 percent; and local tax withholding, $2\frac{1}{2}$ percent. If a worker works 48 hours a week for two consecutive weeks, she will take home
   - (A) $314.69
   - (B) $580.97
   - (C) $629.39
   - (D) $693.16
   - (E) none of these

11. A court clerk estimates that the untried cases on the docket will occupy the court for 150 trial days. If new cases are accumulating at the rate of 1.6 trial days per day and the court sits five days a week, how many days' business will remain to be heard at the end of 60 trial days?
   - (A) 168
   - (B) 184
   - (C) 185
   - (D) 186
   - (E) none of these

12. A criminal investigator has an appointment to meet with an important informant at 4 P.M. in a city that is 480 kilometers from his base location. If the investigator estimates that his average speed will be 40 mph, what time must he leave home to make his appointment?
   - (A) 8:15 A.M.
   - (B) 8:30 A.M.
   - (C) 8:45 A.M.
   - (D) 9:30 A.M.
   - (E) none of these

13. A program analysis office is taking bids for a new office machine. One machine is offered at a list price of $1360 with successive discounts of 20 percent and 10 percent, a delivery charge of $35 and an installation charge of $52. The other machine is offered at a list price of $1385 with a single discount of 30 percent, a delivery charge of $40 and an installation charge of $50. If the office chooses the less expensive machine, the savings will amount to just about
   - (A) .6 percent
   - (B) 1.9 percent
   - (C) 2.0 percent
   - (D) 2.6 percent
   - (E) none of these

14. An assignment is completed by 32 clerks in 22 days. Assuming that all the clerks work at the same rate of speed, the number of clerks that would be needed to complete this assignment in 16 days is
   (A) 27
   (B) 38
   (C) 44
   (D) 52
   (E) none of these

15. The paralegals in a large legal department have decided to establish a "sunshine fund" for charitable purposes. Paralegal A has proposed that each worker chip in one-half of 1 percent of weekly salary; paralegal B thinks 1 percent would be just right; paralegal C suggests that one-third of 1 percent would be adequate; and paralegal D, who is strapped for funds, argues for one-fifth of 1 percent. The payroll department will cooperate and make an automatic deduction, but the paralegals must agree on a uniform percentage. The average of their suggested contributions is approximately

   (A) $\frac{1}{4}$ percent

   (B) $\frac{1}{3}$ percent

   (C) $\frac{1}{2}$ percent

   (D) $\frac{5}{8}$ percent

   (E) none of these

16. A federal agency had a personal computer repaired at a cost of $49.20. This amount included a charge of $22 per hour for labor and a charge for a new switch that cost $18 before a 10 percent government discount was applied. How long did the repair job take?
   (A) 1 hour, 6 minutes
   (B) 1 hour, 11 minutes
   (C) 1 hour, 22 minutes
   (D) 1 hour, 30 minutes
   (E) none of these

17. In a large agency where mail is delivered in motorized carts, two tires were replaced on a cart at a cost of $34.00 per tire. If the agency had expected to pay $80 for a pair of tires, what percent of its expected cost did it save?
   (A) 7.5 percent
   (B) 17.6 percent
   (C) 57.5 percent
   (D) 75.0 percent
   (E) none of these

18. An experimental anti-pollution vehicle powered by electricity traveled 33 kilometers (km) at a constant speed of 110 kilometers per hour (km/h). How many minutes did it take this vehicle to complete its experimental run?
    (A) 3
    (B) 10
    (C) 18
    (D) 20
    (E) none of these

19. In one Federal office, $\frac{1}{6}$ of the employees favored abandoning a flexible work schedule system. In a second office that had the same number of employees, $\frac{1}{4}$ of the workers favored abandoning it. What is the average of the fractions of the workers in the two offices who favored abandoning the system?
    (A) $\frac{1}{10}$
    (B) $\frac{1}{5}$
    (C) $\frac{5}{24}$
    (D) $\frac{5}{12}$
    (E) none of the these

20. A clerk is able to process 40 unemployment compensation claims in one hour. After deductions of 18 percent for benefits and taxes, the clerk's net pay is $6.97 per hour. If the clerk processed 1,200 claims, how much would the government have to pay for the work, based on the clerk's hourly wage *before* deductions?
    (A) $278.80
    (B) $255.00
    (C) $246.74
    (D) $209.10
    (E) none of these

END OF PART C

CORRECT ANSWERS FOR MODEL EXAMINATION 5

BOOK A

PART A—NAME AND NUMBER COMPARISONS

1.	B	11.	B	21.	B	31.	B	41.	A
2.	D	12.	E	22.	A	32.	D	42.	C
3.	E	13.	E	23.	A	33.	A	43.	E
4.	A	14.	E	24.	A	34.	E	44.	A
5.	E	15.	B	25.	E	35.	E	45.	E
6.	A	16.	D	26.	E	36.	E	46.	B
7.	A	17.	A	27.	C	37.	A	47.	C
8.	C	18.	A	28.	E	38.	E	48.	B
9.	D	19.	C	29.	C	39.	A	49.	D
10.	B	20.	C	30.	B	40.	A	50.	C

Explanations

1. **(B)** The first two names are exactly alike, but the third name has a different initial.

2. **(D)** In the second and third names, the surname is Moru. In the first name, it is Moro.

3. **(E)** The given name is alike in the second and third names only; the surname is alike in only the first and second names.

4. **(A)** All three names are exactly alike.

5. **(E)** The middle initial in the second name is different from that of the other two. In the third name, Francis becomes Frances.

6. **(A)** All three numbers are exactly alike.

7. **(A)** All three numbers are exactly alike.

8. **(C)** The "254" of the beginning of the second number is different from the "245" opening of the first and third numbers.

9. **(D)** The "243" ending of the first number is different from the "423" ending of the second and third numbers.

10. **(B)** The "2798" opening of the third number is different from the "2789" opening of the first and second numbers.

11. **(B)** In the third name, the surname changes from Tenenbaum to Tanenbaum.

12. **(E)** The surname is different in each of the three names.

13. **(E)** Again, all three surnames are different.

14. **(E)** "Robert J." of the third name is the reverse of "J. Robert" of the first two names; the spelling of the surname in the second name differs from that of the first and third,

15. **(B)** "Fernand" of the third name is different from "Fernando" of the first two.

16. **(D)** The "630" ending of the first number is different from the "360" ending of the second and third.

17. **(A)** All three numbers are exactly alike.

18. **(A)** All three numbers are exactly alike.

19. **(C)** The "287" beginning of the second number is different from the "278" beginning of the first and third numbers.

20. **(C)** The "861" ending of the second number is different from the "681" ending of the first and third.

21. **(B)** "Courtnay" of the third name is different from "Courtney" of the first and second.

22. **(A)** All three names are exactly alike.

23. **(A)** All three names are exactly alike.

24. **(A)** All three names are exactly alike.

25. **(E)** The second name is "Sr.," while the first and third names are "Jr."; the third surname begins with "Mac," while the first and second surnames begin with "Mc."

26. **(E)** The three numbers end: 2976, 9276, 2796.

27. **(C)** The first and third numbers end, 1695; the second ends, 6195.

28. **(E)** The three numbers end: 0527, 5027, 0537.

29. **(C)** The first and third numbers are identical; the second number differs in a number of digits.

30. **(B)** The last two digits of the third number are reversed.

31. **(B)** "Randolphe" of the third name is different from "Randolph" of the first two.

32. **(D)** The surname of the second and third names, "Johnson," is different from the surname of the first name, "Johnston."

33. **(A)** All three names are exactly alike.

34. **(E)** The middle initial of the third name differs from the other two. "Asheton" of the second name differs from "Atherton" of the other two.

35. **(E)** The given name in the second and third names is "Owen" while in the first it is "Owens." The surname of the first two names is "McVey" while in the third it is "McVay."

36. **(E)** The three numbers end: 5690, 6690, 5609.

37. **(A)** All three numbers are exactly alike.

38. **(E)** The last two digits are, respectively: 41, 47, 14.

39. **(A)** All three numbers are exactly alike.

40. **(A)** All three numbers are exactly alike.

41. **(A)** All three names are exactly alike.

42. **(C)** The first and third names are exactly alike, but the second name inserts an "n" in the surname.

43. **(E)** The given name is different in all three names.

44. **(A)** All three names are exactly alike.

45. **(E)** The surname is different in each of the three names.

46. **(B)** In the third number, the fifth and sixth digits are reversed.

47. **(C)** In the second number, the fifth digit is "6" while in the other numbers the fifth digit is "0."

48. **(B)** In the third number, the last two digits are reversed.

49. **(D)** The last digit of the second and third numbers is "6"; the first number ends with "8."

50. **(C)** In the second number, the order of the fifth and sixth digits is reversed.

PART B—READING COMPREHENSION

1.	A	7.	D	13.	E	19.	D	25.	B
2.	B	8.	C	14.	C	20.	C	26.	C
3.	B	9.	E	15.	B	21.	E	27.	C
4.	C	10.	B	16.	E	22.	E	28.	E
5.	E	11.	D	17.	C	23.	A	29.	C
6.	C	12.	A	18.	B	24.	C	30.	D

Explanations

1. **(A)** The essential information from which the answer can be inferred is found in the second sentence. Since *a uniformed member while out of uniform* (in other words, an off-duty member) *may **not** indulge in intoxicants to an extent unfitting the member for duty,* it follows that the same member may drink liquor in moderation. Response B is incorrect because it directly contradicts the first sentence. Response C is incorrect because it introduces a concept not addressed in the paragraph—that of the uniformed member who reports unfit for duty. Response D is wrong because it reverses the meaning of the second sentence—the uniformed member in civilian clothes may drink only to the extent that the member remains fit for duty. Response E is incorrect because it raises a topic never mentioned in the paragraph—that of the civilian member of the department in a uniform (what uniform?).

2. **(B)** The paragraph makes the statement that the technician may sign that which it is not required that the specialist personally sign and states the rules that apply to the technician: name and title of tax law specialist followed by "by" and the name and title of the tax technician in ink. Response B is incorrect in that the assistant does not have authority to sign all papers. Responses C and D are incorrect because they address topics not mentioned in the paragraph—redelegation and requisitions. Response E is incorrect; the tax law specialist's name may be affixed by rubber stamp.

3. **(B)** The first clause states that the retiree is entitled to an annuity; the second clause tells of the pension that is the equal of one service-fraction of final compensation multiplied by number of years of government service; and the last clause describes an additional pension that is the actuarial equivalent of any reserve-for-increased-take-home-pay to which the retiree might at that time be entitled. Response A is incorrect because it does not complete the explanation of the basis for the second pension. Responses C, D, and E are all hopelessly garbled misstatements.

4. **(C)** In effect, the paragraph is saying, "When in doubt, check it out." Ignorance of the nature of the material to be mailed or of how the law pertains to it does not excuse the mailer if the material was indeed subject to a prohibition. Response A misinterprets the role of the postmaster. The postmaster is the final authority as to mailability. Response B is incorrect in its direct contradiction of the paragraph, which states, "Ignorance is no excuse." Responses D and E both interpret beyond the paragraph. The paragraph places all burden on the mailer.

5. **(E)** The last sentence makes the point that *any and all training* is valuable, *but only as it pertains to the position for which the applicant applies*. Responses A and D miss the point. Any training or education is valuable *if it contributes to knowledges, skills, and abilities needed in the particular job*. Responses B and C make statements unsupported by the paragraph.

6. **(C)** The second sentence tells us that heart disease is an illness of late middle age and old age. Response A is totally wrong. Since heart disease is an illness of older people, the odds of a person with heart disease being over 30 are much more than 50%. The fifty-fifty statement refers to the likelihood of persons over 30 sometime developing heart disease. Response B confuses death from *all causes* with death from *all other illnesses*. Response D makes an unsupported assumption that only the rising birth rate contributes to the number of people above a certain age. Actually, the longevity rate is much more crucial to this figure. Response E makes a statement that, whether true or false, is in no way supported by the paragraph.

7. **(D)** If people want what they can't get through legitimate, entirely legal channels, they will turn to those who supply those products or services. The consumers of less than legitimate products or services are unlikely to betray their suppliers. Response A is incorrect. Since racketeers deliver goods and services for money received, they are not engaged in theft, but not all "non-thieves" are engaged in legitimate business. Response B is incorrect because both racketeering and theft involve objects of value; the differences are along other dimensions. Response C makes no sense at all. Response E is unsupported by the paragraph.

8. **(C)** The first sentence tells us that the problems of the housing authority are legion, that it faces all the problems of private developers and problems peculiar to a public authority. Being *watched by antihousing enthusiasts* is one of these problems. Response A makes an unsupported statement. The paragraph does not enumerate the problems of private developers. Response B is incorrect. It is the antihousing authorities who watch for errors and cost overruns and then bring them to the attention of Congressional committees. Responses D and E make unsupported statements that do not make much sense as statements.

9. **(E)** *The peculiar threats to security in governmental organizations* to which the paragraph alludes are factors related to partisan, electoral politics. Other factors—job needs of the marketplace, interpersonal relationships, and internal power plays—affect private and public employees in about equal proportions. Response A is unsupported by the paragraph. Response B directly contradicts the paragraph. Responses C and D are entirely unsupported by the paragraph.

10. **(B)** Some people develop allergies to antibiotics so that although those specific antibiotics might be the drug of choice to counter illness, the antibiotics cannot be used for those people. Response A makes a categorical statement that is unsupported by the paragraph. Response C is incorrect because antibiotics do not cure allergies; they may cause allergies. Response D is incorrect because the organisms do not become allergic to antibiotics (people become allergic). Response E is incorrect because there would be no need to search for new drugs if the existing ones were unfailingly effective. We need new drugs precisely because some organisms have become resistant to current ones.

11. **(D)** The paragraph clearly states that *in the competitive class every applicant must meet minimum qualifications….* There may or may not be a pass/fail examination, but there most definitely are minimum qualifications that must be fulfilled. Response A is a distortion of the first sentence. The sentence means that there are no reliable exams for noncompetitive positions, not that noncompetitive positions are filled by unreliable exams. Response B is incorrect because the paragraph states that there *may* be an exam, not that there will be an exam. Response C is incorrect because if there is a test, the applicant must pass it. Response E goes beyond the scope of the paragraph. The paragraph does not state that *all* positions for which there are minimum qualifications are in the noncompetitive class.

12. **(A)** The paragraph defines a comma splice as the joining of two main clauses by a comma without a coordinating conjunction. Response B is incorrect because a ran-on sentence is defined as two independent clauses sharing one sentence with no connective. Response C is incorrect because the paragraph suggests that a semicolon used as a connective can stand alone. Response D touches on a subject not addressed in the paragraph. Response E reverses the intent of the paragraph. A comma splice *is* a bad remedy for a run-on sentence.

13. **(E)** In *some* positions overtime is earned for time worked beyond the set number of hours; *other* positions offer compensatory time for overtime. Compensatory time is an alternative to overtime pay. Responses A, B, and C make unsupported statements. Response D combines the additional payments for two different classes of services. Overtime pay is for hours in excess of the standard number; weekend differentials are for work on weekends, even if within the standard number of workweek hours.

14. **(C)** The paragraph makes clear that applicants may take the test before their backgrounds and qualifications have been investigated. If qualification is not even prerequisite to testing, certainly a qualified applicant will not be barred from the exam. Response A is incorrect in assuming that all persons admitted to the test are unqualified. The paragraph indicates only that their qualifications need not have yet been verified. Response B contradicts the paragraph. Response D is incorrect. The investigation is made to verify satisfactory character and reputation. Response E is unsupported by the paragraph.

15. **(B)** Since it is illegal to continue employing an undocumented alien hired after November 6, 1986, it must not be illegal to retain an employee who was hired before that date. Response A is incorrect. It never was illegal to *deny* employment to undocumented aliens; it is now illegal to employ them. Response C misinterprets the paragraph. The paragraph applies only to undocumented or unauthorized aliens. Aliens who have authorizing documents or "green cards" may be employed legally. Response D is incorrect. Penalties are for "knowingly" hiring illegal aliens, not for inadvertent hiring. (You must limit your answers to the material presented in the paragraph, even though you may know of the burden on employers to verify documentation or face penalties.) Response E is in contradiction to the paragraph.

16. **(E)** COBRA provides for the continuation of health and welfare benefits upon payment of 102% of the group premium. Response A misinterprets the variation in the length of continuing coverage to depend upon the reason for termination of coverage rather than upon the reason for continuation of coverage. Response B is incorrect because it is the cost to the subscriber that jumps to 102% of the group rate, not the extent of the coverage. Response C is incorrect because the law requires the employer to offer the opportunity to continue health coverage; it does not require employees, retirees, or their families to continue that coverage. Response D is wrong because under COBRA terminated employees and retirees can continue coverage, but they cannot acquire new benefits.

17. **(C)** Recorded history is short relative to the time span between major earthquakes; therefore, history is inadequate as a predictive tool. Either a much longer period of recorded history or a much shorter span between major earthquakes would enhance the predictive value of historical data. Response A is not supported by the paragraph. Responses B and D are not only unsupported, but also make no sense. Response E makes an assumption that goes beyond the paragraph.

18. **(B)** Basically, the last sentence of the paragraph is saying that if we know the rules of construction of a language, we can understand it. Response A contradicts the paragraph. The paragraph states that the number of rules is finite. Response C twists the second sentence, which states that definition of a language by listing its strings is impossible because the number of strings is infinite. Response D introduces unnatural languages, which is not a subject of the paragraph. Response E makes an unsupported statement.

19. **(D)** Just as *agreement of testimony is no proof of dependability,* so agreement of testimony is no proof of undependability. Response A is incorrect because the thrust of the paragraph is that people's perceptions are sometimes in error. Response B contradicts the paragraph. It is reported that a number of witnesses may report the same erroneous observation even apart from collusion. Response C misses the point. Since witnesses can make mistakes, they are just as likely to have not noticed the truth as to have "observed" that which did not happen. Response E is a misstatement.

20. **(C)** If a contract is changed by a rider, both parties must sign the rider. The basic contract should note that a rider is being attached, and both parties should initial and date the notice in the basic contract. Response A is incorrect in that it creates a rider without necessarily having created a contract. A mutual agreement to refrain from an act may be a first point of agreement and not a change. Responses B and D are both incorrect because there can be no change unless both parties agree. Response E is incorrect because if there is to be no change there is no call for a rider.

21. **(E)** The third sentence of the paragraph states that *it is not true that all organizations are structured so that workers can be dealt with as individuals.* From this statement we can infer that *some organizations are not structured so that workers can be dealt with as individuals.* Response A contradicts both the third and fourth sentences by ignoring the information that *in some organizations, employees are represented by unions, and managers bargain with these associations.* Responses C and D are incorrect because they generalize some to mean all. Response B is unsupported because the paragraph gives no information about working environments other than organizations.

22. **(E)** The third sentence states that *all mechanical explosives are devices in which a physical reaction is produced, such as that caused by overloading a container with compressed air.* From this we can safely conclude that *some* devices in which a physical reaction is produced, such as that caused by overloading a container with compressed air, are mechanical explosives. We cannot infer response A because the paragraph does not provide sufficient information to enable the conclusion that all explosives that have been restricted to military weapons are nuclear weapons. It may be that other explosives that are not nuclear weapons also have been restricted to military weapons. Responses B and C contradict the paragraph. Response D is wrong because the paragraph provides no information at all about whether or not mechanical explosives are restricted to military weapons.

23. **(A)** *Every level of government is a link in the economic process.* It can be deduced that its contradictory statement, *some levels of government are not links in the economic process,* cannot be true. Response B is not supported by the paragraph because it goes beyond the information given. It cannot be concluded that dictatorships observe more than one principle in common with other governments. Responses C and E represent incorrect interpretations of the information that *every level of government is a link in the economic process.* It cannot be inferred from this statement that *all links in the economic process are levels of government,* only that some are. We know that the category "all levels of government" is contained in the category "links in the economic process," but we do not know if other links in the economic process exist that are not levels of government. Response D is not supported by the passage; there is nothing to suggest that the contributions of some levels of society do *not* need to be evaluated.

24. **(C)** The first sentence presents two mutually exclusive alternatives—*all property is classified as either personal property or real property, but not both.* The second sentence states that *if something is classified as personal property, it is transient and transportable in nature.* The fourth sentence states that *permanent buildings and land...are fixed in nature and are not transportable.* From that we can conclude that since permanent buildings and land are not transient and transportable in nature, they are not personal property; they must, therefore, be real property. All other responses contradict the paragraph in some way.

25. **(B)** The essential information from which the answer is to be inferred is contained in the second sentence, which states that if an Act of Congress has been deemed unconstitutional, then it is voided. In response B we are told that an Act of Congress is not voided; therefore, we can conclude that *it has not been deemed unconstitutional by the Supreme Court.* Responses A and C are not supported because the paragraph does not indicate whether an Act of Congress is voided *only* when it has been deemed unconstitutional or if it could be voided for other reasons. Responses D and E contradict the paragraph.

26. **(C)** The last sentence states that *some special programs for broken families are offered when parental care is temporarily or permanently unavailable.* If this statement is true, then its negation cannot be true. Response A contradicts the paragraph. Responses B and D cannot be validly inferred because the paragraph does not provide sufficient information to support the inferences made. Response E is wrong because the paragraph states that *all child-welfare agencies are organizations that seek to promote the healthy growth and development of children.* There is no way of knowing from this statement whether or not there are organizations other than child-welfare agencies that seek to promote the healthy growth and welfare of children.

27. **(C)** This answer can be inferred from the information presented in the last sentence of the paragraph, which says in part that *all document depots have the capacity to provide a great range of user services*. In view of this statement, it is clearly the case that *no* document depot lacks such a capacity. Response A goes beyond the information given in the paragraph. Response B contradicts the information presented. Response D draws an overly general conclusion from the information presented. One can infer that *some* document depots are information centers, but one cannot infer that *all* information centers are document depots. Response E goes beyond the information that is implicit in the last sentence.

28. **(E)** The last sentence says that *if an expression is a familiar one...then it is a nonhyphenated compound*. Therefore, if an expression is a hyphenated compound, it cannot be a familiar one. Response A contradicts the information. Response B is incorrect because the paragraph does not give us information about *all* nonhyphenated compounds, only those that are familiar expressions. Response C is incorrect because the paragraph does not give us enough information about all unfamiliar expressions. Response D cannot be correct because the paragraph provides no information about compounds that have suffixes.

29. **(C)** The second sentence tells us that *some general types of land use are activities that conflict with the purpose of wildlife refuges and botanical reservations*. The third sentence explains that *all activities that exhibit such conflict are...excluded from refuges and reservations*. Therefore, we can conclude that *some activities excluded from refuges and reservations* (the ones that conflict with the purpose of refuges and reservations) *are general types of land use*. Response A is wrong because the paragraph does not give any information as to whether all activities that conflict with the purpose of refuges and reservations are general types of land use. Response B cannot be inferred because the paragraph does not give enough information about *all* activities that are excluded. Response D is incorrect because it is too inclusive. Response E is based upon insufficient information.

30. **(D)** The third sentence states that *if a computer programming language is a machine language, then it is a code that can be read directly by a computer*. From this statement it can be seen that all machine languages are codes that can be read directly by a computer and that if a computer programming language is not such a code, then it is not a machine language. Response A goes beyond the information presented in the paragraph. Responses B and C contradict the paragraph. Response E is incorrect because the paragraph does not say whether or not computer languages that are *not* machine languages are codes that can be read directly by a computer.

PART C—ARITHMETIC REASONING

1.	C	5.	A	9.	A	13.	A	17.	E
2.	D	6.	C	10.	C	14.	C	18.	C
3.	B	7.	B	11.	D	15.	C	19.	C
4.	E	8.	A	12.	B	16.	D	20.	B

Explanations

1. **(C)** The first 12 clerks complete $\frac{6}{18}$, or $\frac{1}{3}$ of the job in 6 days, leaving $\frac{2}{3}$ of the job to be completed.

   One clerk would require $12 \times 18 = 216$ days to complete the job, working alone. Sixteen clerks require $216 \div 16$, or $13\frac{1}{2}$ days for the entire job. But only $\frac{2}{3}$ of the job remains. To do $\frac{2}{3}$ of the job, sixteen clerks require

   $$\frac{2}{3} \times 13\frac{1}{2} = \frac{2}{3} \times \frac{27}{2} = 9 \text{ days}$$

   The entire job takes 6 days + 9 days = 15 days.

2. **(D)** Let x = cost of a child's cleaning

   Then $2x$ = cost of an adult's cleaning

   $$
   \begin{aligned}
   2(2x) + 3(x) &= \$49 \\
   4x + 3x &= \$49 \\
   7x &= \$49 \\
   x &= \$7
   \end{aligned}
   $$

   $7 is the cost of a child's cleaning; $2 \times \$7$ or $14 is the cost of an adult's cleaning.

3. **(B)** First determine the total annual tax:

   $$\$424 + \$783 + (2)\$466 = \$424 + \$783 + \$932 = \$2139$$

   Divide the total taxes by the tax rate to find the assessed valuation.

   $$\$2139 \div .132 = \$16{,}204$$

   To find what percent one number is of another, create a fraction by putting the part over the whole and convert to a decimal by dividing.

   $$\frac{\$16,205}{\$87,250} = \$16{,}205 \div \$87{,}250 = 18.57\%$$

4. **(E)** The correct answer, not given, is five additional days.

   Four assistants completed 336 cases in 42 hours (6 days at 7 hours per day). Therefore, each assistant completed $336 \div 4$, or 84 cases in 42 hours, for a rate of 2 cases per hour per assistant.

After the first 6 days, the number of cases remaining is

$$756 - 336 = 420$$

It will take 6 assistants, working at the rate of 2 cases per hour per assistant, $420 \div 12$ or 35 hours to complete the work. If each workday has 7 hours, then $35 \div 7$ or 5 days are needed.

5. **(A)** Add what the family spends

$$30\% + 8\% + 25\% + 4\% + 13\% + 5\% = 85\%$$

Since it spends 85 percent, it has 100 percent − 85 percent = 15 percent remaining for savings.

$$15\% \text{ of } \$500 = .15 \times \$500 = \$75 \text{ per week}$$
$$\$15,000 \div \$75 = 200 \text{ weeks}$$

6. **(C)**
$$\text{Commission} = 42\tfrac{1}{2}\% \text{ of fares}$$

$$42\tfrac{1}{2}\% \text{ of } \$520 = .425 \times \$520$$
$$= \$221 \text{ commission}$$

$$\text{Tips} = 29\% \text{ of commission}$$
$$29\% \text{ of } \$221 = .29 \times \$221$$
$$= \$64.09 \text{ tips}$$

Weekly earnings:

$$
\begin{array}{r}
\$221.00 \\
+ \quad 64.09 \\
\hline
\$1140.36
\end{array}
$$

Monthly earnings, based on four-week month

$$
\begin{array}{r}
\$285.09 \\
\times \qquad 4 \\
\hline
\$1140.36
\end{array}
$$

Earnings in a month a few days longer than four weeks clearly fall between $1100 and $1200.

7. **(B)** Take this problem one step at a time. Of the 60 employees, one-third, or 20, were clerks. 30 percent, or 18, were machine operators. 22 were stenographers.

The clerks earned $12,750 ÷ 12 = $1,062.50 per month
Machine operators earned $13,150 ÷ 12 = $1,095.83 per month
Stenographers earned $13,000 ÷ 12 = $1,083.33 per month

20 clerks × $1,062.50 × 2 months = $42,500.00
18 machine operators × $1,095.83 × 4 months = $78,899.76
22 stenographers × $1,083.33 × 3 months = $71,499.78
$42,500.00 + $78,889.76 + $71,499.78 = $192,899.54 total cost

8. **(A)** The government worker drove 336 miles, and his car got 24 miles per gallon; therefore, he used $336 \div 24 = 14$ gallons for which he paid \$1.419 per gallon or $\$1.419 \times 14 = \$19.87$. All other information is irrelevant; disregard it.

9. **(A)** There are 360 minutes in a six-hour day. If each seat is occupied all day there are $105 \times 360 = 37,800$ minutes of seating time to be divided among 486 people. $37,800 \div 486 = 77.77$ minutes of seating time per person = 1 hour 17.7 minutes per person.

10. **(C)** The worker earns \$8.60 per hour for two 40-hour weeks or $\$8.60 \times 80$ hours = \$688 and \$12.90 per hour for an additional 16 hours ($\$12.90 \times 16$ hours = \$206.40), so her gross pay is $\$688 + \$206.40 = \$894.40$. From this are deducted: FICA at 7.13% = \$63.77 and the three withholding taxes at the combined rate of 22.5% = \$201.24. Add the deductions: $\$63.77 + \$201.24 = \$265.01$, and subtract the sum from the gross pay: $\$894.40 - \$265.01 = \$629.39$.

11. **(D)** Since the court does one day's work per day, at the end of 60 days there will be $150 - 60 = 90$ trial days of old cases remaining. New cases are accumulating at the rate of 1.6 trial days per day; therefore, there will be $60 \times 1.6 = 96$ trial days of new cases at the end of 60 days. 96 new trial days added to the backlog of 90 trial days would make the total backlog 186 trial days.

12. **(B)** A kilometer is $\frac{5}{8}$ of a mile.

    $480 \text{ km} \times \frac{5}{8} = 300$ miles; $300 \text{ miles} \div 40 \text{ mph} = 7.5$ hours

    Subtract 7.5 hours from the required arrival time of 4 P.M. to find that he must leave at 8:30 A.M. (noon to 4 P.M. is 4 hours + 8:30 to noon is $3\frac{1}{2}$ hours).

13. **(A)** Calculate the cost of the first machine:

    $\$1360 - 20\% = \$1360 \times 80\% = \$1088$

    then

    $\$1088 - 10\% = \$1088 \times 90\% = \$979.20 + \$35 + \$52 = \$1066.20$

    Calculate the cost of the second machine:

    $\$1385 - 30\% = \$1385 \times 70\% = \$969.50 + \$40 + \$50 = \$1059.50$

    The second machine is $\$1066.20 - \$1059.50 = \$6.70$ less expensive; $\$6.70 \div \$1066.20 = .6\%$ savings by buying the second machine.

14. **(C)** The proportion is $32 \times 22 = x \times 16$

    $16x = 704$

    $x = 704 \div 16 = 44$

15. **(C)** Add the suggested contributions and divide by the number of paralegals to get the average.

$$\frac{1}{2}\% = \frac{15}{30}$$

$$\frac{1}{1}\% = \frac{30}{30}$$

$$\frac{1}{3}\% = \frac{10}{30}$$

$$+ \;\; \frac{1}{5}\% = \frac{16}{30}$$

$$\frac{61}{30}\% = 2\% \div 4 \text{ paralegals} = \frac{1}{2}\%$$

16. **(D)** Compute the following:

$$\frac{49.20 - (18 - (18 \times .10))}{22} = x$$

$$x = \frac{33}{22} = 1.5 \text{ hours or 1 hour, 30 minutes}$$

The cost of the switch after the government discount of 10% is applied is $18 - (18 \times .10)$ or $16.20. This amount, when subtracted from the total charge of $49.20, leaves $33, which represents the charge for labor. A charge of $33 at the rate of $22 per hour represents 1.5 hours, or 1 hour and 30 minutes, of work.

17. **(E)** The correct answer is not given as one of the response choices. The answer can be obtained by computing the following:

$$\frac{\left(\frac{80}{2} - 34\right)}{40} = x$$

$$x = \frac{6}{40} = .15$$

$$.15 \times 100 = 15\%$$

The expected $80 cost for a pair of tires would make the cost of a single tire $40. The difference between the actual cost of $34 per tire and the expected cost of $40 per tire is $6, which is 15% of the $40 expected cost.

18. **(C)** Obtain the answer by setting up a simple proportion:

$$\frac{110\,\text{km}}{60\,\text{min}} = \frac{33\,\text{km}}{x\,\text{min}}$$

Solving this proportion, we obtain $110x = 1980$; $x = [1980/110] = 18$.

19. **(C)** Compute the following:

$$\frac{\left(\frac{1}{6} + \frac{1}{4}\right)}{2} = x$$

This simple arithmetic averaging of two fractions can be accomplished by first finding their lowest common denominator:

$\frac{1}{6} = \frac{2}{12}$ and $\frac{1}{4} = \frac{3}{12}$

The sum of $\frac{2}{12}$ and $\frac{3}{12}$ is $\frac{5}{12}$. This fraction, when multiplied by $\frac{1}{2}$ (which is the same as dividing by 2) gives the correct answer:

$\frac{5}{12} \times \frac{1}{2} = \frac{5}{24}$

20. **(B)** Compute the following:

(1) $.82S = 6.97$

and

(2) $\frac{1200}{40} \times S = Y$

The clerk's net pay of $6.97 per hour represents .82 of his or her gross pay (100% − 18% = 82% or .82). Solving equation (1) we find that the clerk's hourly salary *(S)* before deductions is $8.50. Substituting this figure in equation (2), we compute the total number of hours of work involved (1200 forms divided by 40 forms per hour equals 30 hours of work), and then multiply 30 hours by an hourly wage of $8.50 to get $255.00, the amount the government would have to pay for the work.

SCORE SHEET

NAME AND NUMBER COMPARISONS: Your score on the Name and Number Comparisons part is based upon the number of questions you answered correctly minus one-fourth of the questions you answered incorrectly (number wrong divided by 4). Calculate this now: Number Wrong ÷ 4 = .

Number Right − Number Wrong ÷ 4 = Raw Score

_____ − _____ = _____

READING COMPREHENSION: Your score on the Reading Comprehension part is based only on the number of questions you answered correctly. Wrong answers do not count against you.

Number Right = Raw Score

_____ = _____

ARITHMETIC REASONING: Your score on the Arithmetic Reasoning part is based only upon the number of questions you answered correctly. Wrong answers do not count against you.

Number Right = Raw Score

_____ = _____

TOTAL SCORE: To find your total raw score, add together the raw scores for each section of the exam.

Name and Number Comparisons Score   _____

    +

Reading Comprehension Score   _____

    +

Arithmetic Reasoning Score   _____

    =   _____

Total Raw Score   _____

Self Evaluation Chart

Calculate your raw score for each test as shown above. Then check to see where your score falls on the scale from Poor to Excellent. Lightly shade in the boxes in which your scores fall.

Part	Excellent	Good	Average	Fair	Poor
Name and Number Comparisons	43–50	35–42	26–34	19–25	0–18
Reading Comprehension	25–30	20–24	15–19	11–14	0–10
Arithmetic Reasoning	18–20	15–17	12–14	9–11	0–8
Total Score	85–100	70–84	51–69	31–50	0–30

BOOK B

Book B is set up to look like a multiple-choice test and it is timed like a test, but it is not a test at all. There are no right or wrong answers, and there is no score. You cannot study for Book B, and your only preparation can consist of gathering statistical records from your school years and thinking about what you achieved and when.

Book B consists of 122 questions to be answered in 40 minutes. Questions ask about your best and worst grades in school and about your favorite subjects. They ask about your extracurricular activities and about your participation in sports. There are questions about attendance, part-time jobs, and leadership positions. Some questions ask you how you think your teachers or employers might rate you. Similar questions ask you to suggest what your friends might say about you. Still other questions ask how you rate yourself against others. Answer honestly and to the best of your ability.

MINI-MODEL BOOK B

1. My favorite subject in high school was
   - (A) math
   - (B) English
   - (C) physical education
   - (D) social studies
   - (E) science

2. My GPA upon graduation from high school (on a 4.0 scale) was
   - (A) lower than 2.51
   - (B) 2.51 to 2.80
   - (C) 2.81 to 3.25
   - (D) 3.26 to 3.60
   - (E) higher than 3.60

3. In my second year of high school I was absent
   - (A) never
   - (B) not more than 3 days
   - (C) 4 to 10 days
   - (D) more often than 10 days
   - (E) do not recall

4. My best grades in high school were in
   - (A) art
   - (B) math
   - (C) English
   - (D) social studies
   - (E) music

5. While in high school I participated in
    (A) one sport
    (B) two sports and one other extracurricular activity
    (C) three nonathletic extracurricular activities
    (D) no extracurricular activities
    (E) other than the above

6. During my senior year in high school I held a paying job
    (A) 0 hours a week
    (B) 1 to 5 hours a week
    (C) 6 to 10 hours a week
    (D) 11 to 16 hours a week
    (E) more than 16 hours a week

7. The number of semesters in which I failed a course in high school was
    (A) none
    (B) one
    (C) two or three
    (D) four or five
    (E) more than five

8. In high school I did volunteer work
    (A) more than 10 hours a week
    (B) 5 to 10 hours a week on a regular basis
    (C) sporadically
    (D) seldom
    (E) not at all

If you did not go to college, skip questions 9–24. Go to Question 25.

9. My general area of concentration in college was
    (A) performing arts
    (B) humanities
    (C) social sciences
    (D) business
    (E) none of the above

10. At graduation from college, my age was
    (A) under 20
    (B) 20
    (C) 21 to 24
    (D) 25 to 29
    (E) 30 or over

11. My standing in my graduating class was in the
    (A) bottom third
    (B) middle third
    (C) top third
    (D) top quarter
    (E) top 10 percent

12. In college, I was elected to a major office in a class or in a club or organization
    (A) more than six times
    (B) four or five times
    (C) two or three times
    (D) once
    (E) never

13. In comparison to my peers, I cut classes
    (A) much less often than most
    (B) somewhat less often than most
    (C) just about the same as most
    (D) somewhat more often than most
    (E) much more often than most

14. The campus activities in which I participated most were
    (A) social service
    (B) political
    (C) literary
    (D) did not participate in campus activities
    (E) did not participate in any of these activities

15. My name appeared on the dean's list
    (A) never
    (B) once or twice
    (C) in three or more terms
    (D) in more terms than it did not appear
    (E) do not remember

16. The volunteer work I did while in college was predominantly
    (A) health-care related
    (B) religious
    (C) political
    (D) educational
    (E) did not volunteer

17. While a college student, I spent most of my summers
    (A) in summer school
    (B) earning money
    (C) traveling
    (D) in service activities
    (E) resting

18. My college education was financed
    (A) entirely by my parents
    (B) by my parents and my own earnings
    (C) by scholarships, loans, and my own earnings
    (D) by my parents and loans
    (E) by a combination of sources not listed above

19. In the college classroom I was considered
    (A) a listener
    (B) an occasional contributor
    (C) an average participant
    (D) a frequent contributor
    (E) a leader

20. The person on campus whom I most admired was
    (A) another student
    (B) an athletic coach
    (C) a teacher
    (D) an administrator
    (E) a journalist

21. Of the skills I developed at college, the one I value most is
    (A) foreign language ability
    (B) oral expression
    (C) writing skills
    (D) facility with computers
    (E) analytical skills

22. I made my greatest mark in college through my
    (A) athletic prowess
    (B) success in performing arts
    (C) academic success
    (D) partying reputation
    (E) conciliatory skill with my peers

23. My cumulative GPA (on a 4.0 scale) in courses in my major was
    (A) lower than 3.00
    (B) 3.00 to 3.25
    (C) 3.26 to 3.50
    (D) 3.51 to 3.75
    (E) higher than 3.75

24. While in college I
    (A) worked full-time and was a part-time student
    (B) worked 20 hours a week and was a full-time student
    (C) worked 20 hours a week and was a part-time student
    (D) was a full-time student working more than 10 but less than 20 hours a week
    (E) was a full-time student

25. In the past six months, I have been late to work (or school)
    (A) never
    (B) only one time
    (C) very seldom
    (D) more than five times
    (E) I don't recall

26. My supervisors (or teachers) would be most likely to describe me as
    (A) competent
    (B) gifted
    (C) intelligent
    (D) fast working
    (E) detail oriented

27. My peers would probably describe me as
    (A) analytical
    (B) glib
    (C) organized
    (D) funny
    (E) helpful

28. According to my supervisors (or teachers), my greatest asset is my
    (A) ability to communicate orally
    (B) written expression
    (C) ability to motivate others
    (D) organization of time
    (E) friendly personality

29. In the past two years, I have applied for
    (A) no jobs other than this one
    (B) one other job
    (C) two to four other jobs
    (D) five to eight other jobs
    (E) more than eight jobs

30. In the past year, I read strictly for pleasure
    (A) no books
    (B) one book
    (C) two books
    (D) three to six books
    (E) more than six books

31. When I read for pleasure, I read mostly
    (A) history
    (B) fiction
    (C) poetry
    (D) biography
    (E) current events

32. My peers would say of me that, when they ask me a question, I am
(A) helpful
(B) brusque
(C) condescending
(D) generous
(E) patient

33. My supervisors (or teachers) would say that my area of least competence is
(A) analytical ability
(B) written communication
(C) attention to detail
(D) public speaking
(E) self-control

34. In the past two years, the number of full-time (35 hours or more) jobs I have held is
(A) none
(B) one
(C) two or three
(D) four
(E) five or more

35. Compared to my peers, my supervisors (or teachers) would rank my dependability
(A) much better than average
(B) somewhat better than average
(C) about average
(D) somewhat less than average
(E) much less than average

36. In my opinion, the most important of the following attributes in an employee is
(A) discretion
(B) loyalty
(C) open-mindedness
(D) courtesy
(E) competence

37. My peers would say that the word that describes me least is
(A) sociable
(B) reserved
(C) impatient
(D) judgmental
(E) independent

38. My supervisors (or teachers) would say that I react to criticism with
(A) a defensive attitude
(B) quick capitulation
(C) anger
(D) interest
(E) shame

39. My attendance record over the past year has been
    (A) not as good as I would like it to be
    (B) not as good as my supervisors (or teachers) would like it to be
    (C) a source of embarrassment
    (D) satisfactory
    (E) a source of pride

40. My peers would say that when I feel challenged my reaction is one of
    (A) determination
    (B) energy
    (C) defiance
    (D) caution
    (E) compromise

There are no "right" answers to these questions, so there is no answer key.

GLOSSARY

base salary   A *basic salary* with *COLA* added.

basic salary   Annual, daily, or hourly rate of pay, as indicated by the salary schedule for the employee's assigned position; excludes *COLA*.

career appointment   An appointment to the postal career service without time limitation.

casual appointment   A noncareer, limited-term appointment to positions used as a supplemental work force.

COLA   see *cost of living adjustment.*

cost of living adjustment   Increase in pay based on increases in the Consumer Price Index (CPI) over a base month; this increase is specified in bargaining unit agreements.

entrance examinations   Tests given to establish eligibility for employment,

grade   Each pay category,

inservice examinations   Tests administered to substitute rural carriers and career postal employees to determine eligibility for advancement and reassignment; also used to establish qualification for enrollment in certain postal training courses.

Merit Promotion Program   Provides the means for making selections for promotions according to the relative qualifications of the employees under consideration.

performance test   A procedure in which the applicant is directed to carry out a certain work activity related to the position under consideration.

promotion   The permanent assignment, with or without relocation, of an employee to an established position with a higher grade than the position to which the employee was previously assigned in the same schedule or in another schedule.

quality step increase   An increase in addition to a periodic *step increase,* granted on or before expiration of required waiting periods in recognition of extra competence.

rated application   Applications and other required documents that provide a basis for evaluation against an established rating standard; based on this application, a final rating is established for each competitor.

reassignment   The permanent assignment, with or without relocation, to another established position with the same grade in the same schedule, or in a different schedule.

register   A file of eligible employees' names arranged in order of relative standing for appointment consideration.

step increase   An advancement from one step to the next within a specific grade of a position; this is dependent on satisfying certain performance and waiting period criteria. See also *quality step increase.*

temporary appointment   A noncareer, limited-term appointment up to, but not exceeding, one year in a position that includes the performance of duties assigned to nonbargaining units.

temporary assignment   The placement of an employee in another established position, for a limited period of time, to perform duties other than those in the position description.

veteran preference   Granted to eligible applicants to be added to the ratings on examinations.

NOTES